Just plain *Chet*

The History of Krause Publications

---

by Michael J. Goc

Cover Photo: Larry Mishkar
Cover Design: Phil LaFranka

KRAUSE
PUBLICATIONS
EMPLOYEE
STOCK
OWNERSHIP
PLAN

PARTNERS IN PUBLISHING

Published by

Krause Publications
700 E. State Street, Iola, WI 54990-0001
Phone: 715-445-2214

Library of Congress: 92-74073
ISBN: 0-87341-231-1
Printed in United States of America

Contents

Preface

The history of Krause Publications reads like the legendary American success story: a farm boy leaves home and, relying on skills and values acquired from his parents, a country school education and his home community, conceives and builds a thriving, dynamic business.

The legend of the country boy who makes good has deep roots in the United States. It is as much a part of the national heritage as moms who bake apple pie, kids who play sandlot ball, and war veterans who salute the flag on July 4. Like all great legends, it contains large elements of truth. If it did not, it would not strike so deeply at the core of American identity.

In the case of Chet Krause, it is all true. Chet was a farm boy from a solid, talented family. He did attend a one-room school, and his formal education ended when he graduated from Iola High. Instead of college, he entered the U. S. Army for World War II, then came home, rolled up his sleeves and went to work-as a carpenter.

In 1952, he acted on a hunch and started publishing what he called a "trader's paper" dedicated to the "isolated collector" of coins. Numismatic News was the first Krause publication, and this book was commissioned to mark its 40th anniversary. But Krause Publications, and this book, consist of more-much more-than the story of Numismatic News. In fact, the News is only one example of the real and cumulative accomplishment of the past forty years.

The success of Krause Publications is not in its individual publications, but in its system. Over the years, slowly at first, Chet and his staff developed a strategy for recognizing specialty publishing niches to which they could apply a standard formula. They began with numismatics in the 1950s and '60s, then diversified into antique automobiles in the 1970s. The 1980s were the years of greatest growth and diversification. Music, comics, toy, firearm, and sports card collectors became target audiences for Krause Publications. The sports card division was the company's greatest success. Starting as little more than an experiment in 1981, publications devoted to baseball and other sports cards were, by the end of the decade, dominating their market, with the largest circulations and profitability of any Krause product group. In the late '80s and early 1990s, Krause continued to diversify by moving into trade publishing for agriculture and construction and into the recreational niche with hunting, fishing and fantasy baseball publications.

The Krause formula starts with a "trader's" paper concentrating on classified and display ads for collectibles. Next comes a magazine with hobby news, features and ads, primarily for newsstand circulation. Third comes a price guide with timely quotes on items for sale. Not necessarily last comes a giant "telephone book" catalog featuring exhaustively complete listings of virtually every collectible hobby item. Not every hobby is large enough to support separate publications for each one of these four components, so they may be combined into two publications, or even one, but they are present in every hobby division.

The publication formula is only part of the system. Krause has also developed a marketing and promotional capability that sets a newly created publication on a strong footing and has more than once reinvigorated a stagnating product. In terms of the sheer volume of items created and delivered, marketing and promotional efforts are arguably Krause's largest publishing function.

Publishing at Krause has also meant a willingness to experiment, to take a chance on a good bet. In early 1992, Krause was publishing 27 periodicals. Over the years, it has created or acquired, then killed or sold, at least as many newspapers and magazines. Recognizing that birth and death are essential to growth, the company has consistently probed the boundaries of old hobby niches and examined new hobbies to see if they can support a new product.

In the course of four decades, Krause has played a leading-and largely unrecognized-role in the technological transformation of the print medium. Starting in the days of the hot-lead Linotype and proceeding to the era of computerized laser light, Krause has continually ranked among the first publishers in the world to make use of new communications technology.

Krause has also built and maintained a reputation for square dealing and honesty. It is vital to an operation that depends on the trust of readers, traders and advertisers. Early on, Krause declared that all its advertisers must keep their promises and checked to make sure that they did.

The company has also not forgotten its roots and role in its community. The small-town ethic of self-help combined with neighborliness is best illustrated by the Old Car Show. Inaugurated, nurtured and promoted by Krause Publications, with work performed by community groups, the Old Car Show has brought well over $1 million to non-profit organizations in the Iola area. Krause has done more than just donate to local groups. It has given the entire community a chance to work together for its own benefit.

Along similar lines, Krause has also brought more than 300 jobs to a community with a population of just over 1,000. While most evident in Iola, Krause's success dispatches a ripple of economic development that creates jobs, stimulates investment and helps maintain communities well beyond the borders of its home village. The conversion of the family-owned corporation to employee ownership has-as well as anything might-insured that the company will not fall prey to corporate predators, that it will remain in Iola and it will continue to create wealth where it was born.

The operation that began with the man who called himself "just plain Chet" has been the work of many hands. Hundreds of people, not all of them in Iola, have worked for the company over the years and have helped build the successful publishing system. Most important are the readers, traders and advertisers who purchase and use the final products. To their passion for collecting and other pastimes and to their loyalty to the company's publications, Krause owes its success.

Like Krause Publications, this book has been the work of many hands, and a word of thanks is owed to all of them. Iola writer Jim Bach researched and wrote a manuscript covering Krause's first twenty years, and Carol Ann Podoll of the New Past Press assisted with Krause's last two decades. Many friends of Krause, as well as current and retired employees, sat for interviews, answered questions, supplied information and tracked down photos for the project. Chet and Cliff Mishler provided general editorial guidance and, along with Bob Lemke, read and commented on the manuscript. Their insights have been incorporated here. A special word of thanks is owed to Krause Public Relations Coordinator Nora Sebora, whose cooperation and assistance kept the project running smoothly.

While this book could not have been produced without help from all these good people, all errors are my own.

"On time, every time" is the Krause slogan. The people who give meaning to those words have been doing it for forty years. May they continue to do it for forty more, and another forty after that.

Michael J. Goc

April 1, 1992

Chet as a soldier during World War II.

Foreword

The year was 1952. As a thirteen-year-old-kid I was interested in many things — snakes, rocks and minerals, Scouting — you name it. One day, while visiting a local collector of rocks and minerals, I was shown an album of Lincoln "pennies" — including a rare 1909-S V.D.B. for which the owner had paid the awesome sum of $10. Convinced that I could find one for myself in pocket change, I jumped into the hobby — and before long was immersed in the lore of mint marks, Proof coins, obverse and reverse, and other terminology — thus launching an interest, and, soon, a career which extends to the present day. Now, in retrospect, and in having handled some of the largest collections and most valuable coins ever to be bought and sold, I have often expressed thanks that I was so fortunate to discover numismatics. I cannot envision any hobby area, any business that would be more interesting, or have more fascinating people, or be so rewarding in so many ways as that of coin collecting.

Unbeknownst to me in 1952, out in Iola, Wisconsin, Chet Krause was making his own beginning — not in coin collecting (as he was already an established collector), but in printing and publishing, The result, as they say, is history — an American dream come true — *Numismatic News* and Krause Publications.

I do not recall when I saw my first copy of the *News*, but it was probably around 1953 or 1954. At the time, the *Numismatic Scrapbook* magazine, published in Chicago, was the leading coin collecting periodical, followed by *The Numismatist*, official organ of the American Numismatic Association. *Numismatic News* was third in the lineup, probably a distant third as it was just beginning to get on its feet, for numbers one and two in the hobby had been established in 1935 and 1888 respectively.

I recall that around 1955-1956 *Numismatic News* was the primary source for information concerning the 1955 "Shift" Lincoln cent, as it was called — a curious variety made when a die was created in error, with doubled lettering on the obverse. Instead of reading LIBERTY the coin inscription was blurred and appeared as LLIIBBEERRTTY. During the era, the *News* primarily consisted of classified advertising, which was given free to each subscriber.

As time went on, *Numismatic News* continued to prosper. Its size increased as did its subscription base. Chet Krause became an ever more familiar figure at conventions and other gatherings of collectors. By the early 1960s it became apparent that Chet was indeed a "people person" — an astute businessman, to be sure, but a person who beyond that was interested in the people who bought, sold, and collected coins. In a word, Chet *cared*.

I recall one incident a few years ago when I was attending a rather obscure event, a banquet held by the New England Numismatic Association in

Worcester, Massachusetts. The number in attendance was in the dozens, and few if any came from outside the boundaries of New England — except for one, Chet Krause, who traveled all the way from Iola to give an Ambassador Award (an honor given to worthy recipients who have significant accomplishments in the furthering of the numismatic hobby) to an NENA member. He could have easily sent a staff member, but, no, Chet wanted to do it himself.

As the years went on in the 1960s and 1970s, the coin market underwent many changes. The *Numismatic Scrapbook* ceased publication, and in the next decade its founder, Lee Hewitt, passed away. *The Numismatist* changed editorship several times over the years. *Coin World* came on the scene (beginning in 1960) and prospered, becoming a weekly publication — a schedule which *Numismatic News* soon adopted.

As time went on, the Krause Publications empire expanded, other publications were added, and the staff went from a few to dozens to hundreds. However, the "down home" style of *Numismatic News* didn't change, nor did the personality of its founder. Chet Krause still found time to attend business and other meetings of the American Numismatic Association and on occasion to prepare "white papers" giving insight and suggestions for the ANA.

From the beginning, Chet conducted his business by the Golden Rule. In times when he certainly could have used all the money he could get from advertisers, he turned away those who were marginal or unethical, while certain of his competitors didn't care. Once accepted, an advertiser in *Numismatic News* or another of the Krause coin publications had to maintain an excellent record of customer satisfaction, or out he or she went. As a long-term advertiser I always appreciated this — for in certain other publications people would advertise misleading "bargains" consisting of overgraded and misrepresented coins, making it difficult for ethical dealers (such as I consider our firm to be) to compete effectively. Not so in *Numismatic News* — ethics prevailed.

Today in 1992 Chet Krause can be very proud of his accomplishments. *Numismatic News* is now in its fortieth year and has served as an information and market guide through some of the most exciting and formative decades of the hobby. If a roster were to be published of staff members and contributors to *Numismatic News*, it would read as a virtual *Who's Who of Numismatics*. Beyond reciting current events and items from numismatic history, the *News* was active in hobby improvements and changes — including grading interpretations, suggestions for new commemoratives and other coinage, and more.

Beyond *Numismatic News*, his other publications in coins and in other fields have brought joy to millions. It would be difficult to envision numismatics without Chet Krause — he certainly has been a cornerstone in the hobby. More important, while numismatics has been good to him and has helped launch his publishing empire, he has been important to numismatics. I believe it is correct to say that he has put more into the hobby than he has taken out of it. Any success he has achieved is justly deserved. May Chet Krause enjoy many more years in numismatics and his other interests, and may Krause Publications continue to prosper.

It has been nice knowing Chet.

Q. David Bowers

June 22, 1992

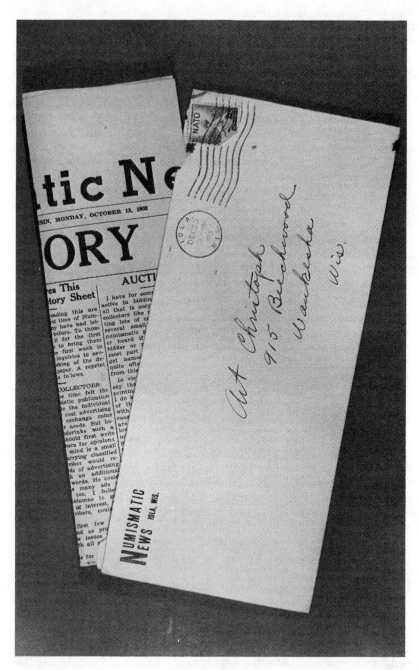

Krause Publications began with a single page of print, an envelope, a stamp and a 600-name mailing list. Working on his mother's dining room table in October 1952, Chet stuffed the envelopes and mailed the first issue of **Numismatic News**. *The rest is, well, history.*

Chapter 1

1952

"The News found its beginning not in a fancy office, but rather on a writing desk in an upstairs bedroom of our home. Our mailing room was on the dining room table."   Chet Krause

In October 1952, a young man named Chester ("just plain Chet") Krause sat at the dining room table in the family home in Iola, Wisconsin. He was writing addresses on envelopes to be stuffed with single sheets of tabloid newsprint: 600 sheets, printed on one side, 600 addresses written by hand. Chet and his mother, Cora, who had volunteered to help so she could have her dining room table back, finished the addresses, sealed the envelopes and stamped them for mailing. It was mechanical, nearly dumb labor, but necessary, since it was also an act of faith. For Chet Krause, sending out the first issue of the newspaper he called *Numismatic News* was an expression of faith in his ideas, his aspirations, and ultimately in himself.

Krause was well-equipped to make a statement of faith in himself. Like all men and women, he was a product of his time and place, and he was doubly fortunate in these two circumstances. In the 1920s and '30s, when Krause was growing up, Iola, Wisconsin, and the farm community surrounding it was a good place for a young man to prepare himself to shape his own future.

Iola was a farm market village of not quite 700 people, tucked into the folds of the gentle glacial hills of east-central Wisconsin. Yankee pioneers had built a water-powered saw and grainmill on the South Branch of the Little Wolf River in the 1850s, and the logging and farm trade it brought stimulated the growth of the village that some say was named after a mythical Indian princess.

Iola was a place of cliches come to life-gabled Victorian houses painted white, barefoot boys with cane poles fishing at the mill pond, retired farmers lounging in the storefronts jawing over last year's news. Visitors told the standard small town jokes about Iola. It was a place so devoid of excitement that the sidewalks were rolled up at night, so isolated that a dog could fall asleep on Main Street at midday and not be disturbed until the cats squealed at night, so unchanging that Rip Van Winkle could awake after a forty-year doze and not know he had been asleep.

The standard jokes fit Iola, as they do other small towns, but they are only part of the basic truth about the place as it was in the 1930s and '40s. Americans have always ridiculed small town life, but they have also relished it and tried to recreate it wherever they settled — in city, suburb, or country. In fact, the traditional values of Iola at mid-20th century were the values that most Americans admired in the middle of the 19th century and that they still uphold in 1992.

Iola was a safe, comfortable, stable place for children, with families close-knit and supportive. Because of the image of rural life as backward and slow, children growing up in Iola were often uncomfortable when they left the community. Many feared that, when judged by standards different from those they had known from birth, they would not measure up. Those who stayed, however, knew they had a place in this world, however small, and that they would be welcomed there.

Iola was an informal, shirt-sleeved community, where folks enjoyed the outdoors. Fishing and baseball, gardening and dancing were more popular than sedentary pastimes such as chess and coin collecting. Iola was a straightforward place that required of its residents a modicum of honesty and good conduct, since lies and other crimes could hardly be hidden. Feedback came quickly in Iola, whether to the boy whose misthrown baseball shattered the neighbor's window or to the merchant who was slow to respond to his customers' complaints.

At the same time, life in Iola taught tolerance for human foibles, since eccentric neighbors might be the only neighbors, and any neighbor was better than none at all. Along with that tolerance came a respect for the opinions of others, no matter how half-baked they appeared to be.

The work ethic was also much in evidence in Iola, and nowhere more so than on the farms-like the Krause place-surrounding the village. Manual labor was just that-work performed by hand and muscle in the farm field and the farm house-and there was plenty of it. No child grew up on a farm near Iola without becoming very familiar with a manure fork, gravel shovel, axe, crosscut saw, pump handle and water bucket. They also learned how to repair machinery that broke down and make do with equipment that was a little bit old, a little bit crotchety, and in constant need of tinkering. The hard times of the Great Depression contrasted sharply with the prosperity that accompanied and followed World War II, but both experiences taught lessons of patience, persistence, and the value of hard work. They also encouraged self-reliance, and the exercise of seat-of-the-pants judgment. There were plenty of Jacks-and-Jills-of-all-trades in Iola, where folks were not raised to rely on experts, since there were so very few experts around.

Despite abundant evidence of their own native abilities, Iola folks were unassuming. Most of them subscribed to the common belief that small town folks were somehow inferior to their big city kin. It is an old myth that still has its adherents in 1992, despite facts to the contrary presented by people like Chet Krause. Iola's values seem shamefacedly innocent to a cynical observer who has not experienced them. But they were, and are, real. To understand the values of mid-century Iola, Wisconsin-family-centered, honest, tolerant, square-dealing, self-reliant, hard working and unassuming Iola-is to understand Chet Krause and his publishing house.

He was born on the family farm a few miles east of the village in the Town of Helvetia. His grandfather, Ludvig, had emigrated from Prussia in 1842, served in the Civil War and tried homesteading in the West, but ended up buying land in Helvetia in the early 1870s. Ludvig Krause was a German living in a township with a Swiss name bounded by Norwegian communities such as Iola and Scandinavia. A few miles west could be found one of the largest Polish settlements in the state, while Yankee, Irish and Danish settlers had occupied the land near Waupaca to the south. The American melting pot did not cook only in the big cities. On market Saturdays in farm communities like Iola-even with its predominantly Norwegian make-up-could be heard the immigrant languages of the Upper Midwest-Polish, German, Swedish, and English in any variety of heavy accents.

Chet's father, Carl, was born on the family farm, and he bought his bride, Cora, there after their marriage in 1910. Like most couples of the time and place, the Krauses had a big family. Five children were born on the old home farm prior to 1923, and the place soon grew too small for the family. Carl and Cora moved their brood about two-and-one-half miles down the road to a farm conveniently located next door to the district school.

Chet Krause, child number six, was born here on Dec.16, 1923. Cora Krause had worked as a teacher prior to her marriage, and she made sure her children were well-prepared when they started classes at the one-room school next door. Carl had made sure the school was well-prepared for his children, since he was the building contractor who supervised its construction.

Carl was an accomplished stonemason who built foundations for houses, barns and schools. He also built the sturdy stone silos that in the 1900s were the symbols of progressive farming, and laid up graceful stone arches for bridges on the improved roadways that marked the outset of the automotive age at about the same time. It was at his father's side that young Chet learned the rudiments of construction work. He mixed mortar, hauled stones, drove nails into 2 x 4s, and acquired organizational skills that served him well in the years to come.

The Great Depression was part of his first memories. The rockbottom farm prices of 1931, the Farm Holiday milk-dumping actions of 1933, the great northern drought and dust storm of 1934, the record heat of the summer of 1936, were witnessed, endured and remembered. For all the real hardship of the Depression years, farmers who remained on their land were spared the worst of the hard times. They might have absolutely no money, but they could raise all the food they needed to eat. A diet heavy in milk, potatoes and home-made bread might not have been very exciting, but it was nutritious. The Krauses, like most of their neighbors, survived the Depression intact.

The election of Franklin Roosevelt as president in 1932 brought hope of better times to all Americans. For Chet Krause, it also helped bring a new interest. Roosevelt was an avid stamp collector. A photograph of the popular president working on his collection brought philately to the nation's consciousness and stimulated interest in numismatics as well. About the same time, the father of his best friend got Chet started in stamps and coins. Collecting was a logical pastime for a thoughtful young man living on a farm near Iola in the 1930s. There wasn't much of anyplace to go and there wasn't any money to spend once he got there anyway.

In the late 1930s, a ritual was established at the Krause home. Carl would come home from work, eat supper and settle into a chair. Chet would inevitably ask to see the coins his dad had in his pockets. Since the Depression was still not over, Carl Krause might not have any coins at all, but when he did, he shared them with his son.

Chet later recalled that "I expect I got interested in the hobby in much the same way as a large percentage of collectors do...I began collecting...as a school boy. At that time we used the old Whitman boards as a housing unit. Perhaps the biggest thrill I got then was finding a 1931-S cent. It was the lone coin in my father's pocket on a Sunday afternoon when I queried him to look at his change. I still have the coin." During quiet evenings at home, and with help from his family, young Chet Krause laid the foundations for his life's work.

Iola itself became part of his everyday life when Chet entered high school there in 1937. In those days it was not automatically assumed that an eighth-grade graduate of a country school, especially a boy, would go to high school. Wisconsin law said that children had to attend school only until age 14 and, until the 1950s, only about one-half of rural school children completed high school. Had Chet stayed at home and farmed, or joined his father in the construction business instead of going to high school, few eyebrows would have been raised outside the family. Within the family, however, there was never any question of Chet's not completing high school. Cora and Carl both believed that their children should finish high school no matter how useful the kids might be on the farm or the building site. Chet was one of a class of twenty to graduate from Iola High in June 1941.

There were no school buses in Iola then, so Chet traveled into the village in a series of jalopies he and his brothers cobbled together and nursed down the road. If the Krauses didn't have a car that ran, some neighbor boys would, and they all crowded together for the ride into school. Like most farm kids, all of the Krause boys were shade-tree mechanics who tinkered with their dads' tractors and his old Model T. In the process, Chet acquired a dirty-knuckled knowledge of mechanics and an affection for old cars that has lasted a lifetime. He also acquired a passion for coin collecting. The family home burned down during his junior year in high school. The blaze incinerated his stamps, but left his coins undamaged. He did not try to replace the stamps or to collect replacements. The lesson of the fire was obvious. His future was not in flammable paper but in durable coin. Many years later, after he established himself in numismatic publishing, he assembled a type collection of United States stamps.

Chet's future was soon put on hold because of World War II. The Japanese attacked Pearl Harbor and other American bases in the Pacific in 1941 about a week before Chet's eighteenth birthday. A little more than a year later and shortly after his nineteenth birthday, Chet was drafted. The United States Army found a place for the mechanically inclined farm boy in the motor pool of the 565th Antiaircraft Battalion.

The 565th was sent to France in December 1944, and took part in the German counterattack on the Allied advance known as the Battle of the Bulge. The unit became part of General George Patton's Third Army and helped defend Patton's headquarters in Luxembourg. After the Germans were turned back, the Third Army went on the offensive and swept across the Rhine.

By the time hostilities halted in May 1945, the 565th was in the Regensburg area of southeastern Germany. His unit did not return home immediately after the shooting stopped so Chet had some leisure time to fill. Not surprisingly, he used his six months stay in Europe in 1945 to travel a bit and, of course, to collect coins. In February 1946, three years after leaving home, he was discharged and came home to Iola.

There he faced the problems of readjustment to civilian life confronting all veterans. Employment was the urgent concern of ex-soldiers in 1946 and fear was genuine that, without the economic stimulus of a war, the United States would slip back into the Depression. The problem was particularly acute and frustrating for people in the building trades. They were ready to work, they had customers ready to build, but materials were nearly impossible to obtain.

The manufacturers of basic materials such as cement, shingles and nails had yet to shift production to meet civilian demand, so even though there were dozens of newly married couples in the Iola area who were willing and able to build new houses, and an equal number of farmers who wanted new barns and sheds, builders such as Carl Krause and his son Chet were hard-pressed to find work. They made do with small remodeling work, but waited for the big jobs that would really put them back in business.

The situation remained tight until 1947, when Chet and his father built a house in Iola. Then they were on their way, as 1948 was a banner year for construction in the Iola area and throughout the United States. Chet was twenty-five years old in '48, an agile young man in his prime who soon acquired a reputation as the fastest framing carpenter in his neck of the woods. Over the next ten years, but especially in the first five, Krause would complete many construction projects, including twenty-five houses and two churches.

For leisure, Chet had his coins. "My favorite uncle gave me a free trip to Europe during World War II. It is since my return my collection really started," he wrote in the first issue of *Numismatic News* in 1952.

He was one of tens of thousands of amateur collectors throughout the United States and Canada. They were people who, as Chet went on to write, were "Far away from the coin clubs, far away from coin shops." There were "thousands of collectors who rarely see another person whose interests are in harmony with his. His collecting is known to only a few and these are not especially interested except that he has so much money."

The words are an accurate description of a man with a passion looking for kindred souls with whom he might share his knowledge and love of coins. They were few and far between in Iola and other small communities. Had he lived in a larger community, Chet probably would have joined one of the approximately 125 coin clubs in the United States and been a regular shopper at his local coin dealer. But he lived in Iola and he wasn't about to move. He did not even belong to the American Numismatic Association, whose 10,000 members relied on *The Numismatist* to learn about coins and collecting. Only occasionally had he read periodicals like *The Numismatic Scrapbook Magazine*, the *Philatelic Press, Hobbies Magazine* and *Rainbow Hobby News*, which were the primary publications then serving the hobby.

None of these periodicals spoke directly to Chet Krause and the thousands of collectors like him. The overwhelming majority, whom Krause correctly identified, learned to live with their isolation. They retreated to their solitary work tables while the rest of the family listened to the parlor radio, occasionally interrupted by a curious youngster with a short attention span. It was with this collector that the man from rural Iola identified; and it was this collector that Chet Krause wanted to reach.

He thought he knew how to do it, too. On the days when construction work was slow, Chet spent a lot of time target shooting with his brother, Neil, and his friend, Jim Dimmock, with whom he also shared an interest in coin collecting. Target shooting was a popular pastime in rural communities like Iola, and the trio was at it quite a lot in the early spring of 1950. Dimmock was a gun collector and he subscribed to a periodical called *Shotgun News*. Founded in 1946, *Shotgun News* ran classified ads for readers who were buying and selling guns, ammunition and other shooting supplies. It had a broad national distribution and reached a handful of readers in a thousand different places like Iola. Isolated fans of shooting sports who bought and sold equipment could reach each other through its pages. Maybe no more than three of the 900 people in Iola read it, but three readers multiplied by the tens of thousands of communities like Iola all across the country added up to a respectable circulation figure. The ability of *Shotgun News* to place the advertising message of one isolated reader in the hands of thousands of others made a strong impression on Chet Krause.

"Jim and I often talked about how enjoyable and rewarding it was for us to have *Shotgun News* available," he recalled. He then made the logical jump. "If such a concept worked for guns...it seemed to us that it could be applied even more perfectly to the coin collecting field."

Here was the means for the coin collector from Iola to end his isolation. He could reach thousands of other people like himself with a specialized publication designed to meet their own specialized needs. A generation later the concept would be called target marketing and it would be the basis for a multibillion dollar advertising industry. For Chet Krause in 1950, it was just seat-of-the-pants common sense, the kind of simple wisdom he had heard at family supper or on Main Street, Iola. What separated Krause from everyone else with an equal share of common sense is that he intended to act on it.

In the way of friends, Chet and Jim chewed over their scheme, always ending the conversation by saying, "...one day we'll give it a try." One day came early in 1952, when Chet said he was ready to take the plunge and asked Jim to jump in too. Dimmock declined.

"As a family man, Jim found constraints on both the time and money that might be required to pursue this goal," said Chet. "No such restraints were present to inhibit me."

There were a few other restraints that might have inhibited him, most notably his total lack of experience in advertising, graphic design, publishing, printing, and distribution. It helped that he did not even know how much he did not know. If he had, he might never have begun.

Begin he did, and in characteristic small-town style. He wrote a letter. Then he rewrote it, and rewrote it again. It was plain, forthright and typically Chet Krause:

Fellow Coin Collectors:

I have for some time felt the need of a numismatic publication that would provide the individual collector with low cost advertising to buy, sell, or exchange coins of their particular needs. But before I would undertake such a project I felt I should first write you as well as others for opinions.

What I have in mind is a small size newspaper carrying classified ads. Each subscriber would receive 20 free words of advertising each month with an additional charge for extra words. He could, however, have as many ads as desired. Dealers too, I believe, could use the columns to good advantage. News of interest, submitted by subscribers, could be passed on also.

However, that is for further discussion. What I would like to know now is, would such a publication be desirable?

Sincerely,

Chester L. Krause

On the Memorial Day weekend of 1952, with an extra day off from work, Chet sat down at the dining room table and addressed 300 envelopes by hand, inserted the letters and mailed them off to "every coin club, every dealer and every collector whose names have come my way during the past years."

Although he was not aware of it, Chet was inventing (for himself at least) the practice of surveying a potential market before investing in production. Market surveys and test marketing of products had not yet become standard practice in American business, but no one had enlightened Chet Krause on the subject. In Iola it was only logical to ask if anyone was interested in an idea before you went through with it. Once again, what Chet didn't know only helped him.

He was also inventing for himself, if for no one else, direct mail marketing. The kind of letter Chet Krause sent out from his mother's dining room table in 1952 would be duplicated by marketing people over and over again in the next forty years. Political candidates, charities, churches, the advocates of countless causes, and vendors of every product from alphabet soup to zirconium jewelry would ultimately flood the mailboxes of America with messages that are only superficially different from Chet's homespun note.

The response he got would have been more discouraging if Chet had known that for a direct mail solicitation to be called a success, it had to garner a significant percentage of positive responses. As it happened, "Several rather anxious days passed and then I began to receive answers. As I recall, the answers were not great in number, but most encouraging." Although it was not the tidal wave of support he hoped for, the response was enough to keep his enthusiasm afloat. "Thus plans began to take physical shape in preparing an introductory sheet."

The few pieces of return mail he received in response to his testing-of-the-waters note helped the would-be publisher keep his feet wet. He was also aided by a change in newspaper publishing that had begun earlier, but had not really spread across the country until after World War II. Free circulation papers, or shoppers, that contained only ads and no editorial material were popping up in communities large and small throughout the land.

Iola had yet to have one in 1952, but it would in a few years. The shopper, usually printed on a tabloid sheet, delivered ads and nothing more, thus sparing advertisers and readers the expense of an editorial staff. It dispensed with the conventional newspapering philosophy that people only looked at ads accidentally, that they really wanted to read the articles. As it turned out, in community after community all across the country, people were quite happy to pick up a tabloid devoid of news and full of ads, and advertisers were happy to support it. The shopper, along with radio and television news and advertising, profoundly changed newspapering in the United States, and put many small-town weeklies out of business.

Although Chet had no plans to put anyone out of business, he was proposing a fundamental change in hobby publishing built on the shopper concept. He hoped that, just as the publishers of local shoppers were finding readers who did not need news articles, he could find collectors who did not need to read feature articles about coins. Other periodicals could supply the news and features, Krause would give readers a place to buy and sell coins.

"...this publication will not carry too many feature writeups and so on. We have several publications in this field already that are doing a marvelous job," he wrote. He did want feedback, so he also declared that "...the columns of this paper are open to any news, comments, feature articles, announcements or any other news matter that subscribers care to submit."

The annals of business are full of prescriptions for success, many of which apply to Chet Krause. "Find a niche and fill it," says one expert. "Find a need and meet it," says another. "Look for the itch and scratch it," says yet another. Chet expressed the same ideas differently when he talked about those "thousands of collectors who rarely see another person whose interests are in harmony with his.... This collector has been neglected." They would be neglected no more, thanks to Chet Krause and his *Numismatic News*.

The first issue of the new paper left Cora Krause's dining room table in October 1952. It was that single tabloid sheet, printed on only one side, sent to a mailing list of 600, in which Chet stated his editorial creed:

"It will be through the columns of this paper that all collectors will have an opportunity to trade and correspond with one another from coast to coast. We shall be able to buy or sell or trade with collectors who have duplicated accumulations, etc. which they would gladly part with to get hold of something they might add to their collections."

He also included a detailed description of how the process would work. He would publish two more free issues and he invited "...all collectors to place at least one free ad...as many as you like...." Ads received would be classified in four categories: For Sale, Wanted, For Trade, and For Sale or For Trade. Right from the beginning Chet realized that some method of organization was essential. It didn't mean much at first, but the concept would prove to be invaluable as the paper grew.

Chet was also setting up a system based on customer response and he took pains to explain how it should work. "Upon reading an ad that interests you," he continued, "write the party, ask if the coin you want is still available. If it is, he will then write you to forward your money and (or) merchandise, he will then ship you your coin.... It is just good sense that the person making a proposed deal send his merchandise or money first." Here was the basic ground rule for buying/selling/trading by mail, one that answered the initial question: Who goes first? It is deceptively simple common sense, but without it the whole system, and *Numismatic News*, could not function.

Yet another component of what would become standard practice for Krause publications was present at the beginning, i.e., giving something away. In 1952, it was two free issues and free classified ads. In years to come, Krause would give away coins, medals and other premiums in order to build circulation. Chet was aware of and utilized this basic marketing motivator at the very start.

Chet also addressed the display advertisers whose support was vital if the *News* was to become a working newspaper. He offered "... to the dealers who feel they too would like to accept...free advertising...4 inches in one column." Ads at no charge were only fair, since Chet was publishing a paper that might have no readers. However, after the first two free issues were out, display ads would cost 70 cents a column inch.

The entire system, for both classified and display advertisers, was based on honesty. As Sears and Montgomery Ward had been pointing out since the 1880s, mail order buying and selling was popular, especially in rural areas. It was another concept with which the man from Iola was familiar and ready to adopt. In 1952, however, mail order also had an unsavory air about it, similar to sales pitches on late night television in 1992. Isolated consumers, like folks in Iola, were vulnerable and had to be careful. With that seemingly inherent understanding that he brought to his work, Chet addressed the problem right at the start.

He declared that "most people are honest, at least I have found it that way," and "...this paper is endeavoring to carry ads from honest collectors and dealers. The fly by night dishonest and unethical advertisers will be refused space. We shall always be on the alert for these people. It will be with your help that their ads are not printed."

Again, right from the start, Chet was announcing a principle that would remain a part of his operation. It was the basic commitment to honesty and plain dealing with which he was raised. It was also plain common sense. If readers could not trust the ads in *Numismatic News*, why should they read them and why should the paper continue to publish?

Chet also asked for subscriptions, which included a free 20-word classified ad each month and would cost $2. They would start in January 1953, after everyone on the mailing list received two free issues. After forty years of inflation, a $2 subscription to any publication seems like a steal, but even in the era of nickel Cokes, *Numismatic News* was a bargain. Chet had little idea of what it would actually cost to produce and distribute a regular newspaper. In deciding on the subscription price, he estimated what he thought would sell in Iola. If it worked there, it would work anywhere in the United States. And it did.

Finally, Chet introduced himself. He started with that simple five-word declaration that says more about the man than a carload of verbiage.

"I am just plain Chet.

"...a man who is from an isolated community.... He is only a collector and has long felt the need of a paper such as this. His interests are your interests. He is not a printer or a coin dealer. In fact, I am only a carpenter...."

He may have been "just plain Chet," the carpenter from Iola, but he had obviously thought a great deal about how to operate a newspaper, run a mail order business and deal with people. The basic operating principles that have guided Krause Publications for forty years can be found in the single page of the first issue of *Numismatic News*.

Not quite forty years later, in the late 1980s, one of America's best-selling books was titled "All I Really Need to Know I Learned in Kindergarten." Chet Krause could have written that book, but he would have had to change the title. His book title would read, "All I Really Need to Know I Learned In Iola." Firmly rooted in the values he learned living in a small community in rural Wisconsin, Chet Krause was ready to shape his future.

Chapter 2

1953

*"This paper is really and truly a publica-
tion by a collector, for the collector."*
Chet Krause

Forty people succumbed to Chet's initial sales pitch for subscriptions to *Numismatic News*. These brave souls, Krause Publications' first paying customers, received their starting issue in January 1953. Chet consoled himself with the thought that forty was better than none and remembered what he learned on the construction site: Even the biggest house begins with only a pocketful of nails. As a magnet to lure more readers, he enlarged his original mailing list and sent an additional 2000 copies to potential subscribers.

The January issue ran six pages, four of which were advertising. Among the classifieds were listings from Oregon's Robert Zucher, who was still advertising forty years later, and South Dakota's Arnold Thorsen, who suggested that Chet join the American Numismatic Association, which he soon did. Display advertisers who would become regular customers were Melvin E. Came, John J. Smies, Copley Coin, Byron Cook, Paul Slosson, Pete Forester, Carl Curcio, Philip Rosenbaum, Andy Scott, Hesperia Art, Thomas J. Settle, "Buffalo" Bill Behringer, Norman Shultz, and Mike Kolman's Federal Coin Exchange.

A reader had asked Chet, "Why did you start a publication openly admitting no professional connection with numismatics?" He responded with the proverb about "fools rushing in where angels fear to tread," and then continued to rush into fearsome places.

He proved it in January by publishing what he called the first standard statement of coin grading and the first results of a mail auction. Chet had announced his attention to publish both in the very first issue of the *News*.

"I would like to set up some standard as far as the grading of coins goes. It would be printed in each issue. If any of you would like to submit such a system or suggestions along this line it would be greatly appreciated."

Here is the self-confessed, non-professional, isolated collector expressing the reality of the hobby as he had known it.

Without a uniform, understandable grading system, how could an individual gauge the quality of his collection? How could he buy, sell or trade with other collectors he had never met? If Chet had spent a lot of time with other collectors, this issue would have been no less valid, but it might have been less important to a new publisher. However, he was the man from Iola who needed to know that the standards he judged his coins by were identical to the standards used in Boothbay, Maine, and Bodega Bay, California.

In January 1953, he announced "...a standard grading system. Beginning in this issue is the nucleus for just that. It has always been our idea that everyone would be very receptive to a standard for which to grade coins, but heretofore no one has ventured towards that goal."

Chet ventured.

He based his grading system on two assumptions. "First that collectors like coins to be graded into five or six grades rather than a dozen. Second, that most dealers use only a general grading system rather than one for each individual series. Therefore, we have used first a general picture for grading and second comments on each series or design of coin."

He listed seven grades, or, what are more accurately called statements of condition: Proof (Pr), Uncirculated (Unc.), Extra Fine (XF), Fine (F), Very Good (VG), Good (G), and Fair (Fa). He also added special notes to help collectors judge the condition of several type series including the Mercury dime, Lincoln cent, and the Standing Liberty quarter.

The new system would meet several goals. As Chet wrote, it was intended "...to be used by the advertisers of this publication." All traders would then presumably be talking the same language. A Washington apple would not be confused with a Florida orange. Since Chet's goal was to serve the thousands of amateur collectors who, like himself, might not be fully knowledgeable about coins, his insistence on a standard grading system was, once again, plain common sense. So, it becomes obvious that, right at the beginning, when he had no more than forty subscribers, Chet was creating an operation that would serve more than twice 40,000, as it ultimately did.

The grading system would keep buyers and sellers talking straight. It would also "provide for the junior collector a guide as to the condition of a coin he desires." The hobby had grown considerably in the postwar years. Chet recognized it and hoped his grading system would make it easier for beginners, young and old, to understand their hobby. This was also the self-taught former farm kid speaking, who in his mind's eye may have seen a kid nuts about coin collecting, but baffled about how to do it well. A simple, universal grading system would make it easier.

The system had not sprung fully born from Chet's head. Those who examined it would "...readily discover that it is more or less very similar to that of a reputable dealer. We have not tried to change the grading system of coins to any great extent, but tried to standardize the grading set forth by dealers. In preparing this grading system we have selected information from all dealers' lists that were available, information that has been recorded by prominent numismatists, and comments that were sent direct to us by the readers of this publication."

He also admitted his own lack of expertise and invited comments. "It would indeed be vain to hope that this grading system was perfect in every detail. As somewhat of a junior in the field of numismatics, we do not profess to be an authority on this subject, only a melting pot for the ideas put before us...we are not trying to set up any dictatorial power or pressure, but to aid in the improving of the coin collecting world as a whole.

"To the best of our knowledge there is no other publication that carries a standard in which to grade coins, but we will welcome any that are set forth by them, or any coin group, or dealers organizations that are endeavoring to accomplish the same ideal as we are, 'Better dealer-collector relations.'"

As the facilitator of those improved relations, *Numismatic News* would position itself in the center of the coin trading network.

Chet jeopardized his own relations with some dealers by publishing auction results. He committed himself to full disclosure of auction prices in his first issue and never stepped back. His commitment was based on his own experience.

"I have for some time been quite active in bidding auctions. After all, that is only one of the ways collectors like myself have in getting lots of coins. I have bid on several small auctions listed in numismatic papers and have never heard if I was a successful bidder or not. I believe for the most part these are only ads to get names for mailing lists as quite often I would receive lists from this or that dealer."

The square-dealer from Iola was understandably unhappy to be manipulated and disappointed when he could not obtain the coins he had bid on in good faith.

So in the first issue of the *News* he made it clear to his readers, "...if you would like to advertise auctions, go ahead. But if I hear any complaints, further ads will be rejected." And he promised to publish lists of results.

Later on, when commenting on his negative experiences with small auctions, he wrote, "The fact is I'd like to see every auction [large or small] publish a result list, it not only furnishes proof of good faith, but is a handy reference for future bids."

"To get to the bottom of this let me first explain my stand," he answered his critics. "An auction is a 'Public Sale.' Now at a true public sale all bidders are at hand and have the right to increase their bids to any extent they desire. In the case of coin auctions, the bidders are all mail bidders or at least in part mail bidders...they have no way of hearing or examining the bids. I maintain they have every right to expect a result list. It not only furnishes proof of good faith but is a handy reference on future bidding...an auction establishes the true selling price of a coin. I mean that at auction a coin is actually sold. On fixed price lists coins are only offered for sale, whether they sell or not one never knows, unless he is the one offering them."

Therefore, Chet had concluded that he had "...more or less established the fact that I would not be favorable to printing auctions not furnishing a result list."

Some dealers objected to Chet's position. They pointed out that printing auction results required space in the newspaper and space in the newspaper cost money.

Growing up in Iola, Chet learned that integrity did not come free or even cheap. He responded to auctioneer concerns about costs by saying that "...many auction dealers have taken exception to my statement, and have pointed out that the cost of such a result list would prove too expensive to make auction sales profitable.

"Therefore this paper is going to print all result lists of auctions published free, as a service to the readers. It shall be mandatory of all those publishing auctions to furnish us with this information."

The policy became permanent as of January 1953. In that issue Chet published the headline, "Auction Results." The sole listing reported on Mail Auction Number 76, held by the Numismatic Gallery, Beverly Hills, California. It listed prices of 22 lots of coins sold the previous December. A precedent was set for the entire hobby. Those isolated collectors sending in auction bids could now see how close they were to the final selling price. They could learn how to bid accurately and how to assess the value of their own and other collections. In addition, much of the suspicion was removed from auction sales. It was harder for someone who did not send in the highest bid to claim foul play. With this cloud removed, the sky was cleared for more auction sales.

Changing the terminology also helped. The practice of referring to mail sales of coins as "auctions" was common in the early 1950s. *Numismatic News* gradually dropped the term and started calling them "mail bids" or "mail bid sales," and the practice passed into common usage in coin collecting and other hobbies as well.

Chet had also shown that honesty and persistence pay off, and not just in Iola. His newspaper soon became known as the regular publisher of mail bid sales results, and collectors who wanted to read them were soon buying and reading the *News,* and more of them everyday.

Many of those new readers were in Canada. Chet had rightly reasoned that many Canadian collectors were as isolated as any in the United States and fit into the "neglected" category of people he wished to serve. Also, many Americans collected Canadian coins and would also read his new "North of the Border" column.

The *News* broadened its coverage further beyond the borders of the United States in October when it published its first full-page ad. Felix Chruszcz of Hamburg, West Germany purchased the page to market ancient Greek and Roman coins.

As the full page ad would indicate, the *News* was getting larger. April saw the first eight-page issue. In November came the first ten-pager. It was packed with thirty-seven display ads and 301 classified ads — "more than all other numismatic publications combined" — as Chet was happy to announce.

He closed his first full year as a publisher with a number of positive accomplishments. He had established a standard grading system for coins; determined that mail bid sale advertisers had to publish the results of their sales; expanded coverage to regularly include news of Canadian coins and collecting; and built the largest classified advertising section of any numismatic publication.

They were all justifiable sources of pride. Chet had proved early on that he would take a controversial stand if he thought it would best serve his readers. As it turned out, his best was excellent. However, taking an editorial position, no matter how worthy or controversial, is the easy part of publishing and something that many novices do very well. What Chet had yet to prove was that his ideas would survive in the marketplace. For if the *News* could not stand on its own financial legs, it would be nothing more than an expensive hobby for a man who made his living as a small town carpenter.

As Chet later recalled, "The first year and a half was not a profitable or well organized business venture...the bridges were many and crossing difficult...."

Kinda strong for cleaning coins ain't it.

*Ed Rochette's first "Numismapest" cartoon appeared in the July 1954 issue of **Numismatic News**. One of Krause's first editorial staffers, Rochette went on to pursue a distinguished career in numismatic journalism. In hiring Rochette, Chet established the policy of finding hobby experts and keeping them on staff at all his publications.*

Chapter 3

1954

*"Always do right. This will gratify some
people, and astonish the rest."*
                              Mark Twain

The year began with the *News* crossing more bridges but making easier
passages. The January issue contained not one but three two-page ads.
Chicago's R. Green and two New Yorkers-Coin Galleries and Thomas J. Set-
tle-each purchased a "double truck," as two-page spreads were dubbed in
those days.

Editorial content was also improving. The *News* had started printing illustrations in 1953. The first image was a graphic of a coin holder in an ad purchased by Roy A. Miller of Racine, Wisconsin. The first photo of a coin
appeared soon after. It was not until February 1954 that an originally commissioned photo appeared in the News. Chet's brother Neil jury-rigged a photo
board out of desk lamps, strapped his trusty Leica to a home-made mount and
shot a photo of (what else?) a coin. Neil used the Krause family living room
for a studio, thereby presenting further proof that the *News* was growing. It
was now claiming space in the living room as well as Chet's bedroom and
Cora's dining room.

In the early 1950s, printing by means of offset lithography had yet to be
developed. The letterpress, which used ink spread on raised type to transfer
words to paper, was still in its heyday. Photo reproduction was difficult and

expensive, and most newspapers-large and small-restricted the number and size of photos they used. Consequently, Chet's decision to print any photo no matter what its source, was a step more significant than it might seem in 1992. Printing a photo was another way for the *News* to show that it was becoming a real newspaper.

The actual typesetting and printing of the paper took place at the shop of Firman Cooper's *Iola Herald*. A weekly newspaper with its own print shop was common in small towns in the 1950s, and the friendly presence of the *Herald's* staff eased the birth of the *News*. Chet was working with people he had known for many years, such as typesetters Bill Cooper, Dick Munson and Dolly Hoffman, press operator Toby Aasen, and Firman Cooper himself, always busy and always chomping on a half-smoked cigar. Were he starting a newspaper in 1992, Chet would have had to travel out of the village to find a printer and the atmosphere might not have been so nurturing to a neophyte.

The *Herald* set type on an old-fashioned hot lead Linotype machine. The operator sat at a keyboard similar to that of a typewriter and punched out an article just like a typist. The Linotype keys, however, were connected to a set of dies that cast the letters, reversed, on a lead slug from molten metal. The slugs-one line at a time-were then fed into a form which made up a metallic image of the final page-in reverse. The ability to read words backwards was part of the printer's art in those days, but it is now as obsolete as the Linotype itself.

The Linotype had been around since the late 1880s, and was a quantum improvement over the traditional method of setting type by hand. It had revolutionized the reproduction of the printed word in the 1890s in much the same fashion as computers would in the 1980s. The clanking machines whose mechanical music had been the hymn of publishing for seventy years had all but created the great age of the mass-circulation newspaper and the general interest magazine. That age was coming to an end in the 1950s. Radio, which was already established; television, which was starting to penetrate even small town markets in 1953 and would soon dominate mass communication throughout the world; and specialized print media such as *Numismatic News* and other Krause publications, would inherit the audience once claimed by *Collier's*, The *Saturday Evening Post* and countless big city newspapers. So it was appropriate that the Linotype was around to help launch Krause Publications.

It was needed, too, for in March 1954 the *News* had grown to 18 pages and would have to be printed in two sections. The *Herald's* equipment could handle sections no larger than 16 pages. Whenever more pages were needed, they had to be printed in two or more smaller sections, which were then folded together for mailing. By September the *News* would hit 24 pages and grow beyond the means of the *Herald* print shop. The old hand-fed flatbed press couldn't turn out papers fast enough, so Chet took his printing to the more modern plant of the Waupaca Publishing Company, located 13 miles away down Highway 49 at the county seat.

Pre-press work, where decisions about content and layout were made, remained in Iola. Weighty trays of lead type were made up at the *Herald,* then loaded into a pick-up truck for delivery to the printer. Pre-press work has always been done in Iola, although, as the company grew, typesetting has been occasionally contracted out, almost exclusively for most of ten years from the late '50s to the late '60s. Improved technology has made it easier for pre-press work to be performed in editorial offices in out-of-the-way places, but in the old days the *News* was doing it the hard way-and still succeeding. And that success would foster the growth of the entire company. Also, although it was still young, the *News* was already showing signs that it would outstrip its Iola roots and, if it was to stay, would ask the community to grow with it.

New growth was certainly evident in the mailroom of the *News.* March 1954 was the last issue to be prepared for mailing on Cora Krause's dining room table. As Chet told his readers, "This month (February) has marked the opening of a small office to be used exclusively in connection with this publication and will, after March 1st, have a full time employee in it. This together with the time yours truly will spend here, should help in giving you the best."

Chet had taken the step that was an essential sign of progress for a home-grown business. He had moved downtown to an office he would share with Iola insurance man Leland Johnson. The two budding businessmen split the rent and the salary of their first employee, Lila Aasen Aanstad. Johnson paid the rent. Chet paid Aanstad. A few months later, Alice Wolberg also came to work as a part-time receptionist for the *News.*

The editorial staff also grew in the summer of 1954. A young fellow from Worcester, Massachusetts, named Ed Rochette saw his first cartoon published in the July issue. Rochette's graphic comments on numismatics were soon titled "The Numismapest" which became a regular feature of the paper.

Rochette would become one of Chet's first full-time employees and he set a precedent for accomplishment that would take him to the position of executive director of the American Numismatist Association. In 1954, he was just starting out and was impressed with what was happening in Iola.

In a 1991 interview, Rochette reminisced that "*Numismatic News* played an important part in bringing to the attention of the average collector that he was not alone in collecting coins-that it was a hobby thousands like him shared.

"The *News* made collectors aware that they did not necessarily have to belong to the elite clubs of the day; that their collections could be just penny boards and folders, that this was a hobby that welcomed paupers as well as princes."

Committing the *News* to making a payroll, even to free-lancers like Rochette, was another statement of progress. It was also a sign of a new confidence Chet was feeling about his whole publishing venture. The first eighteen months had been rough for the carpenter who, as he admitted, "had never been exposed to the rigors of publishing and printing." In that time he had taken the first steps towards wisdom by learning how much he did not know. By June 1954, two years after he had sent his letter to fellow collectors, he had been exposed to the rigors of publishing and he had mastered quite a few of them. The amount he did not know had been considerably reduced.

When he looked into the future now he could see *Numismatic News* as a stable, growing entity. He had lost $1,432 in the first twenty months of operation. It represented a considerable chunk of the wages he had earned the hard way- by mixing mortar, driving nails and running a small business-but he was not disappointed at the loss. Instead, he viewed it as the fee he had to pay in order to learn the ropes of publishing. It was an investment in the future, not a sign of failure. This realization marked a turning point, the most important point since his decision to get started at all. Now he took steps to ensure that his vision of stability and growth would materialize.

In the June 1954 issue he wrote, "This, our 21st issue of the *Numismatic News*, represents somewhat of a turning point with us. When we began nearly two years ago to play with the idea of turning the *News* into a reality, many questions confronted us. As we had never had any experience with publishing or mail contact, it was our belief that if we failed we must have a security for those brave enough to trust subscriptions with us." Here is the square-dealer from Iola talking.

"At that time," he continued, "we felt that it would be to our advantage to encourage only one year subscriptions so that we could feel the willingness of our subscribers to renew within our second year, rather than the third or fourth year. We would like here to thank our subscribers for the support and confidence they have given us through their first subscription and later renewing their subscription.

"In view of this we are making effective immediately these new subscription rates: one year $2.00; two years $3.50; three years $5.00. We are offering these new and cheaper rates as we now feel we are definitely in the field to stay....

"It may also be of news to our advertisers that we are in the process of adjusting our advertising rates, so that we can offer contract space to you."

Long-term survival in publishing, and other businesses, depends on long-term stability. By building a stable subscription list, Chet could deliver a dependable market to advertisers, who could then reciprocate by becoming regular advertisers. Chet had made the intellectual jump from thinking about publishing on an issue-by-issue basis to thinking of publishing as a continuing process. Ironically, thinking six, twelve or thirty-six issues down the line actually made the production of each individual issue easier. For example, once he built his list, he could tell advertisers the minimum number of readers the *News* would have in, say, six months, and they could place advertising accordingly. Knowing how many advertisers he would have down the line gave him a handle on how big the paper might be and what his cash situation would be like. With his offer of long-term subscriptions and long-term ad contracts, Chet showed how much he had learned.

He was still doing a balancing act, though. He still had to deliver the readers to the advertisers, and the advertisers to the readers, then keep them all happy.

Keeping them happy was not always easy. The auction controversy flared again in the fall of '54, when both bidders and auctioneers were failing to live up to their commitments. Sellers were complaining that high bidders were not completing their purchases as promised and were ignoring follow-up requests. Readers were complaining that promised auction results were not appearing in the *News.* Chet was in the middle so he decided to treat both sides equally.

"We would hate to have to cancel subscriptions to bum bidders," he wrote in September 1954.

In October, he reported on "...a matter we have slipped up on. Guess we trusted or failed to impress our advertisers to the fact that when an auction is listed in our columns they are to furnish results lists of said auction for publication in a future issue. These results lists are published free as a service to our readers. In any event we have up until now trusted that these results have been sent to us, and were quite surprised when in the month of September we began to get letters wondering why certain results had never been published...."

"In some cases we have purposefully held up new ads because we felt those results were due our readers, and wanted to have the situation aired first...." This was a courageous act for a struggling publisher who was still building houses in order to put bread on his own table. He was, in effect, putting off paying customers. However, Chet had committed himself to publishing auction results. His integrity was on the line and he wouldn't compromise. As it turned out, the honest course was also the right course. Readers came to trust auctions advertised in the *News,* and auction sellers could feel confident that bidders would pay for their purchases.

He resolved the immediate question in the fall of '54 and kept his advertisers by announcing, "...inasmuch as we are a bit late in informing auction advertisers that certain results were delinquent, it is our intention to accept future ads from them as long as results of these new auctions are furnished, and we shall strive to obtain results that have not previously been published."

A simple record-keeping process was established to make the system work, since "...all complaints, no matter how minor, [had to] be investigated....

"It was a simple matter to check and see whether a certain party had previously been complained about or had previously complained. Too, all correspondence pertaining to the situation was at hand for quick reference."

In 1988, Chet reflected on the outcome of the 1954 controversy. "We developed the first code of ethics in the hobby," he said.

Another small-town boy who made a big splash in publishing would have agreed with the man from Iola. "Always do right," as Mark Twain said. "This will gratify some people, and astonish the rest." Chet astonished a few, gratified many, and did right. Therein lay his success.

The U. S. Treasury's decision to close the San Francisco Mint in 1955, and postpone the release of 1955-dated Franklin fifty-cent pieces until 1956, stimulated interest in coins and collecting. What was good for the hobby was good for Krause Publications. Circulation swelled and **Numismatic News** *doubled its page count in this period.*

Chapter 4

1955

*"...we have gotten back up where we can
see daylight again, and have obtained
many a new friend both by mail and personal contact and have learned the hard
way about the publishing business and the
people who make up this great country of
ours."* Chet Krause

The most interesting news of 1955 came not from Iola, but from the federal mints. The San Francisco mint closed, thereby ending a decades-old
link to the California gold rush of 1849. Even before it halted operations, San
Francisco, and the Denver mint as well, had not produced any 1955 half-dollars. Philadelphia had struck halves that year, but they were not issued until
the summer of 1956.

Most people take coinage for granted. It is a constant of civilized life, and
any variation from a constant makes news. The closing of the San Francisco
mint, the reduction in the number of halves, and the postponement of Philadelphia's 1955 issue of half-dollars focused attention on coins and collecting.
After reading a news article, or watching a TV news spot, that pointed out
how 1955 halves, and all coins with a San Francisco mint mark, were going to
be more valuable, more folks took a different attitude toward the change in
their pockets. An increasing number of them realized that a penny could do

more than just buy three sticks of licorice, and that the right dime could be traded for more than a big bottle of Dr. Pepper.

This discovery was good news for the hobby. The *News,* with its hospitable approach to neophyte and amateur collectors, was the first place many new hobbyists turned for information about coins. Page counts grew throughout the year as the paper filled with auction results and classified ads. New readers were signing on because they wanted the information on coin quality and pricing that the *News* supplied.

Coin price guides were rare in 1955, and the auction results printed in the *News* constituted a market report that was as up-to-date as possible. Collectors could see what their coins were selling for throughout the country and keep track of where prices had been and where they were heading. *Numismatic News* was becoming the *Wall Street Journal* of the coin market and, thanks to its down-to-earth editorial voice, did it without intimidating readers. Quite to the contrary, a raw beginner could pick up the paper, feel comfortable with it, and see how he could learn from it.

The February 1955 issue hit 36 pages in three sections and the April issue hit 40 pages. By the end of the year, the *News* would have 4,100 subscribers and the press run would cross the 5,700 mark.

In three years, the readership of the paper that Chet had started with the hope "that maybe 200 or 300 collectors might like my idea of a collector's publication," had multiplied 100 fold. The 40 paid subscribers of January 1953 had become the 4,100 of January 1956.

The year was a period of grueling production work in which Chet and his little staff developed the process of turning out a newspaper on a regular basis. The attitude behind the Krause motto, "On time, every time," was developed in the tiny office on Main Street, the shop of the *Iola Herald* and in Chet's home at night. It was hard, but exciting too, as each trip to the post office brought more subscription orders, more ads and more auction results to fill more pages of newsprint.

Exciting or not, the work was not without its toll. As Chet told his readers, "...your publisher is just another fellow like yourself, a builder by trade, his days are spent swinging a hammer....Rainy and rough days are spent on the *News,* along with most evenings and weekends."

Chet was still working full-time as a builder, then working more than full-time as a publisher. The paper had already outgrown its first printer and needed more office space as well. It also needed a publisher who could devote all his working time and energy to it. The time was approaching for Chet to make a choice. He would have to lay down his hammer or lay off the *News.*

Chapter 5

1956

*"All in all it has been and still is a most
interesting line of endeavor and it is our
sincere hope that we shall through continued growth be able to give you a paper
that you will honor and trust."*

Chet Krause

Chet was a builder. He was also a publisher who needed a bigger office. It was logical that he would want to build his own office. However, the press of work for both jobs meant he spent much of 1956 trying to figure out when Chet the builder would find time to work for Chet the publisher.

"Our office consists of one room, 12' x 14', which houses all records, offices etc. We anticipate a new office this summer...." he optimistically announced in the issue of February 1956.

In the meantime, page counts and press runs for the *News* continued to grow. March ran 52 pages in four sections. July had a 7,000 press run with 5,800 subscribers. In six months the paper had acquired 1,700 new subscribers, an increase of roughly 25 percent. All of those new names and addresses had to be recorded, the dates noted when the subs started and expired, and stencils for the addressing machine typed and loaded. All of this work was performed by what had become a three-person circulation department.

They also made up the advertising department, kept track of new classified and display ads, and did a little sales work when they could. Auction sale ads were printed, records kept of whether or not the results were submitted, and then those results had to be made ready to print. Editorial material had to be collected and assessed for inclusion in the paper.

And there were always more classifieds, more display ads, more auction results. The October issue required 56 pages and the November issue needed 60. The paper contained so many ads that Chet decided even he needed an index to keep them straight, and so did his readers. By the end of the year, this feature, which became standard for Krause periodicals, was in the paper.

About the only part of building a new office Chet could find time for was the purchase of property for it. By November, with winter coming, he was forced to postpone the project until the spring of 1957.

"We have made mention of the fact that we are anticipating building an office building to house our business," he wrote. "As key materials did not arrive we will not begin construction of it until the weather permits next Spring, but it's a definite step in our future plans. This should represent another first for us as I do not believe a building has ever been built to primarily house a numismatic publication...."

Chet had already acquired the habit of recording at least one *first* for every year he was in business and it was obvious what the *first* for '57 was destined to be. Less obvious is that it was also destined to be the last building Chet Krause ever built.

After he drove the last nail for his office building on the corner of Water and Washington Streets in Iola, Chet hung up his carpenter's hammer. Choosing publishing over building was the most important decision of his life and one that he never regretted.

Chapter 6
1957

"On time, every time."   Chet Krause

Chet considered his new office building to be "a guarantee of what we feel is a permanent entrance into the field" of publishing. It had taken five years for that guarantee of permanence to appear. Five years is the period of time in which the standard wisdom says that a business destined to fail will fail. The *News* hadn't failed and it didn't look as if it was going to fail.

Like the paper, Chet didn't look like a failure, either. He had just about completed the transition from amateur collector and professional carpenter to numismatic publisher. It was a path well trod by others who had turned a pastime into a business. Robert Frost, the poet of the American countryside, gave words to the process when he wrote that he wanted to "make of his avocation, a vocation." That is, he wanted to turn his hobby into his life's work. Many people share that aspiration; few realize it. One who did was Chet Krause.

The *News* couldn't wait for Chet to complete his transition. Early in 1957, the office moved out of its 12 x 14 - foot shared quarters to take up residence in an abandoned dairy bar across the street. It remained there until the weather turned and Chet could finish building a better home for his paper.

The first issue out of the old dairy bar was a record 64 pages and five sections thick. It weighed more than a half pound, thereby exceeding the post office's limit for third class rates. To keep the postage bill tolerable, Chet split the paper into two mailings. Many readers thought they were receiving an incomplete paper at first, and were still unhappy when the second part arrived late. It was only human nature for a reader to presume that the ad he really wanted to see was in the section that came late. It was also human nature for that reader to overlook the fact that although he was receiving a lot more newspaper, his subscription charge had not increased.

Throughout the summer Chet concentrated on building when he was not putting out more and bigger newspapers. The August 1957 press run hit 8,500 and Chet took the opportunity to tell his readers about the building project.

"Our new office is progressing nicely and we hope to occupy it sometime the last of August. This building will represent the second which has been built during the past months to aid in the requirement of numismatic publishing. My good friends, the Hewitt Brothers of the *Numismatic Scrapbook* in Chicago, have recently built an addition to their plant and added more equipment to better handle their needs."

Chet's new shop was about twice as large as his original office, but it was still far from palatial. With 400 square feet of space, it was about the size of a small two-car garage. Even so, squeezing two of the big boats that were popular in the automotive world in those days into a 20 x 20 - foot slot would have been challenging. Of course, Chet didn't have to park cars in his new office; all he and his staff had to do was put out a newspaper.

The September 1957 issue marked the end of Chet's career as a carpenter. Although no one would ever again hire him to pick up a hammer or a trowel, his experience as a builder was great training for publishing.

"A lot of my success later was due to my experience in the carpentry business, because you've got to deal effectively with people. You've got to hire people, be organized, have the necessary materials and equipment on hand. We had to be organized and on time. I had good production abilities."

Those good production abilities had sustained him for five years and would enable him to meet the new challenges of a growing operation. Chet and his staff, Ruth Bestul and Carolyn Rice Halverson, moved into their new quarters on the corner of Water and Washington Streets in the heart of Iola on Sept. 17, 1957.

Once he had more room, Chet had to expand his staff. Art Christoph had been Chet's unofficial guide to the Milwaukee coin world since 1950. He had taken part in the initial planning for the *News* in 1951 and '52. After the *News* was up and running, Chet still met Art at coin shows in Milwaukee. On one of these trips in 1957, Art mentioned that he had been laid off from work. Chet told him to come up to Iola where there was an opening in the advertising department of the News.

It was more than just an opening. Art would become the paper's first advertising manager and an integral part of Krause Publications for three decades. "Art has been a part of active numismatics for several years," Chet said in an introductory note in the *News*. "He will add to our organization another source of numismatic information." Art spent the rest of his working life with Krause and did not leave until his retirement in 1987.

The *News* closed out its fifth year of life by taking another important step. Printing was shifted to the Worzalla Publishing Company in Stevens Point. Worzalla was a printer of Polish-language periodicals, as well as a manufacturer and binder of books. It had the equipment to produce tabloids as thick as 64 pages without splitting them into separate sections. Those fat issues of the *News* would now go out in one piece that was much less likely to come apart in the mail.

Worzalla was the largest printer with whom Chet had ever dealt. The Stevens Point operation was a heavy volume shop with a lot of commercial clients from all over the country. Press time was scheduled tight and locked in place. A customer whose material was not ready when it was scheduled to go on the press had to wait, sometimes for weeks, before another opening turned up. By the end of 1957, Chet and his staff were no strangers to deadlines, but meeting the schedule for press time at Worzalla added to the pressure of getting a paper out on time. A misstep could knock the entire publication out of kilter.

The pressure to meet a cliff-hanger deadline, and then do it again and again, proved to be good discipline for the people who put out the *News*. After five years, they were ready for it and they met the deadlines for the three-and-a-half years that the *News* was printed at Worzalla. The pressure also gave birth to another Krause slogan. "On time, every time" became the watchword of the operation in 1957 because there was no other way.

Chet, Art Christoph and friend Ray Jenner in 1957, shortly after Art became Krause's first advertising manager. One of Chet's first friends in the hobby, Art remained on staff at Krause Publications until he retired in 1988.

"Hammerin'" Henry Aaron was a young star of the pennant-winning Milwaukee Braves in the "Happy Days" of 1958. The changes that would come to collecting in the decades after 1958 are symbolized by the sports card hobby. A pastime for children in '58, card collecting would, in the 1980s, become an investment passion equal to or surpassing all other hobbies covered by Krause Publications.

Chapter 7

1958

"If a customer had invested $10,000 to $20,000 with us in 1958, by 1984 he would be a millionaire." Q. David Bowers

Hindsight is always 100 percent accurate. In 1958, the United States was the dominant economic power on the globe. Germany was still rebuilding its war-shattered infrastructure and the Japanese were seeking an American market for low-quality, throwaway products. A semi-skilled blue collar working man could earn enough to buy a suburban house and his wife could spend her days making it into a comfortable family home. They could both feel confident that, upon retirement, their own savings, a company pension, and the Social Security system would provide a modest but comfortable living standard.

Hyperinflation was a term not yet devised. American coinage minus its silver content could hardly be imagined. An economy in which a family required two working adults in order to maintain the standards of middle class life was equally unfathomable. The possibility that the American dollar would lose 75 percent of its value over the next 25 years was inconceivable.

Consequently, in 1958, few amateur collectors thought of their coins as a major lifetime investment. Certainly, every collector expected his coins to grow in value over time. But, many more of them thought of their collection more as a special gift they might pass down to their grandchildren than as an asset to be bought and sold for its speculative value. Coins were fun, and if they earned a little money over time, that was OK, but hardly essential to collecting.

It was in this atmosphere that Krause Publications was born, and it was in Krause's ability to meet the needs of people who collected for fun that its early success will be found. The period between late 1957, when Chet was finally able to devote all his time to publishing, before the *News* entered its period of skyrocketing growth, and the crisis year of 1965, come to mind as a golden age of adolescence for the company and the hobby.

Like an adolescent, Krause Publications was interested in new ventures. In 1958, the company tried something new by publishing a definitive guide to *United States Postage And Fractional Currency, 1862-1876*. Researched and written by Art Christoph and Chet Krause, the guide illustrated and described the currency printed by the United States government to alleviate the shortage of coins during and after the Civil War.

The war was a period of economic uncertainty and coins represented real value in a handy form. They could be hidden and hoarded with ease. So many coins were withdrawn from circulation that merchants could not make change on purchases. The story is told that one hoarder kept so many copper pennies in his room that the wooden floor collapsed beneath them. In order for normal commerce to take place, buyers and sellers devised their own methods for making change, using everything from personal I.O.U.'s and tokens issued by stores to postage stamps. The popularity of stamps led the United States Treasury to print what it called "fractional" currency in one, three, five, ten, fifteen, twenty-five and fifty cent denominations. The currency was issued until 1876, when the postwar economy settled down, and the volume of coinage in circulation returned to normal.

Postal and fractional currency was scarce and eminently collectible. Although various articles about it had appeared in the numismatic press over the years, no comprehensive, illustrated guide had ever been published until Christoph and Krause did it in 1958. Originally a series of articles in the News, the guide later appeared as a booklet, the first of many that would be produced in Iola over the years.

The *News* was still the prime focus of attention at Krause Publications and it continued to grow. As in every year since its birth, the *News* closed 1958 with more readers in December than it had in the previous January. The subscription list increased 25 percent, from 8,000 to 10,000. It was an increase significant enough to warm the heart of the crustiest of veteran publishers, which Chet was not, but it was small compared to what would happen starting in 1959.

Chapter 8

1959

"Circulation just jumped!" Art Christoph

News reaching Iola in '59 was both good and bad. The bad news was that the National League Champion Milwaukee Braves of Warren Spahn, Lew Burdette, Del Crandall, Eddie Matthews and Henry Aaron would lose the National League pennant race to the *Los Angeles* Dodgers. The good news was that the United States Mint was marking the 150th anniversary of the birth of Abraham Lincoln by redesigning the penny. The sheaves of wheat that had graced the reverse of the coin since 1909 were removed and replaced by a likeness of the Lincoln Memorial. The venerable old wheat cent would no longer be minted. As in 1955 and any other time a design was changed, coins and collecting attracted national notice. The attention only added momentum to growth at the *News*.

It didn't seem to need much help, for 1959 was the year of doubles. Starting with a circulation of 10,000 in January 1959, the *News* grew so fast that its circulation hit 20,000 by the end of the year. The size of the paper also grew past the limits of easy digestibility. Before the year was up, the *News* would come out twice a month, doubling the number of issues from 12 to 24.

The increase in issues and circulation was both cause and effect of an editorial change. "With our January issue this year we began what we hope to be a permanent face lifting in the paper's make-up," Chet told his readers. "Almost from the very beginning of our association with the *News*, readers have been asking for a more newsy newspaper. And although we have carried a limited amount of news matter it was scattered in such a manner that it became lost in our bulk. Therefore, it was our decision that in 1959 we would give the news portion of our publication a forward position as a trial."

Giving the news a forward position made the paper look more like a conventional newspaper, with more articles sharing space with ads. Chet was now displaying the same confidence towards editorial matters that he had earlier shown towards advertising policy. He was still "just plain Chet," but Chet had learned a lot about coins and collecting after seven years, and he would show it through his choice of material for the enlarged editorial section of the *News*.

The course of innovation does not always run smoothly, as Chet found out in early 1959. He had another bright idea to improve the *News*. The paper was still being printed in eight- page sections, and it was easy to print one section entirely in a different color. In the black-and-white 1950s, a multi-colored newspaper was a snazzy piece of journalism. It might have been a Freudian slip, but Chet decided that he would print a color section and, of all the colors under the sun, he chose a nice shade of U. S. currency green.

The *News* was also printing a life-size photo of a Series 1923 one dollar bill, and fate decreed that the photo would appear in that section of the paper that Chet was printing in green. These two steps–reproducing a life size dollar bill in green–created an image that was technically in violation of Treasury regulations. "What a mistake!" he recalled a few years later.

All he wanted to do was add "a bit of color to the *News*."

Instead he had printed 12,500 counterfeit one dollar bills smack in the middle of page two. About half of the copies had been collated and stitched together by the time Chet realized his mistake. "It was Saturday, I could have reached the Secret Service Office, but better judgment told me what I had to do. Print it over in black! and that we did. Ripping the green covers [including page two] off those that were done, we created a mess of waste paper that was thrown into a cart...."

Reprinting new pages in black to replace those printed in green wasn't enough, as Chet found out. "When I finally got to the Secret Service chief, I received orders to tear out that portion of the paper containing the note and surrender it to their Milwaukee office. What a job it was!"

And not just for the folks in Iola. When the Milwaukee Secret Service chief told Chet to send in the copies, he thought Chet was banging out a little newsletter that could be inspected and discarded in a few minutes. He later confessed that the sheets from the *News* cluttered up his headquarters for weeks.

"Thus I learned the hard way," Chet later said, "that paper money, in addition to having to be reproduced three-quarters to 1-1/2 times its original size, must also be done in black and white only. I think I hold the dubious honor of being the largest self-confessed counterfeiter in the state of Wisconsin."

His brief fling with counterfeiting over, Chet faced some of the other consequences of his decision to increase the editorial content of his paper. It was fine to print more news and features, but the supply of ads did not diminish. In order to run more articles and fit in all the ads, the *News* had to get even fatter. The October 1958 issue had been 80 pages thick and had to be shipped in two mailings. Complaints were heard again, but this time more readers complained about the size of the paper than about the split mailing. "...the bulk of 80 pages is just too much for the average reader to consume at one time," Chet wrote, as he introduced the first semi-monthly issue of *Numismatic News*, dated Feb. 16, 1959.

"After four months of sparring with various ways of meeting the demand for space in our publication it was the decision that publishing twice a month be given a whirl."

The whirl spun in the right direction. In March, the staff knocked out two 40-page issues; in April they sent out a pair of 44-pagers; December's two issues totaled 104 pages.

While page counts were climbing, subscription numbers also began to soar.

"Chet and I, Ruth Bestul and Carolyn Rice were down at the office one noon just talking about how we could get more circulation," recalled Art Christoph. "Somebody came up with [the idea that] we'd give an uncirculated '55-S dime and cent as a premium. We thought it would get a thousand, maybe. Well, we ended up making address plates for 10,000 or more! Circulation just jumped! I think it was the first giveaway premium."

The 1955-S dimes and cents were valuable premiums because the San Francisco Mint had struck only a limited number of coins that year. It then suspended operations for what turned out to be 10 years before again minting coins. For all anyone knew in 1959, however, San Francisco was closed for good and any coin bearing an S mint mark was eminently collectible.

Readers flooded the Iola post office with subscription orders. The numbers jumped 1,000 a month in January, February, March, April, May and June. Then they slowed a little to finish out the year with only an additional 4,000. The total gain doubled the size of the subscription list.

In July, when the *News* had only 15,823 subscribers, Chet listed them by state. As the entries showed, circulation was widespread across the nation, and the continent, if Canadian readers were included. With a few exceptions, the largest numbers of readers lived in states which then had the largest populations. Pennsylvania, the third largest state, had the most readers of the News. California, number two in the nation, was number two on the *News* readers' list. Ohio, number five in the U. S., had the third largest number of readers, closely followed by fourth-ranked Illinois and New York, the largest state in the Union. New York was out of sync, but perhaps readers there felt that Iola, Wisconsin, had nothing to say to them, or maybe they were exposed to too many other numismatic periodicals.

Except for Wisconsin, which understandably had a disproportionate number of readers for its population, the rest of the list corresponded fairly closely to the state head counts. Nevada, New Hampshire, Vermont and Delaware were near the bottom, just as they were in national population totals.

The chart was important because it pointed out how successful Chet had become at serving his audience-that neglected, isolated collector, far from the big city coin shops. The *News* found them all over the country, in big states and small. The fact that New York, the largest state in the Union, was not the number one state for readers only reinforces this fact. Even if a less-than-average number of New Yorkers read the *News,* farmers in Nebraska, small town dwellers in Indiana, and ranchers in Texas looked to the *News* when they wanted to learn about their hobby and build their collections.

Doubling circulation was not an unfettered blessing. Along with the flood of subs came a flood of free classified ads. High tech in the office of 1959 meant an electric typewriter and a mechanical adding machine. The *News* had the adding machine, but the typing was all done on sturdy but slow manual machines. Keeping track of hundreds of classified ads was also a colossal headache. In addition, the classifieds ran free of charge, like editorial material, which meant that the cost of producing them had to come out of subscription rates or display ad fees. Regular newspapers and magazines price their subs and ad space knowing that the news runs free-of-charge. As the *News* added to its editorial content and its free classified ad space, it also increased the costs that had to be charged to the subs and display ads. Yet subscription prices and ad rates could only rise so much before readership would start to drop and advertisers pull out. Chet was in a bind and to get out of it, he made a tough decision.

"...*Numismatic News* was founded on the basis of offering to its subscribers 20 words of free classified advertising to each subscriber once each month," he explained to his readers in April 1959. "When our circulation was at 6,000 the ad was indeed a bargain..." but "since January 1st, this year, we have been going through a period of drastic change.

"...During the first three months of 1959 we have had an increase in paid circulation of over 3,000 [to 13,000]. When you compare this with the fact it took us six years to reach 10,000 I believe you can readily see the problem it creates....

"...As a result of our having over doubled...it was no longer economically possible to continue [classifieds] absolutely free. Therefore, we felt that by obtaining at least 25 cents per ad we could continue to provide advertising at a very reasonable rate, yet reclaim the cost of clerical help needed to process them."

The days of free classified ads were over, replaced by classified ads at cost. Twenty-five cents covered the cost of the paper the ad was printed on, the typing, typesetting, printing, and mailing, plus the clerical work involved in it all. It was still a good deal for the advertiser who, for that same twenty-five cents, could buy a round-trip downtown on a big city bus, a quart of Coke, or a gallon and-a-half of regular gasoline. The difference was that an ad in *Numismatic News* could open a door to something worth much more than 25 cents.

Growth and change required more staff. Since the *News* had increased its editorial content, it needed a full-time editor. Chet found him at the Neville Public Museum in Green Bay, Wisconsin. Tom Fruit acquired his knowledge of coins while a curator there. He was the first editor of the *News* with professional numismatic expertise, and his hiring set a precedent for Krause Publications. The people who would supervise editorial work all would have experience and expertise in their fields, be it coins, cars, or trading cards. Chet continued to call himself an amateur numismatist, and maybe he was, but he had become a professional numismatic publisher.

By the end of 1959, the *News* staff totaled eight, with Chet as publisher; Tom Fruit, editor; Art Christoph, advertising manager; Carolyn Halverson, incoming mail/bookkeeper; Judy Egeland, advertising assistant; and Lorraine Nellis, Ruth Johnson and Clare Olson working in circulation.

1959 would prove to be one of *Numismatic News'* most exhilarating years, and the excitement continued right until Dec. 31. Chet had chosen the name of his newspaper because *Numismatic News* literally described what the periodical was all about and the repetition of the *N* and *S* sounds was catchy. In its commonly used abbreviated form–the *News*–the title was brief, memorable and definitive. Coin news was news because it was in the *News*. After years of traveling around the country to promote his brainchild, Chet had become known as Mr. *News*.

Therefore he did not look kindly on the advent, in September 1959, of a publication called *Coin News*. Frank Spadone, who had started a numismatic newspaper called the Flying Eaglet in Newark, New Jersey in 1955, had decided in 1958 that a name change would pump up his faltering bird. Chet had protected his right to his paper's name by filing for trademark protection back in 1955, so he was well aware of its value. Spadone had not violated Chet's trademark, but his use of the word *News* could muddy the waters for readers.

In October, Chet wrote an editorial demanding that Spadone find a new name for his newspaper. By the end of the year the *Coin News* had been retitled the *Coin Press Magazine*. It was a fitting closing to a year that had seen more progress than any since the *News* was founded.

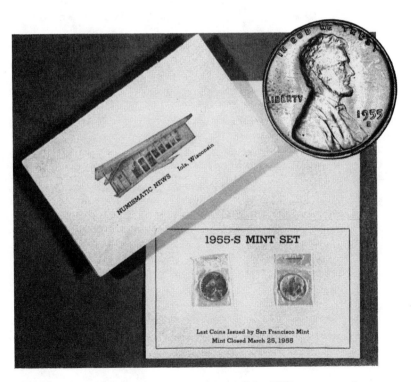

Krause's first subscription premium was a mint set of the 1955 one-cent and ten-cent pieces that were the last coins issued by the San Francisco Mint. The giveaway brought 10,000 new subscribers in 1959. Krause never forgot the lesson and has never stopped using premiums to build circulation.

America's most famous coin for decades, James V. McDermott's 1913 Liberty Head nickel came to Iola in 1960, along with its colorful owner. McDermott believed that collectors should have an opportunity to see the coveted coin and lent it to Chet for exhibition purposes many times.

Chapter 9

1960

*"Optimism and enthusiasm run high in
our organization."*   Chet Krause

The first year of the new decade — the 1960s — whose very name would come to symbolize radical change in American life began with the U-2 spy plane crisis and ended with the election of a new president, John F. Kennedy. Among the changes that would occur in the tumultuous decade was the most radical alteration of American coinage since the presidency of George Washington and the most radical change in the value of paper money since the days of Abe Lincoln. Neither of these transformations took place in 1960. That year was memorable for a less unsettling reason. It merely saw a 1913 Liberty Head nickel come to Iola, Wisconsin.

It was also the year in which the *News* more than doubled its office space in order to add more staff to handle a circulation total that had doubled for the second straight year.

"While you are reading these paragraphs," Chet wrote in April, "masons are at work building an addition to our facilities. This addition will house a new mailing room, an unloading dock and a warehouse. Our present quarters will be remodeled for greater office efficiency."

The addition measured 40 x 60 feet, and every square foot of it was needed. In the first six months of 1960 the *News* had added 9,000 new subscribers. By the end of the year, another 11,000 readers would join the fold and push the total number of subscribers past 40,000.

Page counts also continued to climb: January, 88; February, 112; March, 120. In August the count again hit 120. The growth in subs and page counts proved that Chet's decision to charge for classifieds had no ill effect on the paper. Quite to the contrary, for, as Chet stated, "Only through customer satisfaction can we satisfy ourselves." As the growth indicated, the *News* must have been satisfying customers and its staff.

With the new addition completed, the *News* finally got around to hosting an open house. In July, 375 numismatists found their way to Iola and enjoyed its hospitable atmosphere. Among the big names in coins who attended were R.S. "Dick" Yeoman, publisher of the *Red Book* of United States coins; Ken Bressett of Whitman Publishing Company; and J. V. "Mac" McDermott with his 1913 Liberty Head nickel.

The 1913 Liberty Head nickel was perhaps the most famous and intriguing coin in the collecting world. Only five of the nickels with the traditional Liberty Head design had been struck in 1913 before the mint replaced it with the Indian/buffalo designs of James Earle Fraser. In 1920, the Liberty Heads turned up at the ANA Convention and one was valued at a princely $600. In the 1930s, Depression-ridden dreamers, including Chet Krause, were given food for thought by print and radio ads run by Max Mehl, of Fort Worth, Texas, in which he offered $10,000 for one of the coins.

No unsung, isolated coin explorer ever collected Mehl's reward. The 1913 Liberty Heads in existence were tucked away in the vaults of collectors like Egypt's last king, Farouk, who purchased coins by the bucketful until he was overthrown in 1953. James V. McDermott, a knowledgeable and generous coin dealer who started out as a working stiff, acquired one of the coins. Instead of locking it up in a safety deposit box, McDermott placed his Liberty Head in a clear plastic holder and displayed it at every gathering of collectors he could attend. He brought it with him to Iola in 1960, at which time McDermott was turning down offers of more than $20,000 for the coin.

McDermott was one of numismatic's first "populists." He wanted the average collector to see his coin. It was fitting that he and his nickel should come to Iola, since it was probably the most widely known individual coin in the United States and, thanks to McDermott's down-home personality and his practice of displaying it whenever he could, it showed that collecting was not just a pastime for elitists. The hobby could be mastered and enjoyed by anyone willing to learn its ways, which just happened to be the philosophy inspiring the *Numismatic News*.

Further proof that Chet's philosophy was shared by many in the hobby came in August, when the *News* published its first ANA Souvenir Edition. Ed Rochette had covered the ANA's 69th convention in Boston at the end of August and produced both a pre-show preview and a post-show recap. The recap became the *News'* first ANA Souvenir Section. It was printed on salmon-colored newsprint to set it off from the rest of the paper and represented a small step up the path towards greater creativity within the restricted limits of the materials and technology of newspapering in 1960. The Souvenir Section pushed the page count of the Sept. 5 issue to 72 pages. It was the thickest issue since the switch to semi-monthly publishing, and would have been considered fat even in the days of monthly publishing nineteen months earlier.

The Souvenir Section also displayed Ed Rochette's editorial abilities. By the end of the year Ed would move to Iola to become managing editor of the *News,* and add more numismatic expertise to the staff.

Chapter 10

1961

*"There is always room for one more if it
is a good one."*   Chet Krause

When he was inaugurated as president on Jan. 20, 1961, John F. Kennedy urged Americans to ask themselves what they could do for their country. A month later, he asked Chet Krause.

In February 1961, Chet was named to the Annual Assay Commission. This was a group of eminent citizens and numismatists, charged by Congress, who met annually at the mint in Philadelphia to inspect the coinage and make sure that it conformed "in all respects to legal weights and finesses" specified by law. The Assay Commission was a genteel throwback to the democratic traditions of American government, to a time when interested citizens were called on to oversee the work of a public agency and thereby insure the integrity of its work. The work of the Mint was the manufacture of coinage cleanly struck and containing a true value of precious metal. The Assay Commission survived until 1977, when, as if to illustrate how the nation had changed, the interested citizens were replaced by government administrators.

Back in 1960, however, only a few coin "hobbyists" had ever been selected for the Commission, and Chet was the first numismatic publisher to serve on it. He was also the first commissioner to bring a reporter along with him to cover the assay. Ed Rochette went to Philadelphia and afterwards banged out an excellent photo-journalism spread for the *News*. It was one of the first instances in which the work of the Assay Commission had received extensive coverage in any numismatic publication.

For Chet, serving on the Commission was serious fun. A snowstorm prevented four of the fifteen appointees from landing at Philadelphia so there were fewer people to share the work. Chet was named chairman of the Weighing Committee, whose chore it was to randomly select 43 coins struck in Philadelphia and 44 struck in Denver, weigh them carefully, and be sure they were within the tolerances set by Congress.

Their work finished, the Commissioners went on an inside tour of the mint conducted by Leland Howard, acting director of the United States Mint. The tour also became part of Rochette's story for the *News*.

Back in Iola, in what was becoming a happily monotonous litany of growth, the *News* was running bigger issues on a regular basis. A 64-page paper, for a total of 128 pages a month, had now become standard. Bigger papers on a regular basis and the hefty increases in circulation that were still underway made it necessary for the *News* to find a new printer.

In its near-decade of life, the *News* had been part of a process of growth and centralization of newspaper production. The small shop of the *Iola Herald* was adequate for all the printing in town in 1952. By 1961, shops like that of the *Herald* were disappearing and local newspapers were shipping their printing and mailing preparation work out of town. Centralized printing plants in slightly larger communities became production and fulfillment centers for the small town publishers in their region.

The production plant of the *Shawano Evening Leader* is located in a small city about 40 miles away from Iola (if you don't call it Shaw-no, you're not from Wisconsin). In the early 1960s it was becoming a regional center for printing. The Shawano plant was a letterpress shop with the equipment to produce two-color printing, but not the same kind of color printing that made Chet a counterfeiter in 1959. Two-color printing at Shawano meant two colors on the same page. The *Leader* could also bind tabloids and magazines and handle mail preparation. It would produce a *News* with neatly-trimmed 15-inch tabloid pages held together with staples through the spine. Trimming the pages would make a tremendous improvement in the appearance of the *News*. Stapling would prevent the thick bundle of sheets from falling apart in the mail and make it easier for the reader to page through the paper.

Chet called this "...a pleasing, clean-cut paper.... We have always felt that for a tabloid newspaper of large size to be enjoyed it should measure up to these basic standards: 1. It should be bound so that through use it does not lose its initial orderly appearance; 2. It should carry an index reference of where to find what you are looking for, including advertising; 3. It should be trimmed to give it an appearance of having been finished." He concluded by saying that "we have now achieved these three basic physical requisites."

Neatness and organization are the hallmarks of a good coin collection, and it was only logical that a coin collecting publication should be neat and orderly as well. Other improvements were possible now, and Chet took advantage of them.

Second-color printing would brighten the *News* and give it greater graphic punch. The first color in printing, as with Henry Ford's Model T, has always been black, but the second color can be any shade under the sun. An imaginative designer and a good printer can use two-color effects to create the impression of full-color printing. In the actual physical appearance and quality of the product reaching the hands of the readers, the switch to Shawano meant progress for the *News*.

Since the *Evening Leader* also offered mail preparation services, the *News* would be getting to its readers more efficiently and promptly. Previously the papers were trucked from the printer to the *News* office where the staff handled the labeling and mailing. Now, the papers were printed, stapled, trimmed, labeled and made ready to mail in one continuous operation. The *News* office became the place for editorial, advertising and management work, with no pre-press or production work performed on site. This is the work that separates publishing from printing. Editorial, advertising, design, sales, circulation and management constitute publishing, while the actual physical production, duplication and delivery to the post office or other shipper are the printer's job.

Press production work was shifted to Shawano in July and, in August, the *News* exercised one of its new options and printed its first two-color front page. In that same issue Chet announced that Al Varner, another enthusiastic and knowledgeable collector, would join the staff as editor. Over the course of the next year, the staff would help Chet fulfill his promise to produce a "newsier" *News*. It would devote 25 percent of its space to news articles and utilize improved photo reproduction methods to print more and better photos. The classified ads that were the mother's milk of the paper in the early '50s were still present, but were shifted to the rear of the paper. All in all, the *News* of late 1961 was much more attractive, better organized and more interesting to read than the *News* of 1960.

Chet was always receptive to different options that would increase circulation, and he had tried one in August 1959. Coin collections are valuable and even small ones should be insured. Chet figured he could offer a package deal to his readers-a subscription to the *News* and insurance for their coins.

In August, Chet told his subscribers he was not "...running an insurance business as a subsidiary.... There has been a lot said about coin insurance and ability to get it. While discussing this one day with the Home Insurance Company representative, we agreed such a service was needed and desirable. As a result of this meeting, subscribers to the *News* are now being offered opportunity to obtain, from a large, well-respected insurance company, coverage designed to fit their needs. Not only is it offered to subscribers of a national publication by a leading insurance firm, but in the event of loss, adjustments will be made through local adjustment agents of the General Adjustment Bureau. We feel fortunate in being party to such a convenient arrangement."

The arrangement was a little too "convenient" for state insurance regulators. A month later Chet had to report: "They shook their fingers and said you can't do that. That being, sell insurance and subscriptions, as a package deal.... Accordingly, the insurance for coin collectors is no longer exclusively for our readers, but rather for any coin collector. We, at *Numismatic News*, are not licensed and do not sell insurance. But, we urge you to cover your collection whether it be locally or through agents specializing in collection coverage.

"...the *News* entered into what we thought was an equitable means of serving the collectors' insurance needs and presented it.... The reaction to this ad pointed up that, although our intentions were good, that the insurance because of various state laws could not be sold in the manner described. Therefore, all the inquiries to that advertisement were returned with regret."

The insurance plan didn't work out, although it probably helped convince a few collectors that their coins needed coverage, and if so, served a good end.

A good end also came to 1961. Chet had built a going, growing business. *Numismatic News* was a national publication and doing well financially. Chet could have stopped where he was in 1961 and, for all indication at the time, spent the next thirty years as a successful publisher of one newspaper. But somewhere, sometime, he must have heard the adage that says, "If you're not moving ahead, you're falling behind."

In September, he purchased *Coin Press,* the magazine that had begun as the Flying Eaglet and was briefly known as *Coin News.* Chet believed that collectors wanted to read more feature articles about coins than the *News* was supplying. He could have added more pages to the paper, but its focus on news and ads had proven very successful. It was reaching the market to which it was targeted. Perhaps Chet had also heard the adage that says, "If it's working, don't fix it." In any event he decided that the *News* was not the publication for feature articles. They belonged in a magazine that would be marketed to those who wanted more reading material and fewer ads, with both set in a different format.

The years in which Chet had been in the publishing business had seen the rise of television and the demise of the large circulation, general interest magazine. *Collier's,* which had several million readers in the late 1940s, was dead by 1960. *Look, Life,* and the *Saturday Evening Post* were still around, but would cease publishing by the end of the decade. Television could deliver a much larger general audience than these magazines, and national advertisers shifted to the newer medium.

Specialization became the watchword for print media in the 1960s. Chet's decision to retain the focus of *Numismatic News* and not broaden its content was in keeping with the general trend that began in publishing at about this time. With very few exceptions, like *Reader's Digest,* if a magazine was to survive, it had to specialize.

By the end of 1961, *Coins* magazine was born. It started with the mailing list and good will of *Coin Press,* but soon surpassed it. Chet's friend, Robert Strand, economics teacher at Iola High School and a coin collector, left teaching and became advertising manager of *Coins*. Another long-standing colleague and friend, Strand would stay with Krause until he retired as corporate treasurer in 1988.

Coins also started Chet and his company on the path to growth through specialization that would make Krause Publications a textbook example of how a print medium could be successful in a video age.

With the introduction of **Coins** magazine in 1961, Krause began developing its formula for expansion within a hobby niche. As a feature magazine, **Coins** printed editorial material that differed from that of the trader's publication, **Numismatic News**. The first issue of **Coins** also pointed out the next step within the niche — a Standard Price Guide.

*Out of the Standard Price Guide in **Coins** came another publication, **Coin Prices,** which helped Krause fill out the numismatic niche. If a price guide could be a success in numismatics, it could also be a success in other hobbies, as proven by Krause price guides to cars, comics and sports cards.*

Chapter 11

1962

"Yes, I collect coins and so do the others
rounding out the staff here at the Coin
Collector's Capital."   Chet Krause

Chet closed 1961 by buying one rival publication and he opened 1962 by buying another one. *Numismatic Times and Trends* magazine, published by Ken Pierce in New Orleans, was the latest acquisition. Its readers were enrolled on the sub list of *Coins*, which gave the new periodical an infusion of the lifeblood of magazine publishing — paid circulation.

Chet was also bringing lifeblood to Iola. He was creating jobs — skilled, productive jobs — in a small community whose largest employer had been the local electric company. One of those jobs went to William E. Jensen, who became advertising manager of the *News* and *Coins*. He was an advertising pro with both agency and newspaper experience. Bob Strand left the advertising department and moved into finances as company controller, responsible for the unglamorous but necessary work of credit, collection, payroll and accounting.

Lincoln W. "Bill" Higgie III also signed on to the staff of *Numismatic News* in 1962. He had learned the ropes of numismatic journalism from R. S. Yeoman at Whitman Publishing in Racine, Wisconsin, and he immediately added depth and breadth to the staff. He became Iola's first foreign correspondent, since he soon took an extended tour of Europe and compiled a series of articles on world coinage that appeared in the *News*.

With a roving ambassador of sorts overseas, it was only appropriate that Chet follow up on Ed Rochette's suggestion to put up a sign identifying Iola as the "Coin Collector's Capital." The American passion for nicknames had made big towns like Detroit "The Motor City," New York "The Big Apple," and Chicago "The Windy City." Small towns were just getting into the name game in the '60s as a way to attract tourists. Wisconsin already had Boulder Junction, "The Musky Capital" for anglers, and Sheboygan, "The Bratwurst Capital" for sausage lovers. It would soon have Muscoda, "The Mushroom Capital," for mycophiles, and Sauk City, "The Cow Chip-Tossing Capital," for tourists whose taste runs to the athletically eccentric. Nicknames were intended to stimulate identification and lighthearted fun in the name of commerce. Coin collecting was fun and it certainly brought commerce to its new capital.

Probably the most valuable natural gifts Chet brought to publishing were, first, his ability to recognize a special need for information; second, the knowhow to collect and organize that information; and third, the knack for presenting it in a form readers wanted.

Numismatic News presented classified ads, display ads and news related to collecting in a simple, low-cost format. It was aptly dubbed, "A Trading Post for the Collector of Coins." *Coins* magazine was a feature publication targeted to collectors who enjoyed reading background articles about coins, collecting and the people involved with them. *Coins* was printed on glossy paper that lent itself to better photo reproduction and improved graphic design. It was meant to present information and images in a style that was a cut above the basic approach of the *News*. The glossy image and color covers were important parts of the *Coins* package, since it was destined to be sold on newsstands where a "slick" format was vital for sales. The package must have been successful, for newsstand distribution of *Coins* has consistently surpassed subscriptions by more than two-to-one. Each of these publications helped fill the niche for information on coins, collected it accurately, and presented it in a format best suited to its readers.

As soon as he started publishing, Chet committed himself to helping collectors learn more about their hobby. After ten years in the field, in which he had presented volumes of information to readers, he was still dissatisfied about the manner in which collectors learned about coin prices. There were several "clip and paste" guides but they rarely represented a genuine market. For many, real knowledge of coin prices came the hard way when, through inexperience, they paid more than a fair price for a coin. A market is not truly free unless both buyer and seller have a relatively accurate idea of the value of a coin. It was very difficult for a beginner, and more advanced collectors as well, to assess the market value of a coin as well as a professional. Therefore, they were often at a disadvantage when purchasing coins. It was especially difficult to bid by mail, since an individual collector had no way of knowing how his competitors were bidding until after the sale was made and even then only if the sale was advertised and reported on in *Numismatic News*.

Once again, Chet detected a need for information; that was step number one. Collectors needed a gauge to help them measure the value of coins they wanted to purchase. Chet then needed a source for that information and found it by simply asking those who had it; that was step number two. Finally, he presented the information to his readers in the form of his first *Standard Price Guide*; that was step number three. It appeared in the March 1962 issue of *Coins*, and consisted of three-pages of prices for common United States coins.

No one except a buyer or seller had attempted to set prices for coins. Chet's *Guide* was the first attempt by a presumably objective third party to use the timeliness of a periodical to intervene in the exchange between buyer and seller. In presenting his *Guide,* Chet was taking a risk. On the one hand, it would appear that he was championing the little guy who didn't know much about collecting and was at the mercy of unscrupulous sellers. The implication was that dealers would cheat the unwitting collector, and Uncle Chet was playing cop.

Playing cop was never Chet's intention, but if the sellers who paid for advertising in his pages thought that he was implying that they were dishonest or unfair, they would stop advertising, and the *News* would be hit in the pocketbook. Aside from concerns about the company pocketbook, Chet knew that most coin sellers were a scrupulous, fair-minded group, and implying that they were not was simply not accurate.

Accordingly, he announced that the price list in the first *Guide* was "...a retail guide as compiled from current fixed-price advertisements...prepared by the editors of *Coins* as a prelude to receiving price information from a panel of dealers who are active in the retail pricing of coins."

The dealer panel that would compile prices for the future issues of the *Guide* included: Joseph Adamski, Joseph DeBock, Garland Hughes, C.G. Kimberly, E.C. Leverett, William G. Scott, L.C. Shafer and Norman Schultz.

The *Guide* listed prices for coins in five grades: Good, Fine, Extra Fine, Uncirculated and Proof. Among issues covered were: Flying Eagle cents, 1856-58; Indian Head cents, 1859-1909; Lincoln cents, 1909-1960; two-cent pieces, 1864-1873; three-cent pieces, 1865-1889; Liberty Head nickels, 1883-1913; Buffalo nickels, 1913- 1938; Jefferson nickels, 1938-1961; Barber dimes, 1892-1916; Mercury dimes, 1916-1945; Barber quarters, 1892-1916; Standing Liberty quarters, 1916-1930; Barber halves, 1892-1915; Walking Liberty halves, 1916-1947; Morgan dollars, 1878-1921; and Peace dollars, 1921-1935.

Chet also printed a disclaimer that said, "This is a retail price guide as compiled from current fixed-price advertisements. As a guide, it is meant only to help you in evaluating your coins. Actual selling prices may be higher or lower than indicated here."

The *Standard Price Guide* was well received by readers and sellers and was reprinted in the *News*. Chet introduced it in the issue of Dec. 12: "Making its debut is the *Standard Price Guide* developed here at Coin Collector's Capital, the *Standard Price Guide* has been appearing in *Coins* since Spring. Compiled with the aid of a panel of contributors, it has been accepted by the collecting public as the most realistic in the business. It comes to you not as a beginning attempt, but as a proven product. Updated each issue, it will reflect a most accurate guide — indeed indicative of its name, *The Standard Price Guide*."

The introduction of the *Guide* completed Chet's tenth full year in publishing. In that decade he had met and surpassed the goals with which he had begun. He had also evolved a formula that meshed very closely with the trends of the future.

The world economic situation would stimulate interest in coins and the precious metals out of which they were made as objects of investment and speculation. The interest in collectibles that started with stamps and coins would combine with a developing taste for nostalgia and reminiscence to transform seemingly valueless objects — the rusted Model T back in the barn, Grandma's old bisque doll, the baseball cards that kids once clipped into the spokes of their 1950s Schwinns — into valued collectors' items. In publishing itself, the trend towards more specialization to reach more accurately targeted markets would command the field through the next three decades. Publishers who were good at it would thrive, those who were not would close their doors.

After a decade in publishing Chet was in the right position to flow right along with these trends, to take advantage of them and to build his business upon them. He had the right publication to report news and promote sales of coins. He had added another publication for those who wanted to read about them. Finally, in the *Standard Price Guide*, which would evolve into *Coin Prices* magazine by the end of the decade, he completed filling the consumer niche of numismatic periodical publishing.

The formula for success had evolved over the past decade. In the future, opportunities to apply it would arise and Krause Publications would take advantage of them. Chet didn't have to learn anything more about the basics of publishing. He had only to watch for the right opportunity, judge when to take it, and apply his formula. What worked in numismatics in the early 1960s would work for other hobbies in the 1970s, '80s and '90s.

Chapter 12

1963

"It is indeed very encouraging to know that what you offer is accepted to the point where others of far greater knowledge and familiarity in the field of numismatics get behind you and help sell your product."   Chet Krause

Chet had planted the seed for the organization known as the Numismatists of Wisconsin at the *Numismatic News* open house in 1960. He was elected president of the group in 1962 and re-elected in '63. He took the organization and his job seriously and clearly demonstrated that he wasn't a member or an officer just because it was good for business. In the course of his presidency he traveled to thirty individual chapters of N.O.W. doing what he most enjoyed, talking to enthusiastic collectors about coins.

Chet was able to do some of the things he enjoyed because of the quality of his staff. A newspaper interviewer once asked him, "How do you account for Krause Publications' success?" He responded by saying, "We've had the good fortune of hiring the right people and then delegating responsibility to them."- Many of the right people joined the company in 1963, a year that would see the number of Krause employees double.

Clement F. Bailey's first "This n' That" column on "the light side of numismatics" first appeared in January. He was a collector and a journalist, one who specialized in numismatics as an associate editor of *Numismatic Times and Trends*. After eighteen months as a columnist for the *News*, Bailey could no longer resist the allure of Iola, and moved to town to work full time.

Another well-known numismatic journalist, Robert Obojski, joined the *News* in '63. He was an English professor at Western Kentucky State College at Bowling Green, and a stamp and coin columnist for *The Christian Science Monitor*. He had also written many feature pieces for the *News*. He was one example of the kind of people now coming to work for Krause Publications. They combined journalist ability and experience with knowledge of numismatics.

Stephen Maresh was another pro. As Chet said, Maresh "...was needed to round out the *News* staff." He brought experience in editorial, advertising and newspaper production work to Iola.

Another numismatist came on board in '63 when Harry Becker joined the staff. A business education teacher at Iola High School, Becker started as supervisor of subscription fulfillment. Within a year he was named circulation sales manager, a post he held until his retirement 24 years later. The circulation and fulfillment division of publishing is probably the least-known and certainly the least glamorous part of the process that takes a writer's idea or an ad message, puts it onto paper, and then gets it into the hands of a reader. The circulation people are the truck drivers of the publishing world, delivering periodicals and books-on time-to homes, stores, libraries and businesses.

Becker and his staff had to deal with the postal service, newsstand distributors, and, most importantly, subscribers. They had to make sure all Krause publications were shipped at the correct postage rate, that requirements for permits were fulfilled, and all the necessary records kept up-to-date. They also had to deal with the periodical distributors who actually place newspapers and magazines on newsstands. Good relations with distributors can make or break a publication that depends heavily on newsstand sales, such as *Coins*. Many major markets are served by only one distributor who decides what periodicals get on which stands, how many, and where a magazine is placed once it gets there. For example, the hottest-selling tabloids and magazines with the most lurid covers are placed at the front of the newsstand, at the head of the grocery check-out line, or right next to the cash register to encourage impulse buying. Specialty publications, such as *Coins*, if they are carried at all, are placed at the back of the stand, since it is presumed that the comparatively few people who read them will go to the extra trouble to search them out.

Distributors take periodicals on consignment, keep their own records of sales, pay the publisher at a deep discount only for publications that sell, then destroy unsold copies. Bringing a new publication into this system can be a bruising experience for a circulation manager. It is a bit like playing junkyard basketball, where elbows fly to clear space beneath the basket. Keeping space open and making sure that Krause publications are treated fairly in the newsstand game are also parts of the nitty-gritty work of the circulation department.

Most Krause periodicals are sold on newsstands, but subscription sales are usually far more important, and keeping subscribers happy is the ultimate goal of the circulation staff. Magazines or newspapers that are not delivered or that arrive late or damaged, subscription bills that go unpaid, and renewals that are not made must be accounted for. The periodical reader in a faraway place will not care how good the articles are or how many bargains can be found in the classifieds if he or she does not receive the newspaper or magazine on time. The Krause slogan of "On time, every time" applies not just to getting material to the printer, but in getting the final product to the reader.

Circulation had been a very busy part of Krause Publications ever since subscriptions started to soar in 1958. By the beginning of 1963, the *News* had 60,000 subscribers and was still growing. Page counts were regularly surpassing the 100 mark and, starting in January, two more issues per year were added. Instead of coming out twice monthly, for a total of 24 issues a year, the *News* was now published every other week, or 26 times a year. With readers receiving more and bigger papers, the subscription price was increased from $2 to $3 per year. *Coins* magazine was also growing and reached a combined subscription and newsstand circulation of 80,000 by the end of the year. *Canada Coin News*, *Coin Dealer* and, to a lesser degree, *Club News*, added thousands more readers to keep Harry Becker's circulation department busy and growing.

The most notable addition to the staff in 1963 was Cliff Mishler. He was a native of southwestern Michigan who had worked in the building trades and who was not deterred from taking a job with Krause by what he remembered as "a minus 20-degree introduction to Iola," on a chilly February day. His background was similar to Chet's in that he was a builder from a small town who got into hobby publishing on his own. Mishler had self-published a guide titled *United States and Canadian Commemorative Medals and Tokens* for five years and was a founder of the Token and Medal Society.

Token and medal collecting is a close companion of coin collecting. Tokens issued by merchants, banks and industrial firms had been used in lieu of government coinage for centuries. Their history was just as fascinating and their pedigree older than that of coins themselves. Commemorative medals issued to honor the greater — and sometimes the lesser — people, places and events of history also had a heritage as long-standing as that of coinage.

Collectors of tokens and medals represented a market that Krause could easily serve. Mishler was one of the most knowledgeable token and medal collectors in the United States and he brought that expertise to *Numismatic News*. He became editor of the "Token Collectors" page and performed a number of other editorial chores. Mishler would rise through the company hierarchy and, 28 years later, succeed Chet as president of Krause Publications.

Mishler enlarged the editorial tent at Krause in 1963, but his interest in tokens and medals did not represent the largest expansion of coverage that took place that year. In the same issue that announced Mishler's advent on the staff, Chet declared his plans for publishing an "exclusively Canadian newspaper, *Canada Coin News*...to serve the growing interest in Canadian coins, medals, tokens and paper money."

After several months in preparation, the first issue appeared in June 1963. Once again Chet followed his formula of detecting a need for information, then finding out who could best supply it. He found his source for Canadian coins and publishing in Cale B. Jarvis. The coin columnist for the *Toronto Globe and Mail*, Jarvis was also a well-known numismatist. He sat on the board of directors of the Greater Toronto Coin and Stamp Exhibition and was secretary of the Canadian Professional Numismatic Guild.

Chet had floated the idea of publishing a separate Canadian paper to Canadian collectors in a seemingly unlikely place — the annual convention of the Florida United Numismatists in Miami Beach in January 1963. (Considering Canadian winter weather, perhaps it wasn't so unlikely.) Chet later recalled that he had "...talked to a group of Canadian dealers and collectors about the possibility of setting aside our *Numismatic News* Canadian Section to form a strictly Canadian publication to be identified as *Canada Coin News*. Their reaction was 'GO' and that we did."

Using the information compiled by his own circulation and advertising people, and drawing on his own knowledge and experience, Chet gauged that "...the popularity of Canadian coinage deserves better than second class citizenship. It is popular enough to stand on its own feet."

The first issue of *Canada Coin News* appeared on June 3, 1963. Chet was as enthusiastic about it as he was about the initial issues of the *News* a decade earlier. "...We saw a dream come true," he wrote. "Those of you who have since seen the results of that historic moment have, to some degree, shared in this memorable occasion...and we trust you were as proud of it as we were."

The first issue had a press run of 15,000, with subscriptions priced at $3 per year. Coverage had to be broad, since Canadian coinage has always been historically diverse. All of the coins of the colonial era and that of what was still called the Dominion of Canada in 1963 were included. Since the Canadian federal system was much looser than the American, individual provinces — Newfoundland and the Maritimes — had issued their own coinage, which was also covered. Although the question of Canadian bilingualism had yet to reach the boiling point it would rise to in the 1970s, *Canadian Coin News* announced that it would publish a portion of its editorial content in French as well as English.

The new paper was published bi-weekly on an alternating schedule with the *Numismatic News*. Editorial material would be sent from Toronto to Iola, where it would be typeset and pasted up. Next the completed pages were shipped to one of the few Wisconsin printers using the newly developed offset printing process for newspapers.

This system was set up before the days of overnight air delivery services, satellite communications, personal computers and telephone modems and fax machines. The printing industry itself was just coming out of the linotype/letterpress age. Indeed, Chet made it a point to announce that *Canadian Coin News* would use the most modern printing technology, an offset web press, to provide "...maximum quality to all illustrations as well as clean, high-quality general reproductions." Offset was a great way to print, but the benefits it offered to editorial organization were limited. The staffs in Iola and Toronto had to rely on the mail and the telephone to overcome 600 miles of separation.

It soon became apparent that the distance between Toronto and Iola could not be bridged, at least not by a small publisher, with the communication technology of 1963. After five issues, Chet decided that *Canada Coin News* "...would be produced entirely in Toronto." Chet would "...retain a continued interest," but Cale Jarvis would be the publisher.

"In making the move," Chet explained, "certain inefficiencies will be eliminated.... In addition, the one office will provide on the scene service as well as full authority to act and make decisions without referral to the Iola office.

"...Physical production was continued in Wisconsin for five issues — long enough to assure it of a successful launching and to identify it as coming from our family of publications." It was important that collectors know the parentage of the new paper. It would enhance the reputation of Krause Publications and give *Canada Coin News* a leg up.

Moving the entire operation to Toronto was part of Chet's long-range plan for *Canada Coin News*. It just happened sooner than expected. "Although the producing of a truly Canadian numismatic publication by having it edited and printed in Canada was an eventuality," he wrote "Its transfer there came early with issue number six being produced completely in Toronto."

Believing that collectors of Canadian coins would support their own publication, Chet and his friend, Cale Jarvis, introduced **Canada Coin News** *in 1963. With editorial offices in Toronto and production work in Iola, the publication was also an early experiment in long-distance publishing.*

Through the early transfer, Chet gave the new publication to Cale Jarvis. It was a decision he never regretted, since he wanted to make *Canada Coin News* "a truly Canadian publication," and a success.

It was already successful, as Chet had already pointed out. *Canada Coin News* had "...become a symbol of marked success. Produced every other week it now contains 36 pages of well-edited numismatic information about Canadian material with a circulation crowding 35,000...I am happy to have been a part in founding *Canada Coin News* and we at Iola are happy to enjoy the close relationship we have with *Canada Coin News* and the Canadian collector and dealer."

Two years later, in 1965, Chet would write: "This early decision to make *Canada Coin News* a strictly Toronto based operation has proved to be as important as the publication's founding." In 1992, Chet still took pride in pointing out that *Canada Coin News* is still publishing and looking forward to marking its 30th anniversary.

Canada Coin News was not the only new publication to come out of Iola in 1963. Chet took another step towards filling the numismatic publishing niche by introducing *Coin Dealer* magazine in August. This was a monthly trade publication aimed at the "manufacturer, supplier and dealer...published for you and about you... the commercial side of numismatics." The *Dealer's* first press run of 5,000 was mailed free to commercial numismatists in Canada, the United States and Mexico.

Feedback was positive, "...so great we've had to expand our facilities," Chet wrote. "And the requests keep flooding in." So many requests arrived that Chet increased the press run, first to 7,500, and then to 11,000. Distribution remained free and advertising rates were set "at a figure that won't make us rich, and will allow us to give you the break of contracting for advertising space."

With the establishment of *Coin Dealer*, it appeared that Chet had just about all the bases covered, but he didn't think so. In November, Krause Publications produced *Club Report*, a free newsletter covering coin club news and circulating free of charge to the approximately 2,000 coin clubs on the company mailing list.

What was left in the numismatic niche? Krause had the traders, the amateur scholars, the dealers, the suppliers and the club members, with circulation totals surpassing 150,000. The only hole to be found was in the realm of scholarly publishing. A scholarly journal, whose contributors all had Ph. Ds and whose articles were all properly annotated, was the only numismatic publication not coming out of Iola. Chet never tried this side of publishing. He was a popularizer and, by the end of 1963, he had filled the entire niche of the popular coin press.

Chapter 13

1964

"Coin collecting interest boomed as never before and never since.... Our subscription rolls didn't just grow, they mushroomed, topping out in excess of the 80,000 mark...we were wrestling to serve both the advertising and news needs of our advertisers and subscribers with a flood of 128-page issues." Cliff Mishler

Mushrooms may sprout spontaneously in a shady forest, but newspaper subscriptions do not. They take planning, execution and a good hook.

In November 1963, President John F. Kennedy was assassinated. Part of the national outpouring of grief was the renaming of streets, bridges, buildings and airports in his honor. The U. S. Mint joined the mourners by announcing it would replace the Franklin 50 cent piece that had been in circulation since 1948 with a new half-dollar coin struck in honor of the dead president.

Many new coins have been issued over the years, but only a few in honor of recently deceased political leaders. Franklin Delano Roosevelt, who died in 1945, was memorialized with a new dime in 1946. Most collectors and the general public thought it was a fitting honor for the only American who was elected to the presidency four times.

Not even the most avid Roosevelt partisan, nor the most committed collectors of ten cent pieces, greeted the 1946 dime with the fervent anticipation that accompanied the introduction of the Kennedy half-dollar. Not only collectors were wild to get them, so were people who never did anything with coins except spend them. Everyone wanted a Kennedy half and, when they got one, locked it away as a keepsake of the slain leader. No sooner were the first Kennedys issued than the coins became scarce.

Chet and the promotional people at Krause were well aware of the power of a giveaway and had been using them ever since the first issue of the *News* left Cora Krause's tabletop, but no one was prepared for what happened when Chet announced Krause would give away a brand new Kennedy half-dollar for every new subscription to the *News*.

The result was overwhelming, as an article in *Coin Dealer* reported: "The staff of *Numismatic News* has been working with a touch of madness during the first three months of 1964. We don't mind expansion, and any signs of growth are encouraging. But what has been going on around Iola has been a little breathtaking even for us.... A 30-page advertising increase in just a few months is a pretty awesome thing, especially when we were quite comfortable before it happened. And the circulation has increased by more than 15,000 in just the first three months of the year.... To this figure add another 5,000 sample copy requests we've been filling each issue."

The first three months of '64 saw an increased press run of 10,000 every month. Page counts climbed to 120, 124, and, by the end of March, reached 128. Since the post office required that 25 percent of a periodical's space be reserved for editorial material in order for it to qualify for reduced Second Class postage, a jump of 24 pages in advertising automatically meant another seven to eight pages of articles. The *News* would struggle with the problems of this prosperity for the rest of '64.

It was also struggling to fulfill the promises of the Kennedy half promotion. As Chet recalled: "Realizing what the new Kennedy half-dollar would do for the hobby, I incorporated it into a national advertising campaign in early January, only to learn that just four to a customer was to be the rule of distribution. With thousands of commitments, we had many an unhappy customer for a few weeks." Acquiring supplies of the new coins, packaging them for shipment, then getting them out would induce a "touch of madness" to normally serene Iola.

Despite the delays, the *News* had many more happy than unhappy customers. Demand for news about the coin trade was driving the paper to ever larger volumes. In June, the *News* reached its maximum trimmable and bindable size — 128 pages. Even before the 128-page count, many copies of the paper were arriving torn and damaged, and the staff had tried to protect it with a heavy cover sheet. "It serves as a binder around the regular newsprint used in the center sections," Chet told his readers.

The *News* was breaking new ground here. No tabloid relying on mail delivery had ever been so heavy. It was a fat, floppy-paged parcel extremely vulnerable to less than careful handling. The post office was not necessarily negligent; it's just that the *News* was so vulnerable.

In October Chet revealed that the growth of the *News* was a bittersweet problem. "The last issue of the *Numismatic News* again reached a maximum practical production size of 128 pages," he wrote. "We are, indeed, grateful to the great following of advertisers which have joined *Numismatic News*, [they] can be personally thanked for allowing us to expand our editorial content to give you, the readers, the maximum quantity of editorial content that goes into these voluminous editions."

That was the sweet part; the bitter part was that "the maximum quantity" was arriving in damaged form.

By November, a solution to the problem had been found.

"...Our plans have now been completed to deliver the *News* completely wrapped to all mail subscribers," Chet announced. "This will be accomplished by high speed equipment to insure no delay in delivery schedules." The *News* would now be delivered in a sturdy brown wrapper that would protect it from damage en route to the subscriber.

A few jokes were made about how Iola, Wisconsin was now the home of a publication that had to be delivered in a brown paper wrapper, but the simple practicality of the idea was more impressive than the laughter.

The subscribers also accrued another benefit from the brown wrapper. As Chet said, "It will further afford the subscriber delivery of a product that does not reveal the nature of the publication. This has been a point brought out to us on several occasions for security reasons."

The regular arrival of a numismatic publication told all the neighbors where the local coin collector lived. A big, fat *Numismatic News* falling out of the mail chute made many collectors more vulnerable to burglary and theft, and they were understandably uneasy. Wrapping the *News* in discrete brown paper made the subscriber's collection more secure.

Since no one had ever wrapped a fat tabloid before, the machinery was not waiting for Chet in the warehouse. As he wrote in March 1965, "Our regular mail subscribers will find their product wrapped this issue.... In 1963 you averaged an 84-page paper. In 1964 the average was 116 pages per issue. Therefore, in 1964 we began using a better grade paper on the outside section to produce a more durable binding for the staples. Although this was helpful, it was not the answer we were looking for...in the fall of 1964 an order was placed for a wrapping machine. As this machine was custom built for us we had to wait for its delivery...at long last copies of the *News* are arriving at their destination in the same condition they leave our printers."

The wrapping machine took care of one of the problems of growth at Krause. New technology in different forms would help ease the pressure in other aspects of publishing.

"There is a familiar ticking noise in our back room now — that of a teletype," Chet wrote in March. "It is used as a member of the panel who furnishes price information for the *Standard Price Guide*...the machine does in no way replace the panel of price contributors.... It is the combination of the panel who furnish prices as reflected by everyday over-the-counter transactions and mail orders, plus the use of teletype transactions that will make the *Standard Price Guide-TeleQuote* unique. It will gather information from all known sources and mold them into a most accurate cross section of current values."

In the 1980s, people all over the world would develop computer networks using sophisticated fiber-optic cables or satellite links to convey specialized data to those most interested in it. In the early 1960s, when no more than a dozen satellites circled the earth and the term microchip referred to the crumbs left at the bottom of the potato chip bag, they used the teletype. As Chet felt compelled to point out, the teletype was not setting prices, only reporting them as fast as the technology of the times would permit.

The computers were coming; the first one arrived in the form of an IBM 403 billing machine that used punch cards to keep track of 2,500 advertisers and suppliers, plus 125,000 subscribers. The IBM 403 was the equivalent of the Model T of data processing machines, except it was not quite as dependable as Henry Ford's jalopy. Many bugs had to be worked off the system before it ran as smooth as a Ford, or an IBM, for that matter. The 403 did produce nice new mailing labels which featured the post office's latest clue to locating people, the zip code.

Editorial diversification also continued, as Chet announced the formation of a "Reference Book Division." The first product of the new department was Grover C. Criswell's *Confederate and Southern States Currency*. It was a handsome 280-page volume with 415 black-and-white illustrations and 1,300 listings of currency issued during the Civil War.

A few months later the book division brought out *Coins: Questions & Answers*, by Ed Rochette, Al Varner and Cliff Mishler. Intended for the beginning collector, the book answered over 200 of the most commonly asked ques-

By combining the design features of Frank Gasparro's commemorative medal and the Franklin fifty-cent piece, Krause successfully predicted what the new Kennedy half dollar would look like. Coins *then published its good guess months ahead of the actual date of issue.*

tions on numismatics. The company publications were the best marketing vehicles for all Krause books, but *Questions & Answers*, aimed at a market of novices, was also distributed and placed on newsstands next to *Coins* magazine.

Another Krause book hit the newsstands in '64, *Coins-Price Book of United States and Canadian Coins*. As Chet described it: "The most recent book being edited here is a price guide which will be...quite unlike many of those on the market...it will cover coins of both the U.S. and Canada, listing the values of each denomination by year and various grades."

The fact that these two books, one written for beginners, the other concentrating solely on prices, were sold on newsstands indicated how the hobby had grown. Coin collecting was now popular enough for people to look for information about it at the corner drugstore.

The first three books out of the reference division were new titles; number four was a reprint. In 1885, W. S. Baker had written a book titled *Medallic Portraits of Washington*, which described and listed medals struck in honor of the first U.S. President. "The publishers of this book," Chet wrote, "used a paper that became very brittle and, as a result, the bindings of this book gave way and most copies today are merely a pile of loose pages...."

At the suggestion of collector and bibliophile Aaron Feldman, and the Token and Medal Society, Krause decided to reprint the old work and update it. "This momentous task has been done by Dr. George Feld, a well known name in the token and medal field."

These early Krause reference books illustrate the diversity of collecting and the rich vein of information that could be mined about it. A book of questions and answers on general numismatics as it was in 1964 for beginners is paired with a very specific volume on a very limited subject. Readers could learn from both books and it is safe to assume that more collectors came to the hobby after reading *Coins: Questions & Answers*, and more collectors already in the field started to examine medals and tokens after seeing *Medallic Portraits of Washington.*

Formation of the Reference Book Division was part of a general reorganization at Krause. The operation had grown large and diverse enough for Chet and his senior staff people to require and draw up lines of organization based on five departments: Editorial, Advertising, Operations, Circulation Sales and Controller.

The Editorial Department had Chet as overall publisher of Krause Publications; Ed Rochette, executive editor; Al Varner, managing editor, as well as editor of *Coins* and *Coin Dealer*; Cliff Mishler, Editor of *Numismatic News*; and Jerome Kruger, photographer and editorial assistant. Kruger was one of the newcomers, having joined the staff in November 1964. He managed the camera and darkroom work and contributed news items for *Coin Dealer*.

The Advertising Department listed William Jensen, advertising manager; Lyle Kjer, classified advertising manager; James Lyman, display advertising manager; and Doug Watson, the newest member of the advertising staff.

Lyle Kjer had joined Krause Publications in 1961, following a twenty-three-year career as a weather observer and radio operator for the Federal Aviation Agency at Grantsburg, Wisconsin. He was a native of Ogdensburg, just a few miles east of Iola. As classified ad manager, Kjer was the person who did the classifying and editing of the 700-800 classified ads that appeared in each issue of the News.

James Lyman joined Krause Publications in June, after graduating from the University of Wisconsin with a bachelor's degree in advertising. As display advertising manager, Lyman was responsible for the scheduling and layout of all display advertising in the News and Coin Dealer.

Doug Watson was the newest addition to the Krause team, joining the company late in 1964. Watson had performed layout, artwork and photography for the Advertiser, a shopper in Monroe, Wisconsin, and was assigned to the Advertising Department in Iola. As he recalled it, Doug was not just assigned to do layout in advertising. He actually "was the art department" in those days.

The Circulation Sales Department was created when the old Circulation Department was split. Circulation Sales was managed by Harry Becker and "...dealt with the public relations aspects of the organization. It is the department which must bring the various publications to the attention of the public, and keep them there."

The Operations Department made up the other part of the circulation split. It controlled "...the maintenance, operations and subscriber circulation problems [related to] delivery of the various publications to the subscribers, newsstands and coin shops. This department is kept busy maintaining and updating the mailing addresses of nearly 125,000 subscribers. The department was headed by Clem Bailey who had joined Krause Publications full-time in October 1964 after being a regular columnist for the News since January 1963.

The Operations Department also included Eugene I. Olstad who joined Krause Publications in June 1964 as chief of planning and scheduling. Olstad was responsible for printing production, binding and delivery. He was a graduate of the University of Wisconsin with a degree in business administration.

The final department — the office of Controller — was held by Bob Strand. In 1963, Coin Dealer described Strand as "...one of those people who does his job quietly and without fanfare. He's there in the morning and spends a lot of evening time at his office trying to unravel the business dealings some of the rest of us are responsible for." Strand's responsibilities included accounting and bookkeeping-invoicing, payroll, mailing and labeling lists, insurance taxes. He was a graduate of the University of Wisconsin with a degree in business administration. He was a veteran of the Korean War and had taught for two years at Iola High School before joining Krause Publications in June 1961.

Strand was and still is an avid collector of almost anything. His numismatic interests included North American and British coins while his interest in other fields embraced guns, typewriters and mustache cups.

Conspicuous by his absence from the December 1964 reorganization was the very first member of Krause's professional staff, Art Christoph. Chet reported in the Dec. 21 issue that Art "...now serves as manager of a new company associated with us. Appropriately named ...Coin Capital Printers." Chet, Art and other members of the management team set up an independent printing firm to "handle practically all the printing done for us with the exception of the publications' proper."

The reorganization — with 13 full-time professional management people — was completed by the end of 1964, and so was another addition to the Krause building. The ex-carpenter was proud of the 1,800 square feet of new work space and how it was laid out, as was evident in his description:

"We started this expansion last summer, and it is now complete. Now, as you step through our front door you'll find a pleasant reception area with a few mementoes of our 12-year history, and, in addition, a true atmosphere of a numismatic publishing company, in comparison to our previous arrangement which found visitors amid a busy working atmosphere made up of editors and advertising personnel. Our new quarters have now provided adequate space for each department, with isolation from one another. We have also been able to provide improved working area for our accounting and circulation departments."

The people on staff at Krause Publications were immersed in the day-to-day work of producing bigger publications for more readers. Most of them did not have much time to reflect on the broad, general causes of the growth. They were too busy tending the machinery to see whence it had come and where it was going. Nevertheless, Krause Publications did not run in a vacuum, nor was it a solitary engine powering its own progress. It moved, but it was also moved, by many larger processes of development in numismatics and American society.

In the twelve years since Chet started *Numismatic News*, the estimated number of coin collectors in the United States had grown from less than two million to eight million. As its circulation figures indicated, the *News* had both encouraged and benefited from that growth. Even if the majority of these collectors had — like the fans of the Kennedy half — only a casual interest in the hobby, they represented a tremendous increase in the quantity and intensity of interest Americans paid to coins as collector's items.

Many of those new collectors, and a quite a few old ones, were interested in coins only as an investment. Dealers and professional collectors now used the teletype network to play the market just as farm commodities traders bought and sold grain and cattle.

The traditional collector paid attention to individual coins or types but a new style of collecting had become popular in recent years. As Chet pointed out, "...Collecting modern coins, by the roll, by the bag, or in the specially struck proof sets...parallels that of commodity investment as it is traded in bulk [on] teletype networks as well as publications." Coins in a bag, sitting in a collection, or moving around from collector to collector were coins not in circulation.

Investment collecting also changed the public perception of the numismatist. The image of the collector as a slightly eccentric aficionado of arcana was transformed into that of the wheeler-dealer speculator whose commodity of choice was the nation's coinage. This fellow would withhold coins from circulation to make a buck no matter who was inconvenienced. Whether such a character ever existed was less important than the fact that many people — including U.S. Treasury officials and members of Congress — believed that he did.

Not only the nature and public perception of coin collecting had changed since 1952. The American population itself had increased from about 150 million in 1950 to almost 180 million ten years later; it would cross the 200 million mark by the end of the 1960s. These are the people of the much-discussed and analyzed post-World War II baby boom whose sheer numbers would enable them to shape the nation's culture and economy until well into the next century. More people need more money, not just in the abstract sense of the term as a measure of wealth, but in the very real sense of currency and coins in hand, and they put more pressure on the coinage system.

More people would have needed more coins even if American life had not changed dramatically in the 1950s and '60s. In the 1940s, the Pennsylvania Turnpike was the only long distance superhighway in the United States. By the mid-1960s thousands of miles of four-lane expressways criss-crossed the land. Many of them were toll roads with automatic collecting equipment that required drivers to travel with a pocketful of coins.

Parking a car also cost money, as city and village governments attempted to raise revenue by installing coin-powered meters on streets and in lots. State and local governments also instituted or increased sales taxes that were paid at time of purchase and usually in coins.

Vending machines were not new, but their number increased many times over in the period, and a lot of coins that could have been circulating were locked behind the coin slots. A penny could buy a gumball or a handful of peanuts, a nickel was good for a Chunky Chocolate bar, a dime could purchase a full-sized Hershey bar, and a quarter would cover the cost of a pack of Marlboros, minus the Surgeon General's warning. In some states, cigarettes cost less than a quarter, say 22 or 23 cents. Since primitive vending machines couldn't make change, cigarette manufacturers routinely stuffed pennies under the cellophane wrapper or distributors taped them to the pack. Americans were also washing and drying their clothes at coin-operated "laundermats" and cleaning up the family car, tail fins and all, at coin-operated car washes. One observer even pointed out the increased popularity in gambling via slot machines at Las Vegas as another drain on the supply of coins.

All of these factors added up to a genuine coin shortage that numismatists were well aware of before 1964. They had called for the construction of a new mint at Philadelphia in 1962, but Congress would not appropriate the money in time. Instead, Congress enacted legislation to end the shortage by making American coins less collectible. 1965 would prove to be the most tumultuous year in the history of American numismatics and of Krause Publications.

Chapter 14

1965

"...the Treasury Department is for coin collectors."   Robert A. Wallace,
Assistant Secretary of the Treasury

"...I can see very derogatory effects."
Chet Krause

For numismatists the crisis year of 1965 began early. In November 1963, the Treasury Department began replacing Silver Certificate dollar bills with Federal Reserve Notes. The switch marked a fundamental change in how the United States thought about its currency. The traditional approach was very simple. The value of paper money was literally based on the amount of gold and silver in the national vaults, and a nation was as rich as the amount of specie it had stored away. It could devalue its currency — and stimulate inflation — by printing more money without increasing the volume of precious metal behind it. The United States government issued its first real paper money in order to pay for the Civil War and set off a disastrous inflationary cycle that lasted until the Depression of 1873 knocked wages and prices down to prewar levels.

The hardship that accompanied the introduction of paper money during the Civil War made Americans suspicious of it. A paper dollar just wasn't as real as a genuine gold coin or a silver cartwheel, and that impression would linger for many years. By 1914, when the federal reserve system gave the United

States its first permanent national bank, the true value of the national monetary system depended, not on the hoard in the nation's coffers, but on the productivity of the economy. True wealth had always come from astute investment, competent management and productive working people, but most folks still liked the idea of having their money represent something real. Consequently, the United States issued "certificate" currency that was redeemable in gold, until 1933, or silver. Many Americans rested easier knowing that the crinkly paper in their pocketbooks could be traded in for what they believed to be "real" money.

In 1963, U.S. Treasury Secretary Douglas Dillon announced that the United States would stop printing money redeemable in silver. The new Federal Reserve Notes one-dollar notes would be backed, not by a mountain of precious metal, but by the productive prowess of the American economy. A century earlier a similar policy had set off a financial crisis that soured the United States on paper money for years. In 1963, it made barely a ripple in the national consciousness, although the old suspicion of so-called "fiat" money was still strong enough for the Treasury to state that it would continue to back Federal Reserve Notes with gold to 25 percent of their face value. The gold backing didn't matter to most Americans. The United States had been the pre-eminent economic power in the world for twenty years and no one dreamed that it would falter in the foreseeable future. It was as good as gold, and so was its currency.

Replacing the Silver Certificate freed more than $2.2 billion in silver held in government stockpiles. The specie could now be turned over to the Mint, which could convert it to coins and ease the shortage that plagued the economy. In fiscal 1964, which began in July 1963, the Mint issued 4.3 billion coins, and planned to strike 8 billion in fiscal 1965. Treasury Department officials also announced plans to once again mint silver dollars. The United States had not issued one-dollar coins since the last Peace Dollars were struck in 1935 and Treasury wanted to issue 45 million new ones, still using the Peace design, in 1964 and '65. As Secretary Dillon wrote to Congress, the silver dollar "is particularly used as an ordinary and traditional medium of exchange in many Far Western States [and] use of the silver dollar will...alleviate the heavy demands we have had on the quarter and 50-cent pieces."

President Lyndon Johnson signed the bill that included the appropriation for the new Peace dollars, but, except for a 100,000 coin trial run that was soon destroyed, they were never minted. The proposal was lost in the flurry of debate that accompanied other legislation related to coinage that appeared in 1964 and '65.

The most arresting provision of the new legislation called for a "date-freeze" on new coinage. All U. S. coins issued in and after 1964 would bear that year's date and no other. The sponsors of this measure aimed it directly at speculators who were hoarding coins. "Our basic problem," said Assistant Treasury Secretary Wallace, "was not the coin collector but the coin speculator who bought up coins by the roll and by the bag in the hopes of an increase in their value." The date freeze would diminish the value of all future coinage and, presumably, speculators and collectors would return their hoards to circulation.

Other provisions of the new law erased the traditional mint marks from new coins, prohibited the Mint from issuing Proof coins and Mint sets and banned the use of coins as collateral for bank loans.

Collectors found some comfort in an amendment to the date-freeze provisions that was also on the Congressional table. "Should the coin shortage abate either before the beginning of the calendar year (January 1st) or the fiscal year (July 1st)," as Chet reported, "we then have the possibility of 1965 coins...."

He then editorialized, "From our world public relations standpoint, I can see very derogatory effects, for we have a continual dating of coins since 1792 and, inasmuch as we are now viewed as the world's mightiest nation, to break this nearly two centuries of tradition, would reflect [on our ability] to assess our everyday needs."

Chet had a point here, but in the eyes of many influential Americans, the nation's prestige was better maintained by a generous circulation of the coinage than by the stamping of dates on it. Senator Alan Bible, a Democrat from Nevada, was convinced of it. His state had undergone a drastic economic shift in the years since World War II. Gambling had replaced mining as Nevada's leading industry, and gambling depended on coins. As Ed Rochette estimated in 1965, the 18,000 slot machines in Las Vegas and Reno required nearly 400 million coins a day. They had to come from somewhere and Senator Bible wanted to take them from collectors.

In May 1965, he introduced Senate Bill 2012, "aimed at the prohibition of certain practices which create artificial shortages in the supply of U. S. coins." It would become illegal for Americans to: acquire coins in excess of reasonable demands of business or personal use; export coins; buy, sell or make loans on coins at a price in excess of their face value. Exceptions were made for coins that the Treasury Department, not the marketplace, defined as "rare."

The Bible Bill was not accepted as Scripture in Iola. The *News* remonstrated that it "...deals a death blow to an educational and prestigious hobby.... The bill aims to put out of business summarily 8 publishing houses, 3,000 coin shops, 275 coin supply houses and 7,000 coin dealers directly employing about 15,000 people.

"The bill singles out the coin collector as a culprit forcing him to dispose of his collection or 'go underground' with his hobby."

Going underground was not new to some collectors. In 1933, the United States took its financial system off the gold standard and subsequently made it illegal for citizens to own significant quantities of the precious metal. While many people exchanged gold coins for currency, others simply buried them.

In 1965, coin collectors were more numerous and less docile than the goldbugs of the '30s. Collecting was an industry as well as a hobby, both branches represented million-dollar investments, and both were ready to challenge Senator Bible.

They organized the United Coin Collectors Alliance with an avowed purpose "...to conduct whatever campaign is necessary to unite all coin collectors in a solid front to prevent passage of state and federal laws that are detrimental to the hobby of coin collection."

Chet was named Executive Director of Communications for the UCCA and was charged with coordinating "...all publicity in the fight to have this bill defeated." On behalf of over 300,000 subscribers to numismatic publications, Chet pledged to "...stand up and fight."

The *News* urged collectors to "Write today to your senator, your congressmen...tomorrow may be too late...to preserve a stimulating, worthy hobby from the sentence of death." In the *News*, Chet declared, "Only by our emphatic expression will we be able to kill the monster that lurks in the darkness."

The staff members in Iola, whose vocations and avocations were now threatened, set to work. "Tens of thousands of pieces of literature have been prepared at Krause Publications.... The literature has been mailed in the form of informational kits to all known coin clubs, coin dealers and coin columnists in the United States."

With the grass roots activists mobilized, the UCCA went after the head of the problem. The Alliance hired Manford Minzer, a Washington attorney, to direct its efforts in the capital. Chet went to Washington and met his congress-

In 1965, Chet made his first appearance before a Congressional committee in Washington D. C. His testimony against the Bible Bill was the first of many trips to the capital for Krause staff people.

man, Melvin Laird. He also talked with Eva Adams, director of the Mint, and Senator Bible as well.

The trip was an eye-opener for the man from Iola. On his return, he reported that "My visit to Washington has concerned me with one thing. The image of coin collecting needs improving!"

Chet discovered that many legislators thought of coin collectors as coin hoarders who were responsible for the shortage hindering the economy. He thought collecting did not deserve its negative image and urged his readers to polish the glass through which others viewed them. "...Our hobby has been down-graded, and that's where we, the collector, can do much to reflect a proper image. It can be done at the very grass roots of our hobby.

"...Collecting coins is predicated on enjoyment; profit is secondary.... That's why it's so important to sell enjoyment. And, after all, isn't that really what we want in life?"

Enjoying his collection had always been Chet's purpose. The criticism the hobby had received in the mid-1960s showed him that all collectors were not so altruistic. Despite all the pleasure to be found in numismatics — learning the history and lore associated with coinage, appreciating the genuine beauty of individual coins, finding satisfaction in completing a set and meeting a desired goal — coins were also a tax-subsidized commodity eminently suitable for speculation. They were not the sole nor even a major cause, but collectors had contributed to the coin shortage.

Collectors did help defeat the Bible Bill, but the problem of which they were a part did not go away with the senator from Nevada. In the summer of 1965, the Lyndon Johnson administration proposed solving the coin shortage by drastically reducing, and then eliminating, the silver content of United States coins. The United States had minted nickels for over a century, and pennies that contained no precious metals, for many years, but never had the nation proposed entirely eliminating silver from its coins. American coinage was going the way of American currency. It would have no real value in itself, but would merely represent a small chip of the nation's economic power.

The immediate reason for removing silver was to end the coin shortage. The massive coin press runs required to bridge the gap between supply and demand would soon deplete the nation's supply of silver. "That is why it has been necessary for the Treasury to obtain legislative authority to change the metallic content of our subsidiary coins," said Assistant Secretary Wallace. "Had this not been done the Treasury supply of silver would have been exhausted in less than three years."

With the coinage separated from the supply of silver, the Mint could knock out a steady stream of base-metal money to meet the growing national demand for pocket change. For collectors, coins minus silver knocked numismatics into an entirely new dimension.

Collectors who kept coins for the joy of numismatics should not have been troubled, since the new coins would look and feel similar to the old ones. The history and lore would still be there, but the speculative value of the coins would be all but eliminated. Taking the silver out of the coins would divorce collecting from the precious metals market.

The new silverless coins also took the momentum out of Krause Publications and revealed a few facts about the nature of the people who had been driving up circulation figures in the past few years. Were they speculators or collectors? No sooner was the Coinage Act of 1965 passed, then circulation at Krause began to fall. By August the *News* was struggling to break the 100-page mark, even with help from a 32-page special section on the ANA Convention.

As Cliff Mishler recalled twenty years later, the *News* ". . . caught pneumonia . . . by year-end we were sputtering, and more issues were coming in under 100 pages than over. Subscription numbers were sliding steadily. As the year ended, circulation was sliding to the 65,000 plateau."

In 1965, Chet was a bit more optimistic, but realistic as well. He wrote, "Basically, any change that takes place in coinage will popularize our hobby. Such a change receives tremendous play by the national press and is reflected in the interests of clubs, conventions and hobby media. It gives every collector something to seek — not necessarily the new coin, but what the new coin has made obsolete."

Chet was right about the attraction of the "obsolete." Collectors and noncollectors alike indulged in a silver-hoarding orgy in late 1965 and the loss of interest in buying and selling silver coins was a factor in the decline in page counts at the *News*. Those who didn't have silver coins searched in vain for them. Those who had them hung onto them, knowing that the pre-1965 issues would be the last American coins to possess both numismatic and metallic value. Ironically, the congressional measure designed to reduce the hoarding of coins encouraged it. Only the doubling of the Mint's capacity and the banging out of billions of basemetal coins prevented a shortage in the late 1960s far greater than that of the mid-1960s.

The history of American numismatics has crossed many thresholds that clearly separate one period from another. Probably no threshold so clearly identified a break with the past as the Coinage Act of 1965. Collecting was thrust into a new environment where it struggled for several years before it once again became comfortable with itself. One place which saw the hardest struggle was Krause Publications.

Circulation of the *News* and *Coins* continued to decline and *Coin Dealer* went out of publication. *Coin Dealer* was struggling even before the Coinage Act. Hoping to turn it around the staff changed the format, switching from an 8.5 x 11-inch page size to 5.5 x 8.5 inches. As Ed Rochette explained in May, "...We're changing to pocket size so you can handle us easily, carry us around for ready reference, and so your ads gain greater on-the- page exposure, greater display value and impact. On the outside we're changing our cover to one of the rarest and richest you'll find anywhere, and on it featuring brilliant four-color reproductions...we're beefing up our reading content, orienting it to your interests all the way, and presenting it in quick, capsule form to save you time."

Coin Dealer was distributed free of charge to people in the numismatic trade under the presumption that advertising would pay production costs and show a profit. In January 1966, after the Coinage Act became law, the magazine was offered on a subscription basis at a rate of $3 per year. "We knew the change was inevitable," wrote Chet, "if we were to sustain the kind of magazine to which we committed ourselves last May."

Subscriptions themselves would not pay for the magazine. However, advertising in a paid periodical is worth more than it is in a free distribution magazine, and a switch to paid subscription meant that *Coin Dealer* could increase its ad base and income. That is, if the subscribers signed on. As it turned out, in the unsettled atmosphere of early 1966, subscriptions were hard to sell to professional collectors — so hard that Krause saw no future for *Coin Dealer* and, in April, stopped publishing. It was the first Krause publication to fail. Chet and other staff members were used to struggling but winning in the end. Struggling and failing was a new experience for them.

Despite the setbacks, Krause Publications continued to speak up for the hobby and the trade. In August, Chet called for an end to the crisis atmosphere in coins. "By deliberate effort," he wrote, "you do not see large headlines about pending congressional legislation in numismatic publications, as we feel enough of this type of news has been printed for awhile."

Krause also warned collectors to pay attention to their image. After the Coinage Act was passed, Treasury Department officials expressed fears that when the new composite or "clad" coinage became available, collectors would vacuum up every specimen they could acquire and prolong the shortage the new coins were designed to end.

Chet hoped to set the minds of the officials at rest and alert his readers to a new reality when he editorialized, "One thing is certain, we all must strive to improve our image with the lawmakers." He urged "...collectors to put their best foot forward...." [and] "...disappoint these Washington cynics."

He warned collectors not to grab up and hoard the new coins and published the following declaration above his signature: "In cooperation with the Treasury Department, *Numismatic News* announces its intention to refrain from the acceptance of advertising which offers the new clad coins in quantity, until such a time as the coin shortage is abated, and the new coins have achieved normal circulation."

He even suggested that collectors "reassess your collections, take those coins that aren't worth much over face...turn them back into circulation and let your congressman know that you are doing this as your part in the effort of coin collectors [to put] their best foot forward."

Considering the atmosphere of the times, when it was commonly — and correctly — believed that the United States would never again issue silver coins in quantity, any collector returning specimens to circulation was putting forward not just his best, but both his feet. It was a patriotic act that defied practicality, since every person on the street, and certainly every collector, knew that any silver coin would gain value over time and was worth saving. The quick disappearance of silver coins from circulation that occurred in the last half of 1965 only proved the point.

Coins disappearing from circulation were not the only missing pieces of silver troubling Krause Publications in 1965. One October night, a burglar slipped into the office and made off with $13,800 worth of silver dollars and rare coins. It has never been a common practice for Krause to keep more than a few collectible coins on the premises, but the fall of '65 was exceptional. The company had acquired 4,500 silver dollars for use in a subscription promotion and Chet had brought in coins valued at approximately $3,000 from his own personal collection to be photographed for a cover of *Coins*.

When the staff arrived on the morning following the burglary, they found the back door of the office jimmied and two file safes drilled open. A random break-in on the very night the safes held an unusual volume of valuable coins was a bit too coincidental for the local police to accept. They soon suspected one of the employees. Five days later, Iola restaurant owner Harry Finch discovered some of the missing coins stashed beneath some old railroad ties stacked near the old Iola pickle factory. Leaving the coins beneath the ties, sheriff's deputies staked out the site and observed a Krause employee nearby.

Upon further investigation, the police discovered that a man who had joined the staff in the spring had presented false information on his resume and had served time for armed robbery in the 1940s. He was arrested and in the course of the interrogation confessed that he had used his office keys to enter the building and open the file safes. He then removed the coins, stashed them in his garage and returned to stage the burglary. He was convicted and sentenced to five years in the state penitentiary.

The silver dollars and three of Chet's coins were traced to a dealer in New York, who returned them to Iola. The rest of Chet's coins never did turn up, but local rumor holds that anyone wishing to find them should start by excavating the old Iola village dump.

The federal government had profoundly altered the money supply with detrimental effects on numismatics, thirteen years of uninterrupted growth at Krause had ended, and a bungling burglar had lost some valuable coins, but 1965 was not a completely negative year.

Chet took a positive step by incorporating the company. The birth of Krause Publications Inc. was actually overdue, since the size of its operations had long since warranted the protection and prestige accorded by corporate organization. Krause Publications was no longer merely Chet Krause and company, but a group of people — including Chet — working together to sustain and develop a publishing operation. The corporation was a new entity in which staff people could take pride and with which they could identify. They were not merely trading time for money and helping Chet Krause get richer. They were now working for a separate organization that could — legally — stand by itself.

Theories of business operations calling for greater involvement of employees in management were not much discussed in the 1960s. Twenty years would pass before terms like "participatory" or "consensus" management became buzzwords in the boardrooms. Because of his background in Iola, his own unassuming personality and the size of his business, Chet practiced consensus management long before it became popular in larger operations. The step to incorporation in 1965 added a new dimension to the system. Now staff people were participating in the management of an entity separate from and larger than Chet Krause.

Ed Rochette was one of these people, and he had a very good year in 1965. He was executive editor at Krause and had been one of the first professional numismatists on the staff. He was hired in late 1960 in time to accompany Chet to the 1961 sessions of the Annual Assay Commission. It was an omen. Ed's experience in numismatics and his knowledge of coinage was recognized by the federal government in February 1965 when it named him to the Annual Assay Commission.

In September, Ed and Chet traveled to Chicago's Roosevelt University to help launch the nation's first university-accredited course in numismatics. Chet wrote: "Both Ed and myself are advisers to the course, and because of the great importance of the event felt it proper that we should attend.... It was indeed inspiring to be among those present."

On the second anniversary of the Kennedy assassination in November, Krause announced the publication of Rochette's latest book, *Medallic Portraits of President Kennedy*. Since Kennedy's death, over 1,000 varieties of medals bearing his image had been struck all over the world, and Rochette had cataloged them all.

Rochette was also instrumental in the introduction of what would become another regular Krause publication — the annual hobby calendar. Building on the popularity of an in-house calendar generated for 1965, and improving on it, the calendar for 1966 featured full-color photos of the coins that had appeared on the cover of *Coins*. It sold well enough to make hobby calendars a permanent part of hobby publishing in Iola. The antique car and sports collectible calendars of the future had their roots here.

Rochette's success would carry over into 1966 when he was named editor of *The Numismatist*, the ANA's official publication.

After six years with Krause, Rochette moved to his new position at the new ANA headquarters in Colorado Springs. Rochette left many happy memories of his association with Krause and a long record of accomplishment. Among his warmest memories was the response of *News* readers to his suggestion that they donate tokens bearing the image of the ship for display on board the *United States Constitution*. A New Englander himself, Ed felt a special affection for "Old Ironsides." At the 1960 ANA convention in Boston, Chet presented a collection of *Constitution* tokens to the ship's crew and they were still on display when Rochette left Krause Publications in 1967. Ed was also the man who hired Cliff Mishler and many of the other key people who worked for Krause. No matter how great his national renown, however, Ed will go down in history as the man who first suggested that Iola be re-christened as "The Coin Collector's Capital."

The *News* bid Rochette farewell by saying, "...We wish him well in his new setting. Our loss is a gain for the American Numismatic Association, and for this, we as an organization feel honored."

1965 was a memorable year for Ed Rochette, Krause Publications numismatics and the United States. In his final *News* column of the year, Chet summarized it well when he said, "...The year is nearly ended, and what a year it was!"

It was a year of losses, as Chet chronicled: "To those of us who like to save a coin from each mint, each year, 1965 thus far is a total loss to us, save the quarter dollar. It is true that by mid-1966 we will have defacto dimes and halves.... But, the lowly cent and nickel shall never bear the date.

"Too, we have no 1965 proof sets, as a matter of fact, we don't have any 1964 proof sets struck in 1965.

"Added to the earlier arbitrary losses...was the loss of mint marks.

"Through Senator Bible and cohorts, our hobby suffered its greatest losses...."

The 20 percent decline in circulation of *Coins*, the 25 percent reduction in page counts of the News, the demise of *Coin Dealer*, were testimony to the hard knocks Krause had taken and the overall decline of coin collecting.

As Chet summed it up. "1965 ended up in the RED."

Chapter 15

1966

"It was a truly rough year." Cliff Mishler

The coin speculation bubble that inflated in the early 1960s, and the Coinage Act of 1965 that popped it, brought about a fundamental change in coin collecting. The speculative period had dimmed the numismatic aura of genteel reserve, while the Coinage Act removed the silver that had been the very object of that speculation. As 1966 began, the hobby and the industry it supported faced a new dawn.

It was described by Q. David Bowers in his Centennial History of the ANA: "In the offing was a nationwide scramble to pluck all pre-1965 silver coins from circulation, eventually making it impossible to find even a common early Washington quarter, Mercury dime, or other silver coin in pocket change. Already gone was the possibility of going to a local bank and obtaining at face value Morgan silver dollars...or Peace dollars.... Now more than ever, collectors had to rely on purchases from dealers to acquire even a basic numismatic holding. In early 1966, most collectors, if asked, would state that they began their interest in coins by finding scarce dates in circulation. Increasingly, this answer was not valid...."

Chet Krause, Ed Rochette, Al Varner, Cliff Mishler, Doug Watson, and the other collectors at Krause Publications had started out in the hobby by poking through pocket change. This source was now rapidly drying up, as a massive substitution of the coinage was underway. Collectors and hoarders were removing the old silver coinage — dated and with mint marks — from circulation. Just as quickly, the Treasury Department turned up the supply of uniformly dated and unmarked "clad" coins. The semi-silver half-dollars, with 40 percent precious metal content by weight, would soon be replaced themselves by coins with no silver content at all. At the beginning of 1965, the average person could pull a variety of coins of varying ages and mint marks from his back pocket. By the end of 1966, nearly all the coins in hand — excepting cents and nickels — would be less than a year old, bear no mint marks and contain only a small amount of silver. Much of the variety that brought spice to the collector's plate had been stripped from American coinage.

Coin collecting had to redefine itself, and so did the media that served it. *Numismatic News* issued a "Bandwagon Edition" that offered a "...refresher course in basic numismatics." The 120-page issue was filled with features outlining the art, science and joy of collecting. It represented a return to the pre-1960s philosophy that emphasized the coinage and the collecting instead of the speculation. It also returned the hobby — instead of news about politics — to the front page. For several years, the media — in Iola and elsewhere — had been covering issues related to collecting instead of collecting itself. The situation resembled that of the sports publication that devotes more of its coverage to articles about players' salaries, sex life and drug abuse than it does to the sport.

With the "Bandwagon Edition," Krause wanted to return to "the sport." Chet told his readers that he hoped the issue "...would be a rekindling of your spirit, making you a better ambassador for the entire field of coin collecting." He was still sensitive about the image of collectors as hoarders and wheeler-dealers and felt that the best way to improve it was for collectors to stick to collecting.

Coins also attempted to redefine itself. Circulation had fallen drastically, from a peak of 120,000 in June 1965 to less than 60,000 a year later. Even though *Coins* was in serious danger, Krause didn't give up. "We refused to go down without giving the product our best," recalled Cliff Mishler. "Effective with the July issue, we reduced the annual subscription rate from $5 to $3. At the same time we increased the size of the package from 68 pages per issue to 100, thanks to a switch from glossy stock to newsprint body pages." Changing the paper inside allowed *Coins* to put more resources into content and

Congressional action dampened collectors' enthusiasm for circulating coins and inadvertently stimulated interest in commemoratives, as offered by a familiar Krause advertiser, Bebee's, Inc.

less into the package. It was a good financial move in hard times but — as the expanded page count indicates — it also represented a renewed commitment to covering the hobby.

Other publications had to try more drastic measures. The *News* and *Coins* tried to weather hard times by refocusing on collecting. Krause's step-child, *Canada Coin News*, tried diversifying by covering what editor Cale Jarvis called "...two of the faster growing fields in the North American hobby market, antiques and stamps." Jarvis renamed his paper *Coin, Stamp, Antique News* and reached out for a new audience. The market for stamps would remain as narrow as it always had been, but the term "antique" would expand quite a bit in the next few years. In 1966, an "antique" was usually a piece of furniture. Over the next twenty-five years it would grow to cover everything from automobiles to zithers. The expansion of the term and the explosion of interest in collecting all kinds of "antiques" would ultimately insure the success of Krause Publications. But not in 1966, when diversification beyond coins was an idea whose time had not come.

The struggle continued in Iola. *Coin Dealer* was purged. *Coins* was revamped. The *News* was refocused. All to little avail. "Before the year was out," Cliff Mishler recalled, "circulation [of the *News*] had dropped well below the 50,000 level. Only twice, and not even for the ANA convention issue, did page counts breach the 100 mark.... It was a truly rough year."

Chet pointed out the undeniably tough nut that all numismatic publishers now had to swallow. "We would be less than realistic if we did not submit to the fact that there are less coin collectors in...1966 than a year ago." The numismatic publishing niche had decidedly diminished.

Ed Rochette left Iola in November 1966. His responsibilities were turned over to Cliff Mishler, who took the new title of numismatic editor. He would "be responsible for providing numismatic direction to both *Numismatic News* and its sister publication *Coins*."

Cliff's old position as editor of the *News* went to Robert M. Poeschl. He was a retired Air Force officer with experience in military public information work who would learn the ropes of numismatics on the job in Iola.

The year closed with the Krause staff sending out a Christmas card signed by the entire staff. Twenty-five employees had weathered the roughest year ever, and they were happy for any bit of Christmas cheer they could share. Veterans of the battle of 1966 were: Chet Krause, Lyle Kjer, Harry Becker, Clem Bailey, Doug Huntington, Bob Strand, George Blenker, Lola Mae Luttrull, Marie Olson, Darlene Johnson, Bob Poeschl, Edythe Inderdahl, Sally Leer, Rosella Jenson, Clare Oppor, Cliff Mishler, Ed Rochette, Suzanne Olkowski, Doug Watson, Lois Myhra, Evelyn Stoltenberg, Mary Ann Rice, Jerry Krueger, Judy Loken and Bill Jensen. The wishes they expressed for a "Happy New Year" were more meaningful than ever before.

Another expansion within the numismatic niche was the hobby calendar that Krause later extended to other hobbies. The 1967 calendar pictured here featured a color photo of Krause products. It became a collector's item itself after customers noticed four days had been omitted from July.

Chapter 16

1967

*"This is a hobby for the ages. It will pros-
per so long as man and coins exist at the
same time on the same planet."*
Chet Krause

The hobby would exist for ages, but what form would it take and what role
would Krause Publications play in it? The company had been born and
raised on the democratic ideal that collecting could be for everyone. It had
encouraged and benefited from the hobby's growth in the 1950s and early
'60s. Government action in 1965 had altered collecting, and the people at
Krause had spent 1966 battling with the consequences of that alteration. They
would continue to battle in 1967. By the end of the year, they could claim several small victories, and tally at least one major accomplishment, i.e. they had
halted the decline of their publishing company.

Krause had a number of options it could pursue. Federal legislation had
changed the hobby, but no legislation is carved in stone. Laws could be
changed. No one with a grip on reality expected the United States to reissue
solid silver coinage, but other provisions of the 1965 Coinage Act that ham-
pered collectors could be amended. Krause could and did make a commitment
to changing the laws affecting coinage.

The company could also reexamine the coin collecting market, look for new
opportunities within its traditional niche and restructure its periodicals to meet

the new realities. Finally, Krause could recognize its own genius and build on it by applying the publishing formula that had been successful in numismatics to other pastimes.

In 1967, politics came first and mint marks were the first issue. A proposal to restore marks to the coinage had been introduced in Congress in 1966, but it languished in committee until the spring of '67. By then, the new San Francisco Mint was operating, Philadelphia and Denver had been refurbished, and together they were banging out coins at the rate of nine-plus billion units a year. The shortage of '64 was only a memory.

Chet joined other numismatists in Washington to lobby for the restoration of mint marks and proof coin sets. His face was becoming familiar to elected officials and their staff people as belonging to one of the "usual suspects" to be rounded up when they needed citizen input on measures affecting coinage. In 1967, Chet joined R. S. "Dick" Yeoman and other eminent numismatists to testify before the Senate Banking and Currency Committee, chaired by Alabama Senator John Sparkman. The Senate was still dominated by senior members from the southern states in the '60s, and Sparkman was a graduate of the "good ole boy" school of politics. Chet later recalled that he came to Washington armed with a letter to Sparkman from a mutual friend who asked the senator to treat the ole boy from Iola "like a son." With a foster father in the Senate, Chet found political doors open that would have been closed to an orphan.

He didn't have a letter for her, but Chet also knocked on the door of the director of the Mint, Eva Adams. She was no stranger, since she had visited Iola back in 1965. Her position at the Mint and her occasionally negative comments about collectors had given Adams a high profile over the past few years, but she was equally well-known for her down-home manner and Nevada-bred accent. Chet met her for lunch in Washington and asked her about mint marks.

"I like those little S's and D's, don't you?" she replied.

Chet certainly did, and he also liked, C's, CC's, O's, and other marks that have appeared on American coins over the years.

The next day, when an aide to Senator Sparkman asked Chet what Adams thought about the marks, he said that she "liked those little S's and D's, don't you?" The aide and the Senator liked them enough to initiate legislation to restore them to the coinage. Starting in 1968, "those little S's and D's" were back on the coins. Proof sets were also scheduled to come back in '68.

Chet's political work in '67 and in earlier years, and the occasion of the 15th anniversary of *Numismatic News*, prompted the American Numismatic Association to present him with a Medal of Merit. He was one of three recipients honored at the ANA convention that year.

The award certificate read, in part: "...you have contributed to all phases of numismatic work in our association. As publisher of two leading numismatic journals, you have sought to further the aims, ideals and ambitions of our association. You have served on many committees on behalf of the association, in particular, the numismatic terms standardization committee, where specific research on your part has greatly aided the committee in realizing their goal.

"You were most active in Washington, D.C. to gain restoration of mint marks on coins. As an author, you have shared your knowledge with fellow collectors. You have given freely of your time and efforts, and have contributed immeasurably to the encouragement, enjoyment and promotion of numismatics and numismatic knowledge."

Krause had begun the year with a special 15th anniversary issue that included an editorial in which Chet reflected that, "Without a doubt, there has been more happening in the United States with respect to coin collecting in the (past) decade and a half than in the combined years prior to *Numismatic News*. Indirectly, we at Iola have had a hand in things."

A lot had happened over the years, and in Iola they were trying to figure out how to stay on top of the situation. Circulation was still slipping at the *News* and at *Coins*. The *News* would drop to 40,000 and *Coins* to below 60,000 by the end of the year. Yet, as Chet told his readers, "faith in the hobby perseveres at Krause Publications despite the present lull." As always, faith was accompanied by action.

"We worked hard to turn things around, with a strong promotional effort tied to an anniversary theme," Cliff Mishler recalled. "For just $5, the annual subscription rate plus $1, new and renewal subscribers [to the *News*] then received a bonus in the form of specially packaged 'mint sets' containing 1966 or 1967 coins."

Krause had been using premiums of many kinds for many years, but the mint set "bonus" of 1967 was truly unique. Using all available resources to meet the seemingly insatiable demand for coins to meet circulation needs, the U. S. Mint had discontinued the sale of coin sets to the public. Collectors were eager to acquire nominally priced sets of coins consisting of selected examples of current issues, and many of them accepted Krause's offer. The promotion proved to be very popular and productive, and would serve as a model for promotional efforts which would follow through the years.

Editorial content was also shifting, with more coverage of tokens, medals and international coins, and with more feature pieces on coin lore and the pleasure of collecting. The combination of good news from Washington, the subscription giveaway and the shift in editorial content worked. By the end of 1967, circulation figures for the *News* bottomed out. In '68 they would turn around and begin nudging upwards. The *News* would never again reach the heights of 1964 and '65, but it would never again fall to the depths of mid-1967.

Krause also decided to follow the maxim that says, "When the old falters, try the new." The "new" came in the form of two publications. The first was a new magazine initially titled *North American Coins*. It was soon renamed *Coin Prices*, which was a more accurate description of its contents. The *News* and *Coins* had been printing the *"Standard Price Guide"* since 1962. It was one of the most popular features of both publications and had helped spur their growth in the hot years of the '60s.

Coin Prices covered all American coins, Mexican coins since 1905 and Canadian coins from 1864. It was published quarterly and sold on newsstands, presumably alongside *Coins*, so the audience could find it. The first issue, which appeared in the fall of '67, was enthusiastically received. The second issue, which appeared in spring 1968 and was the first to be called *Coin Prices*, was also a flying success.

"We launched *Coin Prices* to give newsstand readers a legitimate price guide," Chet recalled. The changes that had taken place in American numismatics since 1965 had created a greater demand for price information. *Coin Prices* served veteran collectors but it was primarily aimed at the people who had been pulling pre-1965 silver coins out of circulation and now wanted to know how much they were worth.

All grading standards were well-defined and prices were presented for type coins in nine grades of presentation: Proof, Uncirculated, About Uncirculated, Extremely Fine, Very Fine, Fine, Very Good, Good, and About Good, or Fair.

Prices were reported based on teletype sales reports coming to Iola from dealers throughout the United States and Canada. The first price panel, whose sales were reported in the fall of 1967, included: Joseph J. Adamski of Naugatuck, Connecticut; Aubrey Bebee of Omaha, Nebraska; Lauren Benson of Davenport, Iowa; Hy Brown of Painesville, Ohio; Collectors Research of Montreal, Canada; Joseph DeBock of Chico, California; Thomas W. Fruit of Green Bay, Wisconsin; Nick Berbinski of Winnipeg, Canada; Ray Hobin of Stittsville, Canada; Richard Margolis of Teaneck, New Jersey; Chuck Martin of Sudbury, Canada; Ivan Martin of Corpus Christi, Texas; Tom Mowerey of St. Paul, Minnesota; Richard M. Muniz of Miami Shores, Florida; Dean Oakes of Iowa City, Iowa; Roscoe T. Parmley of Mt. Clemens, Michigan; Jess Peters of Peoria, Illinois; Joe Powers of Lynn, Massachusetts; William G. Scott of Wakefield, Massachusetts; Norman Schultz of Salt Lake City, Utah; Leo M. Thomas of Ashland, Ohio; J.C. Wozniak of Sunland, California; and Glenn Wright of Iowa City, Iowa.

The idea of reporting prices based on a national panel and using up-to-date equipment had been controversial when the *News* introduced it in 1962. It still had its critics in 1967. Some collectors felt that one inept but wealthy buyer and one unscrupulous dealer in one corner of the continent could drive up coin prices from Florida to Fairbanks. The threat of the "fool driving the market" had always been a part of coin collecting. It would always be a part of coin collecting, and of other branches of collecting as well, no matter who sets the prices or how they are reported. It was a fact in 1967, when Aubrey and Adeline Bebee paid $46,000 for the McDermott nickel, and it was a fact in 1991, when millionaire hockey star Wayne Gretzky and millionaire hockey franchise owner Bruce McNall paid $410,000 for a Honus Wagner baseball card. The collector's market has always been free and a free market is just that, free. People who participate are free to be as foolish as they are free to be wise. In 1967, *Coin Prices* helped them make a choice.

In his 15th anniversary retrospective editorial, Chet recalled the beginnings of the *News* and its importance to collecting. "The 20 free words of classified ads once offered to a subscriber with his subscription had a marked influence on what evolved," he wrote. "At that time, although I almost went broke fulfilling the bargain, it aroused collectors to trade with one another. Today, as was the case then, the very basis of enjoying your collecting is the ability to buy, sell or trade with one another."

In 1967, Krause Publications returned to the democratic commitment that Chet had made in 1952. It was as much a business decision as a statement of principle.

"...To serve," as Chet wrote, "the specific needs of the average American collector, the collector whose budget does not allow him to ever think of owning such rarities as a 1913 Liberty Head nickel," Krause introduced *Coin Shopper.*

It came with a $2 a year subscription price for twelve issues and a nearly free classified ad rate of four cents a word. As the *News* reported, "...*Coin Shopper* will be concentrated in the area of classified advertising, balanced by the display advertising of dealers, [but] the news angle of the hobby will not be neglected. A special section of the publication will be given over to the presentation of 'Collector Capsules,' brief capsule reviews of the news of the day throughout the world of coins."

The first issue of the *Shopper* appeared in October — eight pages shipped free to 22,000 collectors who were not on any other Krause subscription list. They received a familiar Krause sales pitch, three free issues — October, November, December — the same offer the original readers of the *News* had received in the fall of 1952. A giveaway was also part of the deal. Subscribers could add a dollar to the cost of the sub and receive a shiny 1965 Canadian silver dollar.

The *Shopper* was intended to revitalize Krause Publications by digging down to the grass roots of collecting. The *News* had its readers, now largely reduced to the core of veteran collectors who were around before the '60s. The staff in Iola was looking for a new generation of collectors who were starting as they had, with a surplus of passion for coins and a shortage of resources. The *Shopper* was targeted to bring in new collectors who might not be comfortable with the *News.*

The question to be answered in the next year or so was whether or not a whole new generation of coin collectors existed; and if it did, how large was it? The first wave of a new generation had matured in the fifteen years since Chet had mailed out the Volume I, Number 1, of the *News*. It was the largest, wealthiest, best-educated and most sophisticated group of Americans to inhabit the continent, and the first to have a television set to fill their idle hours. These young people had more leisure time and more ways to enjoy it than their elders had ever imagined. Whether a significant number of the same baby-boomers who loved televised sports, rock-and-roll and Pontiac GTOs was also interested in coins would determine how Krause Publications would develop in its second fifteen years.

One item everyone seemed to enjoy was a calendar. The annual coin collector's calendar introduced in 1965 as a publishing timetable for the staff, and advertisers had proven very popular beyond the confines of the office. The 1966 calendar was the first to be offered as a subscription premium and for sale. It featured full-color photos borrowed from the covers of *Coins* and notes on significant dates in numismatic history compiled by Clem Bailey. Over the years, calendars have proven to be the easiest to manage and the most dependable subscription premiums for numismatic and other hobby publications.

Demand for the 1967 calendar was so great that it required three press runs with, as Chet reported, "...a note pinned to the purchase order: 'We need these yesterday.'" Demand for the calendar was strong, even though the staff, in its rush to be on time, had sent the first run to the printer minus the dates of July 26, 27, 28 and 29. It was a bittersweet error, since, to a collector, a calendar minus a few days is a collectible. As Chet wrote, the 1967 calendar "...was corrected in the second and third press runs, and the errors have now achieved the stature of collector's items."

The mishap with the calendar in Krause's 15th anniversary year harkened back to the wobbly early days of the *News*. In an anniversary editorial, Chet recalled, "Those early years produced many a laugh. I recall that the 'office' was an old library table...in the bedroom. The first piece of equipment was a four-legged secretary's chair.

"One night, long after the rest of the household had retired, I decided to call it quits. I pushed back on my lightweight swivel chair, one wheel caught on a raw edge of floor-covering, and I awakened the entire household with a crashing reverse swan-dive."

He also reflected on how the work had changed. "I was in business several months before anyone felt it important enough to call me on the phone, but once it began to ring, it has never stopped.... The first call I remember was from Blaise Danton (Peachtree Coin Shop) of Atlanta, Georgia. He had sent in an ad which either came too late or we didn't have time to set; things never were on much of a schedule in those early months. In any event, I just laid the ad aside, intending to take care of it in the next issue. Blaise, in all his professional Southern eloquence, proceeded to tell me the facts of life. That day, I was happy he was in Atlanta and I in Iola.

"Harry Forman was (and still is) a great believer in postcards and the telephone, and would call in last minute changes. I thought this was O.K. but he always did it about midnight. I was years in breaking him of that habit. On second thought, I doubt if I ever did! I think he just began working shorter hours. He still holds the record for my longest call, an hour and forty-five minutes."

Whether the hours were long or short, and whether or not the progress made since 1952 would be sustained for another fifteen years, Chet still found great satisfaction in what had been accomplished. "The past fifteen years is not a particularly long period in the reckoning of time, but to us, it has been the most interesting and rewarding of our lifetime."

Chet had no way of knowing it, but the next twenty-five years would be about the same, only more so.

Chapter 17

1968

*"The future climate for the coin collector
in the United States is becoming increasingly promising."*   Chet Krause

The future was looking brighter for collectors in 1968. The U. S. Mint restored mint marks with coins struck on the first working day of the year and "those little S's" from San Francisco brought joy to the hearts of numismatists across the country.

Proof sets also returned in '68. Originally intended as gifts for dignitaries visiting the United States, the multi-coin sets that epitomized the coin maker's art caught on with collectors as soon as they were available in 1936. Production was low in the 1930s and suspended entirely during most of World War II. Not until 1950 did the Mint again strike proof sets. Their return helped fuel the growth of the hobby in the 1950s, as thousands of Americans began to religiously purchase them every year. In 1961, the Mint struck more than three million sets and, despite its own pronouncements about the coin shortage and hoarding by collectors, boosted production to a height of 3.9 million for 1964.

In 1968, proof sets were struck again, at San Francisco instead of Philadelphia, so the new coins bore the San Francisco mint mark. By August the *News* was reporting that 1.7 million sets had been ordered and the Mint was placing a ceiling of two million on production. Demand would prove large enough for the Mint to push output beyond the three million mark by the end of the year.

Canada had celebrated the centennial of its independence in 1967 by issuing a handsome set of silver coins that stirred up interest recently gone dormant in the United States. Demand for Canadian silver was so strong that Krause decided to feature the scene of a coin bag spilling out Canadian dollars on the cover of the spring '68 issue of *Coin Prices*. This was the second issue of *Coin Prices*, with a press run 25 percent larger than that of the first edition. It was fortunate that there were more of them, since newsstand sales of the guide were so strong that distributors were reporting sellouts and asking for more. As interest in *Coin Prices* indicated, the climate for collecting had become increasingly promising.

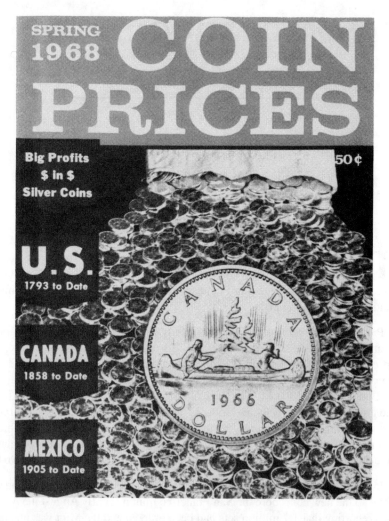

Even though the United States was removing silver from its coins in the late 1960s, interest in silver coins was still strong. This 1968 issue of **Coin Prices** *was targeted on collectors of the popular new Canadian silver coins.*

Although it did not involve coins, interest in collecting and in silver was also stimulated by the Treasury's redemption of silver certificates. Starting in May of '67, the holders of the notes could exchange them for $1.2929, their value in silver, plus a premium based on the silver futures market. By the time the program closed at the end of June 1968, over $150 million worth of notes was redeemed, with another $240 million unaccounted for.

Many collectors held onto their certificates in the hope that they would increase in value after the Treasury's redemption program ended, but as Chet wrote at the time, "no appreciable collectors market was developed." Instead, "the great stir they created has sparked new interest in paper money...an unforeseen but welcome boon to the hobby."

As always, news about coins, currency and silver "was a boon to the hobby" and to Krause Publications. The passing of time also helped. The numismatic world had settled down since the turbulent mid-1960s, which only helped stabilize circulation figures at *Coins* and *Numismatic News*. The decline had bottomed out in the summer, with page counts at the *News* dropping to 48 before returning to and staying in the 64- and 72-page range by the end of the year. Circulation held in the 45,000 range. *Coins* published a steady 68 pages throughout the year, with circulation hovering in the vicinity of 60,000. The numbers were smaller than in 1965, but they were respectable and solid.

The editorial content of *Coins* reflected the new reality of the collecting world. In October, for example, *Coins* ran four feature articles, all by freelance writers. Don Taxay wrote about the early American coins known as the Fugio cents. Larry Stevens put together a farewell photo essay on the old Philadelphia Mint. Carl Allenbaugh wrote a historical review of coinage related to the Olympic Games which was also timely, since the 1968 Mexico City Games were held that month. Finally, Dan Raymond penned a piece about Good Conduct medals awarded by the United States Coast Guard. Only one of these articles was about United States coinage. To be sure, other pages of *Coins* were filled with columns and news about American coins, but the feature section indicated the broadening of interest that was now required in numismatic publishing. The columns made the same point. In addition to the three coin columnists writing for *Coins* — Maurice Gould, Walter Breen and Clem Bailey — was Virginia Culver whose "Token Tales" kept track of collectible tokens.

The *News* was also broadening its coverage. The November issue included a 16-page insert titled "The Medal," which covered collectible medals of all sorts, from the medallions presented to American Indian chiefs at treaty time, to newly minted pieces struck in memory of the recently assassinated Senator, Robert F. Kennedy.

"That the hobby was developing a new face was readily evidenced by a perusal of the pages of the *News*," recalled Cliff Mishler. "Nearly every issue carried ads offering new commemorative medal programs. A bead was being drawn on world coins, emphasized by the marketing of a variety of modern sets and individual coin commemoratives."

Krause's newest periodical, *Coin Shopper*, struggled to find a place in the new numismatic niche. In May, it was combined with *Coin Collector*, a tabloid formerly published in Kewaunee, Illinois which Krause had recently acquired. The people in Iola hoped to duplicate the success they had with *Coins* in 1962. Its initial circulation had been built through the timely acquisition of *Numismatic Times and Trends*.

The new combined *Coin Collector* and *Shopper* offered 32 pages of want ads, display ads and articles for a $3 subscription. Along with the subscription came the opportunity to place one free want ad. It was "Like finding a dollar bill," as proclaimed by the house ad inserted in the *Shopper's* pages. Although the *Shopper* absorbed the subscription list of *Coin Collector*, it had a tough time maintaining circulation in profitable numbers. The Krause people hoped that the acquisition of *Coin Collector* would invigorate the "trader's" tabloid and keep it alive into the 1970s; they had little reason for optimism in 1968.

Ironically, probably the *Shopper's* stiffest competition was right in Iola. As collectors came to rely more on dealers and less on each other to build their collections, the display ads in *Numismatic News* became more important than want ads in the *Shopper*. The whole process of mail order sales that the *News* had worked so hard to successfully establish was reducing the potential niche for the Shopper. In short, the collector of the late 1960s wasn't as isolated as that of the early 1950s, his collection was more sophisticated and he felt more comfortable buying from and selling to professionals.

The *News* made it even easier for its readers to deal with professionals by inaugurating the Customer Service Award. To qualify for the award an advertiser could not be the subject of more than five complaints from readers in a year and could not leave any justifiable complaints unresolved. The award winner was also expected to purchase a minimum amount of advertising on a timely basis. The minimum purchase requirement seemed to be a nice way for Krause to stroke its biggest advertisers while paying lip service to readers, but the CSA was, and is, a sincere attempt to keep the trade honest.

"The last two criteria may sound self-serving, but volume [of advertising] is necessary in order to expose themselves to activity generating the potential of complaints and reflects how they conduct business," said Cliff Mishler in a 1991 interview. It is difficult to gauge how an advertiser deals with customers if he rarely advertises specific coins for sale or purchase. A regular advertiser, by comparison, is running his operation in a business- like manner and his efforts can be monitored. If something is wrong, it turns up via customer complaints. As Mishler said, "In all likelihood a negative trait runs through their fabric and will be exposed."

The idea of working to keep the trade honest has deep roots at Krause Publications. It goes back to Chet's 1953 decision to refuse advertising from dealers unwilling to publish the results of mail sales. Inquiring about and following up on complaints became standard practice at Krause in the 1950s and continued into the 1960s. Krause kept track of its advertisers by placing blind orders, i.e. placing orders via anonymous third parties and then assessing how the advertiser handled the order.

"We are very conscious about the integrity of the industry and our mail order advertisers," said Mishler. "It's important for us to maintain the trust of subscribers."

Maintaining that trust was not only right, it was good business. Krause was able to survive the downturn of the late '60s, in part because it was not losing readers because of dishonest advertising.

Fred Green became responsible for the advertising department at Krause in October 1968. He left *Coin World*, another hobby tabloid, and moved to Iola to supervise advertising in all Krause periodicals. A charter member of the Texas Numismatic Association, Green was — like all managerial people at Krause — a collector and a member of the American Numismatic Association.

Tom Becker also belonged to the ANA. He joined the editorial staff at Iola in August, after working at the National Bank of Detroit's Money Museum. Becker was a numismatic historian who earned the ANA's top literary award for his *History of Minting Methods* in 1966. He had also published other books and many articles that had appeared throughout the numismatic press, including the *News* and *Coins*.

Becker and Green were examples of the kind of people coming on staff on Krause — professionals in publishing and in numismatics.

The year ended with a bulletin from the Treasury Department announcing it would release 2.9 million Morgan dollars for circulation. The coins would be sold on a bid-sale basis in ten different date categories. Well over 100 million Morgan or Liberty Head dollars were struck between 1878 and 1890, and the Treasury's hoard was the last and the largest store of the coins known. The stockpile cast a large shadow over the market for silver dollars. The dates of the coins it contained, their volume and quality, were unknown. Collectors wanted the shoe to drop so they would know how it would affect their own stores of Morgan dollars. Some of the Morgans were released in '69, but it was not until 1970 that the final store was open to collectors.

The announcement of the Morgan dollar sale was a fitting end to a year that had witnessed the end of the depression in numismatics. Collectors now had another 2.9 million silver coins to seek out and trade, and Krause Publications could look to a new year with more promise than any since 1965.

The Richard M. Nixon commemorative medal is a token of the late 1960s. The inflation that began in those years triggered a boom in collecting that created an environment favorable to growth at Krause.

Chapter 18

1969

*"Nearly every issue carried ads offering
new commemorative medal programs."*
Cliff Mishler

The year began with the inauguration of President Richard Nixon. The
Vietnam War was still in full rage, and among the ills it was inflicting on
the United States was economic inflation. Prices rose, the purchasing power of
the dollar diminished, and real goods — antiques, coins, silver flatware —
became more valuable. The energy crisis of 1973 is usually remembered as
the starting point of the disastrous inflation that plagued the United States in
the 1970s and early '80s, but the dollar had already been shrinking for several
years before the price of gasoline tripled.

Stimulated by inflation, interest in collectibles grew rapidly in the 1970s,
and created an environment favorable to growth at Krause Publications. The
company's development, based on the expansion and diversification that
began in the '70s, occurred in a period of inflation and cannot be understood
outside that context. Ironically, the company that began because of its
founder's interest in coinage, experienced its greatest growth only after inflation devalued the entire monetary system and increased the value of a broad
range of collectibles in addition to coins.

In 1969, inflation was already making coins more valuable as collector's
items and arousing the silver market. This circumstance created greater

demand for commemorative medals and other collectibles made of precious metals — all of which was good for Krause.

The inflation that the Nixon administration battled had a general and permanent effect on the economy, collecting and numismatic publishing. One part of the Nixon political agenda had a more specific and timely effect. Dwight Eisenhower died in the summer of '69 and, after reading one of Cliff's editorials in the *News*, Republican partisans began calling for the Mint to strike a coin in his honor. They argued that Franklin Roosevelt had been so honored shortly after his death, as had John Kennedy. Eisenhower, by comparison, was the hero of World War II and a two-term president who had successfully confronted the Soviet Union during the Cold War.

Arguing the worthiness of political leaders — dead or alive — for immortalization on the coinage was a question that the founders of the United States had briefly debated. They decided that placing the image of a political leader, no matter how great a statesman, on the coinage was anti-democratic and unsuitable for the young republic. After all, only kings and emperors had their faces stamped on the coinage. The United States would immortalize great democratic ideals such as liberty or peace on its coins and not some faddishly popular politician.

The nation began chipping away at the democratic tradition in 1909 when it marked the centennial of his birth by placing the image of Abraham Lincoln on the penny. The images of George Washington, Thomas Jefferson and Ben Franklin followed, their presence on the coinage justified because they were founding fathers. Franklin Roosevelt, whose visage appeared on the dime about one year after his death, was different. His accomplishments were great, but had not been tested by the passage of time, yet there he was on the coinage. Once the precedent was set, any national outpouring of grief or affection for a leader could be transferred to the coinage, as in the case of John F. Kennedy in 1964.

By 1969, however, the coinage was covered with statesmen and finding a coin for Ike was difficult. He was too important a leader for a mere limited issue commemorative like the 1946 Booker T. Washington/George Washington Carver fifty-cent piece. His coin had to be in everyday circulation. However, removing Washington from the twenty-five-cent piece would be a national sacrilege, no matter who replaced him. Likewise, Ike couldn't bump Jefferson off the nickel, and even if he could, the Republicans would not allow their hero to appear on a coin of smaller denomination than the Democrats' Kennedy or Roosevelt.

Accordingly, Congress resolved to strike the first new one-dollar coin since 1935. Eisenhower could get his coin without displacing an American hero and the Republican dollar would outrank the Democrat half-dollar and dime. The Congress and the Nixon Administration chewed over the fine points of the Eisenhower coin throughout late 1969 and early '70. The amount of silver it should have, if any, was among the points of discussion. In keeping to its pattern of inconsistency, Congress passed a measure removing all the silver remaining in American coins, then mandated that the new Eisenhower dollar would be produced in both cupro-nickel-clad and 40 percent silver versions. The first Ike dollars bore the date of 1971, and were the first American dollar coins not to be 90 percent silver.

Coinage has always been subject to the whims of politics. The Eisenhower dollar, which halted a forty-year old interruption in the minting of United States dollar coins, was yet another example of how politics sometimes manages the Mint.

Chet says that credit for the Eisenhower dollar "truly belongs to Cliff, but several Washington notables immediately took credit for it once it became law. Frank Gasparro, the chief engraver of the U. S. Mint still [1992] thanks Cliff for having given him the opportunity to design the coin."

In Iola at the start of '69, neither Cliff nor anyone else was paying much attention to inflation or politics. Instead, the staff was busy banging out the first weekly issues of *Numismatic News*. The switch represented what Cliff later called, "solid testimony to our confidence and the enthusiasm of collectors and dealers." Mishler was right when he said it in 1985, and the Krause team was right when they did it back in '69. The *News* held onto its 45,000 subscribers and, sooner than anyone expected, page counts for some weekly issues were larger than that of the average bi-weekly issue.

Switching the *News* to weekly publication also pointed out another reality of the times. The late '60s were years of transition in mass communications and data transmission. The *News* was straddling the gap between the past and the future. As a print medium, it was in the traditional camp, communicating via the printed word as people had communicated for centuries. The process had been considerably expedited, but the transmission of information still took at least one week from arrival in the *News* office to delivery to the reader.

At the same time the *News* acquired information via the most modern means of communication — the telephone and the teletype.

The Telequote page of coin prices was as up-to-date as the technology of the times could make it. Coin prices could be transmitted to Iola minutes after sales were completed. Getting that news out of Iola and to the readers took as long as two weeks. Obviously the bottleneck was in Iola. In 1969, only visionaries foresaw the extension of electronic communication from point to point that came with cable television and computer networks in the 1980s. In Iola in '69, the best way to expedite the transmission of information from source to reader was to publish more frequently.

The *News* became a weekly and was able to relay data in only a few days. Further refinements in information gathering, processing and transmission would occur over the next few decades, but when the *News* became a weekly in 1969, it had gone about as far as a print medium could go in putting news in the hands of its readers as fast as possible.

The *News* continued to provide broader coverage than it had in the early '60s. As Cliff wrote twenty years later, "Nearly every issue carried ads offering new commemorative medal programs. A bead was being drawn on world coins, emphasized by the marketing of a variety of modern sets and individual coin commemoratives."

The appeal of commemoratives was revealed in the *News* editorial content as well as its ads. A major feature on the Philadelphia Mint was paired with an even larger piece on the privately owned and operated Franklin Mint. Increasingly, new issues from Franklin were accorded as much coverage as the output of the United States Mint — yet another indicator of the trend of the times.

The Convention of International Numismatics was scheduled for Los Angeles in '69 and it gave the *News* a chance to focus on world coins by issuing its first world coin supplement in June. "There are 1600 collectible U. S. coins," recalled Chet in 1991, "as opposed to thousands of collectible coins in the world." If U.S. coins had become less interesting since 1965, foreign coins had not. Krause had already been providing regular coverage to international numismatics in *Coins*. The world coin supplement in the *News* in June 1969 represented an expansion that the company would build on in years to come.

One expansion it would not build on was *Coin Collector* and *Shopper*. The paper died at the end of 1969. The numismatic niche had changed and a want ad paper for individual collectors no longer had a place in it.

Another casualty of change was the Roosevelt University course in numismatics that Chet and Ed Rochette had helped start in 1965. Only a few students had registered in '68 and '69, and the Chicago university stopped offering it. It was a disappointment to numismatic veterans. They were already expressing concern over the "graying" of the hobby and some wondered if it would die when the last members of the World War II generation passed on. The *News* and *Coins* targeted some editorial material to young people, and ran features on how to begin collecting on a fairly regular basis, but numismatics was too tame a pastime for most members of the Woodstock generation.

Two men for whom numismatics was not too tame joined the staff in 1969. Rollie Finner signed on as a researcher in April and Glenn Wright became part of the advertising sales staff later in the year. In short time, Wright would be ad manager of *Numismatic News* and, in 1973, he was named Krause's vice president of advertising.

The 1960s had seen more change concentrated in a shorter period of time than any in American history. Coin collecting had gone through the wildest roller coaster ride it had ever known and had taken the little company Chet Krause had started along for an exhilarating and dangerous run. Collecting and Krause Publications had changed, adapted and survived. More roller coaster rides were coming, yet the decade ended on a telling note.

For several years the Treasury Department had been employing a separating machine that sorted coins as they passed through the federal reserve system. The gadget pulled all the silver coins so they could be withdrawn from circulation. By the end of 1969, the Treasury announced that the separator would cease to operate. It no longer had to pull silver coins out of circulation because there were so few silver coins left. No other piece of information so well sums up the decade of the '60s.

Chapter 19

1970

"There's an old saying that victory has a hundred fathers and defeat is an orphan." John Kennedy

A truly useful aphorism has several interpretations. Kennedy's quote points out the normal human desire to claim credit for success, and to disavow failure. It also states the truism that a successful endeavor — like the growth of Krause Publications — is rarely the product of a single cause.

At least three general factors added up to success for Krause. Two of them were beyond the company's control. First, Krause developed in a culture that placed high value on material goods and during an inflationary period which only added to that value. Second, Krause developed in a period when technology was revolutionizing mass communication. The third, and the controllable factor, was Krause's ability to build on the first two. The company was persistent about searching for marketing niches that were growing due to inflation and receptive to the use of up-to-date technology. Building a successful business is like steering a boat on the ocean. The helmsman cannot control what the wind and waves will do, but he can adjust his sails and spin the wheel to take best advantage of new conditions. This is what Krause Publications was doing in the opening days of the 1970s.

New technology came to Iola in the form of an IBM System 3 Series 10 computer. It began as a device for storing addresses and printing mailing labels, but it did it faster and more accurately than any other system yet devised. IBM later developed its circulation application manual on the basis of the Krause installation. It was a prototype for the computerized handling of names and addresses that is the foundation of modern direct-mail marketing. Its use of zip codes was also new, and Krause became only the second publisher in the United States to use the new codes on all its mailings. IBM perfected its systems in Iola, then took it around the world. In 1969, they could have changed the sign near Iola. Instead of declaring that the village was the "Coin Collector's Capital," it could have read, "The Birthplace of Computerized Direct-Mail Marketing."

In time the computer also handled accounting and other management chores. It reduced clerical time and space, eliminated duplicate mailings, and expedited the delivery of all Krause products. Describing the new system at Krause, the *Stevens Point Journal*, said it was, "The blending of modern communication factors with the leisurely setting of the Wisconsin woodlands." The next twenty years would see this blending recur over and again at Krause, until, by the late 1980s, a desk without a computer was a rare sight.

Also in 1970, Krause completed its shift to offset printing. The year's first issue of *Numismatic News* was printed by the new process. The raised-type letterpress system that was invented in the 1500s was replaced by the essentially photographic process of offset lithography. Type could be set faster, page design could be more elaborate while layout work was simplified, and, most especially, a sharper photographic image could be reproduced. The *News* was physically improved when Krause's printer, the *Shawano Evening Leader*, switched its newspaper production plant to offset.

With new technology on line, Krause was still exploring odd corners of the numismatic publishing niche. *Coin Shopper* had died because, as Cliff recalled, "We responded to a cry from readers that they 'don't need that stuff every week.'" Most of the old readers were happy with what they had, but new ones were a bit harder to find. Krause cast a net for new readers by putting together a single sheet tabloid called *Numi-Notes*. It was sold in lots of 100 to dealers, coin clubs and interested collectors, "at the cost of mailing," which came to a penny a copy.

The goal was to place a stack of *Numi-Notes* on the counter of every coin dealer in the country. "How many times have you had interested collectors walk into your shop bubbling over with questions, only to walk away disappointed because you were too busy to answer them?" asked an ad for *Numi-Notes* in the *News*.

The little handout answered "95 percent of the beginners questions, thus creating friends, which in turn are potential customers." The people picking up *Numi-Notes* might also be customers for Krause as well, a fact that the ad acknowledged when it stated that "we have included our advertising message."

Advertising messages for the *News* were important in 1970. Readership was increasing, but advertisers were not; nor were established advertisers running larger ads. The growth curve for ad lineage was nearly flat. Special spring and fall "Bandwagon" editions targeted on coin collecting did well. Performing better were special editions on medals, Canadian coins, and international coinage. Subjects that were once of only secondary interest to American coin collectors were coming to the forefront.

So was silver. The United States removed the metal from all its coins except collector editions of the new Eisenhower dollar, which only helped make silver in foreign coins and elsewhere more attractive to American collectors. In fact, one reason circulation at the *News* rose in 1970 was a successful subscription promotion using uncirculated specimens of the 1966 Canadian silver dollar. For $1.25 plus the regular $5 annual subscription cost, readers received the coin that, as the ad read, "will never be minted again." This was a good deal, since the silver coin was worth more than the $1 Krause was charging and the additional 25 cents just covered the cost of shipping and handling.

As the popularity of the Canadian dollar showed, silver exerted an irresistible force on many collectors. In 1970, producers tried to profit from the force by marketing silver stamped and shaped into a variety of forms. *Coins* and medals were the obvious and traditional shapes for precious metal, but the "bar" was becoming increasingly popular. Calling rectangular-shaped, one-ounce strikings of pure silver a "bar" conjured up an appealing and marketable image of the cache of government specie stacked up at the West Point Bullion Depository. For example, in 1970, Foster Inc., Walla Walla, Washington,

The Eisenhower dollar ended the 40-year-old American hiatus from the minting of dollar coins. Cliff Mishler was instrumental in bringing back the coin.

advertised three ounce bars stamped to commemorate silver mines in the vicinity of Coeur d'Alene, Idaho. Single bars sold for $12 and a five-bar serially numbered set retailed for $59.50. An ounce of silver shaped into a commemorative something and selling for $4 was typical of the times. For Krause, interest in silver, and the proliferation of coins, medals, and bars into which it was formed and marketed, represented new material for editorial coverage, more potential readers, and another source of advertising.

The *News* kicked off the year with a special supplement devoted to commemorative medals. "The collecting of medals has taken giant strides during recent years!" read an introductory piece. "As prices of key coins have continued to climb to unobtainable heights for many collectors, many have turned their attentions from coins to medals. Serving much the same purpose of the now defunct commemorative half dollars, medals — for many — have become a wholly acceptable and adequate substitute."

The lead article of the supplement profiled the leading source of the "adequate substitute." It announced the "new $10,000,000 plant and office facility 12 miles southwest of Philadelphia" of the Franklin Mint. Franklin opened its doors with seven employees in 1964, just when the world of coins and collecting was changing profoundly. Riding the crest of those changes through the close of the 1960s, Franklin became the world's leading producer of commemorative medals, bars, plates and other metallic collectibles. Franklin was a genuine mint that struck coinage for nations too small to have a mint of their own, like Jamaica, Barbados and Panama. It struck coins, bars and plates in gold, platinum, sterling silver, fine silver, brass, bronze, nickel and various alloys, including those of its own invention, like Franklinium and Franklin Bronze.

Franklin worked closely with sponsored commemorative societies, ranging from The Britannia Medal Society to the Legal Heritage Society and the National Commemorative Society. Medals and other items gained value for the artistry they displayed and the precious metals out of which they were wrought. By 1970, Franklin had fifty sculptors working on designs and over 1,500 employees handling production, customer service and marketing. A whole new industry was spawned in these years, and Franklin led it. Throughout the 1970s, driven by inflation, economic upheaval and political instability, the precious-metals commemorative market blossomed and Franklin found itself with many competitors. The market grew so large that Krause and other specialty publishers found themselves competing for ad dollars with mass circulation, general interest periodicals, and with radio and television.

Krause was only one of many players in the commemorative silver game, but its role was very significant for the company. Throughout the 1970s, relations between Iola and the Franklin Mint grew stronger. Medals and bars were, after all, coins in another form, and Krause had been covering collectible medals since the 1950s. The expertise and enthusiasm in Iola naturally led to the publication of the special guides on Franklin's issues which came in the mid-'70s. The groundwork for those books was laid years earlier through the attention paid in Iola to medals in general and the Franklin Mint in particular.

The success of the Franklin Mint also pointed out that interest in commemoratives was still strong in 1970. So did the Eisenhower dollar, which was a commemorative despite the politics involved in its birth. Ironically, the success of Franklin and its imitators also proved that the government did not have to be the only source of products to meet the demand for commemoratives. Yet, the traditional role of coinage as a token of historical distinction would not die. No matter how many beautiful and valuable medals and other commemorative objects mints like Franklin would strike, they did not hold the same cherished cachet as coinage. A one-of-a kind platinum commemorative might sell for more than a St. Gaudens double eagle, but it would not be treated with the same reverence. In 1970, collectors would buy commemoratives, but most of them would agree with one line of the "creed" proclaimed on the editorial page of the *News*. It called for "the return of significant commemorative coins."

"Officials in the Treasury and legislators," editorialized the *News*, "...have forgotten and largely negated the fact that a nation's coinage serves an important secondary function in projecting the heritage of and to its people."

Krause had an opportunity to espouse its creed in 1970 when Cliff Mishler was asked to sit on a panel to study what the United States should do with its coinage to mark the national bicentennial celebration scheduled for 1976. Cliff recalled that "We felt the Bicentennial was a good reason for commemorative coinage...it would provide a boost to coin collecting."

Cliff presented what had been the position of Krause Publications for years. "Issue to circulation like the Canadian dollar commemoratives," and "change all the coins," he said. Cliff and other numismatists in Iola and throughout the country wanted a new set of coins to mark the nation's birth. "First and foremost...numismatic efforts should be aimed at...a reselling of the American ideal...This is the mission which can be accomplished with the offering of a comprehensive bicentennial coinage program," read another *News* editorial.

Cliff knew "it wouldn't fly," but, as he said in a 1991 interview, Krause had been involved in Washington politics long enough to know that if collectors wanted half a loaf, they had to start by asking for the whole bakery. As it turned out, about half a loaf is what collectors got. Treasury's first formal proposal was against any Bicentennial commemorative coinage. After the deliberations of the Advisory Panel were completed, Treasury relented and called for the United States to issue one-dollar and half-dollar coins bearing a Bicentennial commemorative on the reverse. Of course, the battle had only begun in 1970. In the course of the struggle, American Numismatic Association President John Pittman joined Cliff to testify before the Senate Banking Committee. Pittman played the "good cop" to Cliff's "bad cop" and asked that Congress accept the compromise of including the quarter- dollar in the Bicentennial package. The compromise was adopted and three of the six American coins were altered for the nation's 200th birthday.

In 1970, only the one-cent piece was altered, and only by accident. Flukes and errors are part of the history of coinage and the mistruck coin only adds spice to the collector's everyday porridge. Over the years, the lowly cent has brought more than a penny's worth of excitement to the numismatic table. In 1955, collectors took delight in the doubled-die error Lincoln cent, and they enjoyed it again in 1969. In 1960, collectors relished the added flavor of the cent variations known as the large and small date issues. This course was served again in 1970, when the Mint struck large dates on some cents and small dates on others. The difference was important, first because the small date 1970 cent was worth about 100 times as much as the large date, but also because the mistrike was first announced in the pages of *Numismatic News*.

"...Allow us to pat ourselves on the back for breaking the initial word of the 1970-S cent varieties," read a September editorial. The actual discovery had been announced in March "because a careful study of specimens proved the validity." The numismatists in Iola were quite competent to judge the coins and did so, even though they knew controversy would follow. The tempest was brief, however, and, as in the past, good for the hobby. It was also good for Krause because it indicated the validity of another part of the company's numismatic creed, the call for "an international standard of numismatic terms."

For months after the large-date-small-date cents were discovered, collectors argued about what to call them. They were called high 7 and low 7, thick and thin, weak and bold strikes, or wire and round edges. Ultimately the hobby settled on the same "large and small date" terminology that had been applied to the 1960 cents, which was just what the *News* had suggested. Questions of terminology would continue to be raised and Krause, as the place where words and collecting came together, would continue to argue for clarity. The philosophy of straight-talking "just plain Chet" still held sway in Iola.

Other points of the Krause creed were also exhibited in 1970. The company continued to lobby for "liberalization of gold collecting restrictions," and advocate "full-time hobby representation in Washington" as well as "stronger guidance from the national association." For the short term, it wanted the "release of the Treasury's silver dollar holdings," which started to happen in '70. For the long run, it sought "development of a valid national youth program."

The youth program was the hardest hurdle to leap in the heyday of Jimi Hendrix and Janis Joplin. Krause reported news about young people involved in collecting in all its publications, and attempted to attract baby-boomers to the hobby, but with little success. Coin collecting continued to grow gray hairs and would not attract large numbers of the baby boom generation until the 1980s, when the styled pelts atop the boomers heads were themselves going gray.

Chapter 20

1971

"Chet, Bob Strand, Harry Becker and I were on our way to the Twin Cities. As we sat around the table at a truck stop, the idea of Old Cars was born."

Art Christoph

What better place to conceive a periodical titled *Old Cars* than at a truck stop on the interstate highway? Is it surprising that four guys who spent their working lives producing publications about collectibles should look at the autos zipping by on the highway and think about publishing a paper about collectible cars? Of course not, but the decision to move Krause Publications towards its first major diversification took longer to brew than a cup of truck stop java.

"We had been surveying several types of things to diversify into," recalled Chet in a 1981 *Old Cars* editorial, "horses, snowmobiling, sports publications and antique autos." The surveying had begun a few years earlier when the numismatic niche was getting shaky and had already taken one detour in an unlikely direction.

In the late 1960s, Krause marketed typesetting services and zinc halftone printing plates. One customer was the publisher of a struggling equestrian magazine titled *The International Rider & Driver*. When the publisher was unable to pay his bill, Krause acquired the title and the services of its editor, Bill Simpson.

In Krause's 20th anniversary booklet, published in 1972, *IRD* was described as "providing homey coverage of the entire show horse field... by devoting easy-to-read sections to national ratings... [and] by dedicating several issues each year to coverage of specialized classes of show horses.... Hackneys, Stallions, and Shetlands."

The *International Rider & Driver* looked for readers among the lovers of fine-blooded horses and those who bred them. It was a very specialized niche, even for a specialty publisher like Krause, and one that the company chose not to serve. By the end of 1972, Krause was out of the horse publication business.

Horsepower publishing was more attractive. Chet himself had long been interested in the old cars he and his brothers had tinkered with back in the 1930s. He was already spending weekend hours puttering with a 1927 Model T truck and 1923 Model T roadster. It was logical that he should choose to steer his publishing resources down the automotive route. When the staff at Iola was polled on new ventures, collectible autos were on the list, along with professional and university sports. But, as Chet recalled, "the staff was more familiar with cars... not too many sports enthusiasts at the time."

Once the subject matter for the new periodical was agreed on, the name followed and, once again, the just-plainspoken-Chet philosophy prevailed. As Art Christoph mentioned, at Krause, they believed in calling a spade, a spade. So they named a coin magazine, *Coins*, and a tabloid devoted to antique autos, *Old Cars*. "It's better to say just what you mean in plain English," said Chet. The first issue of *Old Cars*, a 36-page tabloid, appeared in October 1971. Dave Brownell was the editor of the monthly, and a year's subscription cost $4.

Good timing is a virtue with which Krause Publications seems to be blessed. Chet got into numismatic publishing just as coin collecting started to experience massive growth. Twenty years later, when Krause decided to introduce its new publication, interest in antique cars was starting to mushroom. Krause brought the first issue of *Old Cars* to the annual show and swap meet of the Antique Automobile Club of America in Hershey, Pennsylvania. Held in October 1971, the show "astounded the hobby... when 2700 vendor spaces were sold...." The Hershey show had been held for years, but never had it attracted so many sellers and buyers of automotive equipment and memorabilia. By 1977, the Hershey swap meet would host 6500 vendors. It was only one example of a large, growing interest in automotive collecting that Krause would help build and benefit from.

As the Hershey meet also pointed out, flea markets and swap meets were becoming all the rage in the United States. In the early '70s, people started spending their weekends buying and selling second-hand goods, with automotive parts and supplies among the most popular items. At the same time, the first major antique automotive auction company held its first sale. By 1977, it would be holding 40 auctions of more than 1,000 cars throughout the United States. Interest in old cars, in buying and selling parts and supplies, and in advertising for them had grown into a substantial market. Krause's *Old Cars* entered the field just as this market started to blossom. By 1977, *Old Cars* would have a circulation of 90,000; its rate of growth surpassing that of *Numismatic News* in its first five years.

Krause had the formula down for building circulation and advertising — give something away. Instead of giving away free classifieds, *Old Cars* offered reprints of historical pieces about cars to potential subscribers and advertisers. The giveaway garnered 105 ads for the first issue. Sample copies of that issue were sent to every person Krause "could remotely relate to the old car field." Among them were 200 antique auto clubs who were planning major swap meets. They were also distributed free to thousands of old car buffs at the Hershey meet.

Just as Chet had to explain how mail sales of coins worked to the first readers of *Numismatic News*, Krause had to show how ads for automotive antiques would look. Dave Brownell concocted one dummy ad that was more powerful than even he expected. It advertised a car for sale from Timbuktu, and got a response. A reader, who apparently thought that a newspaper published in a place named Iola would sell cars from Timbuktu, called and asked about the car. Also in the Krause tradition, the first issue of *Old Cars* contained a reader's survey and asked for feedback on what the new paper should cover.

The old *Numismatic News* formula worked very well for *Old Cars*. Fill as many pages as possible with low cost classifieds to cover production costs and build readership. Make sure the editorial people — on staff or free-lance —

After the crisis in coins of the mid-1960s, Krause committed itself to a major diversification into a new hobby niche. After examining many options, the staff selected automobiles and published the first issue of **Old Cars** *in 1971, just as the hobby was taking off.*

know their subject so readers can rely on their advice and want to read it. Pursue display advertising, keep it honest, and deliver the circulation the advertisers need to stay in business — and keep advertising. Finally, produce it all as efficiently as possible, and put the paper in the hands of readers "on time, every time." How simple the one-paragraph summary seems, yet whole libraries have been written about the subjects covered in each sentence and many publishing companies have gone out of business because they were unable to perform the simple chores outlined there.

The inaugural run of *Old Cars* and the visit the Krause staff paid to the Hershey swap meet had reverberations in Iola. In the summer of 1972, Chet invited other old car buffs living nearby to an informal get-together in Iola. The number of cars was small, but the volume of good feeling was large and boded well for the future. It wasn't long before somebody in Iola was scratching his head and saying, "Well, if they can do it in Hershey, why can't we do it in Iola?"

Another thing they were doing in Iola was still producing numismatic publications. The year was relatively uneventful, with the introduction of the Eisenhower dollar the most significant coin news item. On the speculative front, bags containing $1,000 worth of silver coins were registered for trade on the New York mercantile exchange, and, on the political front, a senator from the silver-producing state of Idaho — Frank Church — surprised no one by calling for the minting of silver coins for the 1976 Bicentennial.

With Chet ushering *Old Cars* into life, the staff, especially Cliff Mishler, was managing the numismatic branch of the business. In that capacity, Cliff was able to experience what he called a rekindling of his enthusiasm for collecting. In his 1986 capsule history of Krause publications, Cliff recalled what had happened and made a definitive statement about collecting that applies to hobbyists in every field and reveals much about what really makes Krause Publications tick. As Cliff wrote:

I'll never forget the stimulating experience of spending two mid-January days in Milwaukee poring through a vintage collection of world coins that had been untouched since the early 1950s. A 'catalog' of that collection featuring rubbings of each and every one of the 2,360 coins numbered in it as of July 25, 1950, prepared by the Milwaukeean who formed it, still rests on a shelf in my office; it is one of those relics of the past I value quite highly, as it embodies the heart and character of one particular old-time collector.

We photographed nearly 2,000 coins from the collection that would illustrate the volume. They effectively rekindled in me a lot of the old enthusiasm for the beauty and intrigue of coin collecting that had dissipated through the previous 10 years of intense professional involvement with numismatics.

"The magnetism of beautiful coins is something very special," I remarked in print at the time, "and very difficult to describe." That regenerated enthusiasm has never flickered in the slightest over the succeeding 15 years.

Chapter 21

1972

"In the most god-forsaken corners of the world, in any country where coins are found, you will find Krause's Standard Catalog of World Coins. Krause has succeeded in gaining the market of the entire world. They have produced the fusion of knowledge of modern world coinage."
Elvira Clain-Stefanelli,
Smithsonian Institution.

The "fusion of knowledge" so graciously alluded to by Elvira Clain-Stefanelli was another step towards broadening the base of Krause Publications. Chet had started the business based on his own interest in United States coins. After twenty years, the interests of the company and the market it served had assumed worldwide proportions.

The first *Catalog* appeared in March 1972. It was a chubby volume, nearly 800 pages thick, that was immediately greeted as a "telephone book" and the "bible" of international coins. It was also a sellout. By the end of the year, two more printings, complete with revisions, were issued. The *Catalog* was introduced in typically understated fashion. "This volume," read the Introduction, "is designed to fill a need which has come into growing evidence in recent years as the expanding interests of the American coin collecting community have been ceaselessly shifting into the arena of world coin issues. The absence of a single comprehensive standard catalog to which collectors could turn as they sought guidance has tempered the growth of that interest.

"That cataloging deficiency is filled with the publication of this tome which covers, by date, the world's coin issues from the mid-1800s right down through 1971."

The *Catalog* was an impressive achievement on several fronts. Collecting the data enclosed required the work of dozens of numismatists, collectors and historians who "researched and compiled revised and original national compilations of coin issues especially for this catalog." Among them were: Steve Album, Albert Baber, Tim Browder, Colin Bruce II, Harvey Bruns, Ray Byrne, James Center, George Falcke, Kent Froseth, Sylvia Haffner, Lee E. Harvey, Pat Hogan, William Holberton, Robert Julian, Mel Kohl, Charles Panish, Harvey Rose, Albert J. Ruh, Robert Saiber, John Scheiner and Richard Trowbridge.

As the Introduction read, the *Catalog* was "basically a compilation of the digested knowledge which students of the numismatic science have contributed to the coin collecting hobby through the years." It took most of 1971 to meet the spring 1972 deadline, and the entire production required the equivalent of volumes of investigation, information tracking, fact checking, coordination and scheduling.

The 15,000 photos between the covers "resulted from a high degree of interest and cooperation" from at least seventeen photographers and collectors. As the "How to Use..." section explained, "To reduce the problems of coin identification to their minimum, one of the primary focuses in assembling this volume... was placed on the acquisition and presentation of actual size photographs of each coin type listed. The objective was virtually achieved with all but about 500 of the more than 8,200 listed coin types being illustrated...." This was meticulous work, since all coins were presented "in actual size," to the nearest half-millimeter for smaller coins and the nearest millimeter for larger types. Acquiring, cataloging, tracking, and making sure each photo was accurate, and then captioning it correctly, was also no mean feat.

Coordinating and organizing the listings, cataloging them according to the numbering system established by R. S. Yeoman, making sure every entry was complete, then proofreading every word, were equally formidable tasks. Chet and Cliff were listed as authors, with most of the hands-on work falling to Chet, Marian Moe and other members of the Iola team. They laid the groundwork for what became a mini-division of the company, as distinct as that of one of the magazines.

The initial *Catalog* is an interesting document that tells much about the company that published it. First, there was its size. It was large enough to be a daunting endeavor for a publishing company with about two dozen employees that was already meeting 95 deadlines to put out six periodicals a year. Second, there was the competition. Krause's *Catalog* was not the first compilation of world coinage, and established references were on sale. The Krause *Catalog* was, however, the largest and would be the best-marketed. Krause used the network of contacts it had built up around the world, as well as the pages of its own numismatic periodicals, to make sure people in "the most god-forsaken places on earth" knew about the *Catalog*. Among coin collectors around the globe, the name of Iola was much more familiar than it was forsaken.

The company's reputation in the international coin market was evident in the list of contributors that appeared in the Catalog, which included dealers who specialized in international coinage from all over the United States.

Incorporated in the *Catalog* was a detachable response envelope that solicited feedback for corrections and additions for a second edition, since the first *Catalog* would not be the only *Catalog*. New and improved versions were scheduled, with each new edition offering new possibilities for greater sales. In essence, the *Catalog* was another periodical, albeit bigger than anything else produced in Iola and appearing less frequently, but still a periodical.

The *Catalog* was the hallmark of Krause's 20th anniversary year. It was fitting symbol of how Krause had grown — from the handiwork of one man with a single interest to a company capable of cataloging the entire world of coins.

The actual celebration of the anniversary came in the fall. Krause celebrated its 20th by publishing a special anniversary image brochure in which Chet employed "The metaphor of fine fabrics" to characterize the work of publishing. "...The material used and the way it is woven together will determine the fineness of the finished product," he wrote. "The big difference will be the element of time. It is much more a critical factor in publishing. Consequently, successful publishing is an effort — a constant war — in fighting that element... the weapons: the sharp point of coordination and the shield of realistic scheduling."

The publication of the first **Standard Catalog of World Coins** *in 1972 completed Krause's formula for occupying an entire hobby niche. Catalogs and guidebooks became regular and important additions to the product line.*

"On time, every time" is an ambitious goal, but, as Chet said, it is realizable — if the elements involved are well-coordinated, and if they come together when and where they should. He went on to list the other ingredients in the mix that had kept the company alive and well in its first twenty years. They are an excellent resource for the history of Krause Publications and a practical guide for the management of any business. They can be called *Chet Krause's Ten Points for Building a Business*. To wit:

1. "A short term idea is to stay up all night and do things yourself. The reason it's a short term idea is that if you continued to pursue it, you'd be dead. The real secret is to get other people to do the work."

2. "Coordination and scheduling...a better answer than aspirin to turning out publication on time."

3. [Keep abreast of new technology] "We were the first publisher in the country to use [the IBM System/3] for the purpose of programming circulation. With it over 100,000 weekly, monthly, and bi-monthly subscriptions are addressed, mailed and renewed."

4. "In doing our own publications, we decided to make sure readers had the benefit of honest advertising. We policed advertiser's products, and still do!

5. "I recall how frustrating it was for me to watch a publication 'bog down' once it came off the press.... I tried what I thought was everything, including complaining. Then I decided to try working with the system... We did things that weren't necessarily hard but things we had never before done or thought of doing."

6. "The heart of a publication is where research and good writing go together to communicate and sell print. We've got people who are honest, hard-working, and creative. Fortunately for us, they also love to write."

7. "Only three things go together to make up a production department: equipment, personnel, and a philosophy for getting work done. I feel we've got them all, including the philosophy of getting work done together."

8. "Don't get something you don't need...there were certain things Krause Publications should not try to do...such as the actual printing."

9. "I have become accustomed to being away from the office days at a time...[after a trip to Israel], I had returned to Iola somewhat apprehensive about being gone so long. This was perhaps the most rewarding return of my life. I found I had created a self-sustaining organization. My only disappointment was the greeting I received when I walked in the door and said, 'Shalom, I'm back!' and the receptionist replied, 'Were you gone?'"

10. "I remember so well the beads of perspiration that flow inside one's mind when he's a small publisher and wants to get bigger... I'll never regret making that decision."

With these ten points, Chet waxed just about as philosophic as he ever gets. After twenty years in the business, he had acquired a store of knowledge and experience and was able to distill it into cogent form. All the basics of business success are embodied in his ten points: Take advantage of new technology; do only what you can do well; find good people who know their field, trust them and reward them well; time spent organizing and coordinating is never wasted — it actually creates more time. The Krause 20th anniversary brochure, with Chet's Ten Points, could serve as a primer for college courses in business management.

By 1972, the senior people at Krause had graduated from the college of experience. The company was entering mid-life but without undergoing a crisis. The system was up and running and waiting for more new opportunities such as the venture into antique automotive publishing that began in '71 and the assault on the world market that came with the *Catalog* in '72.

The inflation driving the American economy was registering in the antique auto business, in world markets, and in numismatics. In '72 the "finest known" 1804 twenty-five cent piece sold for $25,000, an 1804 dollar hit $80,000, a unique 1907 St. Gaudens double-eagle fetched $43,500, an 1894-S dime went for $50,000 and a 1913 Liberty Head nickel hit the fabled price of $100,000. While these prices were for rare and highly sought-after coins, they represented the general trend which was driven by the scarcity of silver coins and an inflating money supply.

"By 1972 very few silver coins were seen in circulation. The seeker of scarce dates in pocket change could no longer experience the excitement of finding a truly rare date," wrote ANA Historian Q. David Bowers. "Now as in recent years, those desiring to put together a representative set of just about anything had to do it by making purchases from dealers."

The dealer-driven hobby was not the hobby that Chet first targeted his publication on in 1952, but it was the hobby that Krause Publications was now serving. Over the years in the *News*, classified ads from individual collectors had been replaced by display ads from dealers. The *News*, along with other Krause periodicals, changed to better serve its market. Circulation and page counts of *Numismatic News, Coins,* and *Coin Prices* held steady with little change since the late '60s.

The economic conditions that were driving up coin prices and keeping dealers in control of the hobby were also changing the attitude of a few governments towards collecting. The United States Mint, Britain's Royal Mint and the Mint of France featured prominent displays at the 1972 ANA Convention. They were not there just to greet numismatists. All three mints wanted to fill the blanks in their budgets with profits made on sales of coins to collectors. This was a significant shift in policy and attitude. In Europe, collectors were respectfully tolerated, but for a great nation to depend on them for income had long been considered a blow to national prestige. Britain and France were not San Marino and Andorra, two tiny nations that financed their affairs through the sale of postage stamps. At least not until the early 1970s, that is, when finance ministers began looking at sales of coins to collectors as a painless way to raise revenue.

The United States Treasury, which once viewed collectors as nuisances, now valued them as customers. The U. S. Treasury had released the "last" of its silver hoard of Carson City dollars and now the U. S. Mint was selling the new Eisenhower dollar at a profit of $4-a-coin. Treasury Secretary John Connally, who had been appointed by Richard Nixon, called the profit "unconscionable," but did not reduce the price or halt the sales. While the idea of the government profiting from the production of coinage may have been a philosophical affront, it was too profitable to abandon. A few years later, when the United States Post Office Department, facing yet another of its perennial financial crises, was "privatized" into the Postal Service, it marketed collectible stamps as hard as it could. While never as aggressive as the Postal Service, the Mint was not above promoting its products beyond their face value.

Whether for stamps, coins or old cars, the market for collectibles grew by leaps and bounds in the early 1970s. The United States had changed tremendously in the years since World War II and Americans developed a fondness for the artifacts of the past. Farmers no longer used horses to work the land, so horse-farming equipment — collars, single trees, cultivators — was collected; so were the early tractors that replaced the horses. Soda pop now came in throwaway bottles and cans that had pop tops — so older returnable bottles, as well as cans that required a "church key" opener, became collectible. Groceries came neatly packaged and processed so the artifacts of packaging and home preservation — colorful flour sacks, fruit crate labels, mason jars, stoneware, sauerkraut cutters — were in demand. While Americans plunged headlong into the future, they looked back and clung to mementoes of the past.

Automobiles were among the most significant of those mementoes. In 1972, the American auto industry was in its muscle car heyday. Camaros, Torinos, Chargers, Grand Prixs, and GTOs with hundreds of cubic inches under the hood ruled the highways. At the same time, Model T clubs were growing faster than ever, shade tree mechanics who had seen the hit movie "Bonnie and Clyde" were restoring 1930s roadsters, and just about everybody took notice when an antique Duesenberg that once belonged to Greta Garbo sold for $90,000.

As the publisher of *Old Cars*, Krause was ready to be a part of the new collectible market. The company had already hosted a small gathering of old car buffs in July of '72. They parked their cars in the village park, took each other for rides in the country near Iola, ate chicken at the Iola Lions Chicken Roast, and talked old cars. It was an enjoyable Sunday for those who came and that was all it was supposed to be.

The *Old Cars* staff, led by advertising manager Bob Lichty, with support from Cliff Mishler, had other ideas. In the course of promoting *Old Cars*, Lichty and editor Dave Brownell had visited many antique auto shows and swap meets. They spent the last days of 1972 laying plans for an old cars rendezvous at Iola that would be more than just an enjoyable day for those who came.

Chapter 22

1973

*"Bob Lichty came on staff... and set the
Iola Car Show on fire because he did a lot
of traveling in the area and talked to a lot
of local collectors."*   Chet Krause

N o one likes conventions more than Americans. As members of trade or
professional associations, as part of local or regional groups, as people
who share a passion for any subject, as well as buyers and sellers of this, that
and the other — more Americans come together in large numbers to gawk and
talk than any other people on the planet.

The Iola Lions Club had been doing it since 1956. On the second Sunday in
July, club members set a few dozen chicken halves on the barbecue, invited
their neighbors to join the picnic, and raised a few dollars for a good cause. By
the early 1970s, the Iola Lions were feeding several hundred people and had
raised many thousands of dollars for civic improvement in the village.

In 1973, Chet and Cliff speculated aloud about what would happen if the
Annual Iola Lions Chicken Dinner were combined with a real old car show
and swap meet. The Lions agreed to see what might happen, since the old cars
would bring to town more people who, once they smelled the chicken roasting
on the grill, would find it irresistible. The staff of *Old Cars* also liked the idea
of hosting an old car show in Iola on the day of the Lions chicken feast. They
figured that, even if nobody showed up to look at antique autos, the chicken

roast would attract enough of a crowd for the car show to be successful. They didn't leave it to chance, however. Bob Lichty personally visited every antique car club and individual owner he knew within reasonable driving distance of Iola and invited each one to the show, while *Old Cars* gave the event national exposure.

As it turned out, no one had to worry about attracting a crowd. The Lions sold all the chicken they could cook — 1200 dinners — and 90 antique cars lined up for display at the Iola Park. Everyone called it a success and made bigger and better plans for the future. Krause made a commitment to pave the way for expansion, undertaking to build a new office/production facility on the eastern edge of the village in 1975 and, in 1976 to move the show there. By 1977, 700 cars were on display, nearly 200 vendors were selling automotive goods, and over 10,000 visitors toured the grounds.

"It's important to us from the an image standpoint," said Chet of the show, "because of the exposure it gives automotive products." By the end of the 1970s, the Iola show was the largest of its kind in the Midwest. It brought thousands of people interested in old cars to the headquarters of *Old Cars* and other Krause automotive publications. It enhanced the prestige of the publishing company in the eyes of its readers and advertisers by showing that the Krause people did more than just talk about old cars. They really did know

In its early years, the Iola Old Car Show was held at the village park. In 1976, the show moved to Krause's grounds on the edge of the village and hosted over 500 cars and 10,000 visitors.

and care about them, as evidenced by the cars they themselves owned and put on display.

The show was mighty good for Iola, too. "It has had a very visible and enduring impact," said Cliff. Over the years, local volunteer groups have raised more than $1 million for good causes in the community. They provide the people who staff booths where visitors spend money that buys athletic gear for the local park, educational material for the schools, medical equipment for the hospital and rescue services, and equipment for several area fire departments. It's been said that Krause Publications has done many wonderful things for Iola. Perhaps the most wonderful is the opportunity the Old Car Show provides for local people to work for their own community, and be successful at it. Krause brings out the crowd. The local people use it to raise funds for their projects.

The Car Show was also a circulation builder for *Old Cars*, which had already become a bi-weekly in early 1973. "It's a good vehicle for exposing the hobby to the public and a good source of new subscribers," said Cliff. With help from the Old Car Show, circulation of *Old Cars* topped the 90,000 mark by the end of the newspaper's fifth year of existence. Throughout the 1970s, the success of the car show and *Old Cars* gave Krause Publications a strong new leg on which it could stand.

Krause's older leg — numismatic publishing — had become more diverse then ever, and was still reflecting a hobby that was subject to politics and driven by inflation. In 1973, the collector's world as served by Krause Publications was divided into many segments. Although collectors' interests overlapped, each segment of the hobby represented a different market. First were the traditional readers who collected United States coins, and would collect them regardless of the amount of precious metal they contained. Second, were the silver collectors whose interest in coins was based first on their content of precious metal. Occupying another niche were collectors of international coins, which may or may not have had silver content. Next were the collectors of both old and newly minted medals and tokens, some of whom were traditional hobbyists and some of whom were precious metal speculators. Last were the silver bugs who bought bars, medals, tokens, coins and other objects because inflation was driving up silver prices. A subgroup of this last bunch might be called the "coffee can collectors." They didn't collect coffee cans, except to fill them with silver coins of little numismatic value and stash them as security against total economic collapse.

All of Krause's coin-related publications served these markets to a greater or lesser degree. The classical hobbyist hoping to fill out his single type collection, the enthusiast fond of collectibles issued by the Franklin Mint, the gloomy doomsayer who believed the world's economy was due to crash and that true security lay in "real" goods such as silver — all had a reason to read *Numismatic News, Coins, Coin Prices* and *The Standard Catalog of World Coins.*

As if to prove it, coin prices were rising fast and hard in 1973. As recounted by Cliff Mishler, "An uncirculated double eagle sold for $60,000...the most expensive United States gold coin ever sold.... Hardly a coin sold at auction through the first six months of the year failed to establish a new record...."

The pace continued throughout the year with "a 1794 dollar enjoying a pedigree from the day of its striking...realized $110,000 at a Superior sale, making it the world's most expensive coin...[until] a Saint Gaudens $20 changed hands for...$125,000, [then] an 1804 dollar [was placed] on the market at $165,000."

These sales represented the top of a market that was rising rapidly and attracting more participants daily. *Coin Prices*, the Krause publication solely devoted to reporting market conditions, became, as Cliff recalled, "the largest circulating publication in the hobby, with a distribution of just under 140,000, six times a year." Nearly every copy of *Coin Prices* was sold on newsstands, and most of them went to readers who cared more about investments than collecting. Interest in the subjects *Coin Prices* covered was so great, however, that it experienced its own mini-boom in '73. It became the most sought-after "hobby" magazine on the market. By mid-1974, interest in the prices of coins and silver had grown enough for *Coin Prices* to become a bi-monthly.

As recorded in *Coin Prices* and reported in other Krause publications, some of the biggest sales of coins in history took place in the fall of 1973. But they were roundly viewed as mere consequences of one of the most memorable and far reaching events of the last half of the 20th century. In October 1973, Egypt, Syria and other Arab states once again dispatched their armies against Israel. Accompanying the military action was a far more significant economic assault on the western industrialized world. Arab and other oil-producing nations declared an embargo on exports and the cost of every oil-based product — as well as the cost of transporting everything from apples to xylophones — skyrocketed. The cost of gasoline tripled at the pump and, as crowds of impatient motorists sat in lines at filling stations, Americans worried about whether they would be able to buy any fuel at all.

The 1973 oil embargo accelerated the inflation already pushing the economy and had a predictable effect on collectibles. "The coin market was becoming very bullish," as Cliff calmly understated the situation. Equally "bullish" was the market for other collectibles, as many Americans, confronted with genuine economic uncertainty for the first time in forty years, sought comfort and value in real goods.

The market for silver was the most bullish of all, and marketers moved to take advantage of it. The Franklin Mint and other familiar producers of precious metal collectibles were joined by unlikely vendors such as *Time* Magazine and Mobil Oil, who were marketing "exact reproductions" of antique coins. "The packaging explained they were reproductions," recalled Cliff, "but if someone took the sets apart and put them in a drawer to keep, and 15 years later someone finds the coins and thinks they're Grandma's keepsakes, they think they have found a rare item worth a lot of money."

In order to "protect enthusiasts," Krause Publications once again took up a highly visible role in the political arena. As a newspaper, *Numismatic News* had always been the most politically aware of all Krause publications. It had long advocated passage of a strict "Hobby Protection Act," which required that the word "copy" be prominently incised in conspicuous *sans serif* type on any "reproductions." Incising the term "copy," i.e., scribing it below the surface of the "coin," would make it much more difficult for forgers to erase. Using modern-style *sans serif* type on the "reproductions" would also send up an obvious warning flag that even the most gullible could identify.

Chet, Cliff and other representatives of the numismatic fraternity went to Washington to testify in favor of the Act. Mishler recalled that congressmen became more favorable to its passage after witnesses explained that the authenticity of campaign buttons, tokens and other political memorabilia was also threatened by "reproductions" and could be protected by the new law. Congress passed it and The Hobby Protection Act was signed into law by Richard Nixon in August. "It was no cure all," as Cliff said, "but it helps eliminate the obvious deceptions."

The "exact reproductions" said something about how coin collecting had developed in the last few years. American coinage no longer contained silver, but some coin-like collectibles did. Economic conditions were reducing the value of money in circulation and inflating the value of collectible coins, on both a numismatic basis and for their content of precious metal. Collecting was no longer a pastime for the hobbyist who read *Numismatic News*, but a speculative venture for commodity investors who read *The Wall Street Journal* and the apprehensive citizen who answered a Sunday's supplement ad for an "exact reproduction" coin or a "commemorative" silver bar.

All these collectors, speculators and pessimists were pleased when, at the end of 1973, the United States Treasury relaxed rules on the ownership of gold by American citizens. In the wake of the oil embargo, gold prices had soared past the $300 per ounce mark, and gold coins were in greater demand than ever, which only added more fuel to the coin price fire. At the end of 1974, all restrictions on gold ownership would end and many a collection of gold coins came out of the closet. Gold joined silver as a commodity for speculators, and the manufacturers of medals, tokens, bars and other marketable collectibles added new product lines to their offerings. The liberation of gold also created a new market for Krause Publications to serve, and one which the company would directly pursue in the early '80s.

In 1973, however the company moved to expand its niche in the international coin world. The *Standard Catalog of World Coins* had shown the people in Iola that interest in international coinage was large enough to warrant a newspaper of its own. Once again, there was nothing subtle about the title of the new tabloid publication that debuted in December 1973. It was called *World Coin News*, a title as plain spoken and direct as the other Krause venues.

"It was designed to supplement and complement the *Standard Catalog of World Coins*," recalled Cliff. It also successfully followed the formula Krause had pioneered with its other numismatic periodicals. As in the early days of the *Numismatic News*, classified advertisers were the first market for *World*

Coin News. "For as little as $1.35," read a notice in the pilot issue, "a classified ad will enjoy the attention of a readership made up entirely of other collectors of world coins. This makes *World Coin News,* the 'bull's-eye' marketplace for those who desire to buy, sell or trade."

Two Krause veterans brought the new publication to life. Bob Poeschl served as editor with Glenn Wright as advertising manager. The pilot issue appeared in December 1973. *WCN* was launched as a quarterly in February 1974, became a monthly in August, and a twice-monthly publication in January 1975. The initial subscription price, for the quarterly edition, was $4, the same as for the first issues of *Old Cars.* In less than two years, subscription circulation of *World Coin News* settled in at the 16,500 mark. Its largest readership consisted of subscribers in the United States, although a few thousand papers were shipped overseas or sold over the counter in coin shops. Unlike *Coin Prices, World Coin News* could not command an audience large enough for general newsstand sales. It did, however, cater to readers with a specific interest in world coinage and delivered them to advertisers who wanted to meet them. The newspaper was yet another example of the diversity of the coin collecting market and how Krause Publications was adapting to meet it. In the late 1980s, professional economists, business leaders and politicians expended a lot of wind talking about a world economy that operates without regard to national boundaries. As the publication of the *Standard Catalog of World Coins,* followed by the *World Coins News,* points out, they were well aware of it in Iola in the early 1970s.

Chapter 23

1974

"We at Iola have long felt these individuals, while recognized for their special contributions to the hobby in the local area, have not received the national recognition that is merited."   Cliff Mishler

Cliff voiced those sentiments at the inception of the *Numismatic News* Ambassador Award in 1974. It was intended to show what hobbies and hobbyists meant to Krause Publications in 1974, what they always have meant, and what they will always mean to the publishing company. The first award was presented in May 1974 to Charles Colver, "a California collector who joined the hobby at the age of seven when his grandmother gave him an English florin." When he announced the award in the *News*, Chet pointed out that recognition of collectors of Colver's caliber was long overdue and well-deserved. "After all, it is their grass roots support that has made our hobby truly national in scope and influence."

Colver had been a collector for 47 years, and had spent many of them teaching and promoting the hobby in his home state. He easily met all the criteria for the Ambassador Award as outlined in the *News*: "a devotion to the hobby, assistance given to other collectors and organizations, integrity and overall knowledge of the hobby."

In one of the coincidences that make for historical irony, the issue of the *News* that carried the Colver story also reported on Richard Nixon's proclamation of National Coin Week. The president was quoted as saying that "since the beginning of history, coins have helped to tell the story of civilization. They frequently reflect the economic development of their country....

"Today more than 10 million Americans collect coins for both profit and pleasure.

"In honor of our Bicentennial years we are changing the designs on the back of three U.S. coins...to serve as reminders of our rich national heritage and continuing dedication to freedom and self-government.

"In recognition of this worthwhile hobby and in honor of the significance of the coins marking the Bicentennial, we do hereby designate the week beginning April 21, 1974 as National Coin Week."

The coincidental publication of both articles in the same issue of the *News* was striking. Charles Colver, and the other recipients of the Ambassador Award over the years, personify the best in all hobbyists, and show why coin collecting was worthy of national recognition.

Later in 1974, the *News* presented another Ambassador Award. This one went to Miriam Gilmore, "a diminutive housewife who seven years ago, single-handedly put over a selling campaign to keep publishing the Texas Numismatic Association's official journal." Gilmore was editor of the TNA News when, as the *News* reported, "the journal ran into financial difficulties.... [Gilmore] put on a drive for funds to continue publication. She put it well into the black and made it one of the most respected [club] collector's journals in the nation."

In 1974, Krause inaugurated its Ambassador Award for distinguished and devoted coin collectors. Californian Charlie Colver accepted the first award from Cliff Mishler that year.

The Ambassador Awards illustrated one unchanging aspect of the coin collecting hobby and other hobbies as well. They are based on the knowledge and dedication of individuals whose rewards are anything but financial.

An aspect of the hobby whose rewards were strictly financial was also covered by the journalists in Iola and was summed up by Cliff when he said, "$22 billion in gold made quite an impressive sight."

Cliff was impressed by the stacks of gold bullion he had seen while touring the United States gold reserves storage site at Fort Knox, Kentucky. He made the trip as part of a press contingent invited to inspect the nation's gold supply. In late 1973 and '74, Americans beset by the effects of the oil embargo and the ominous unfolding of the Watergate Scandal turned to a traditional symbol of wealth and security. As long as Fort Knox was still filled with gold, the United States could endure any shock, many believed. As a representative of the numismatic press on the Fort Knox tour, Cliff saw the gold, and dutifully reported that it was present, safe and sound.

The *News* also reported that the United States had lifted all restrictions on gold ownership by Americans. The act of Congress removing the final limitations was one of the first measures signed by the new president, Gerald Ford, only a few days after he followed Richard Nixon into the White House.

As the price of gold hit $200 per ounce for the first time in history, gold fever quickened and carried silver along with it. The Franklin Mint, on the stroke of midnight, Dec.30, 1974 — the first day on which Americans could own as much gold as they wanted — struck its first gold issues. They were 100 Balboa coins for one of Franklin's regular customers, the government of Panama. The Panamanian coins were the first of many gold collectibles to appear in response to public uneasiness.

The uneasiness was reflected in coin prices. "The list of records was nearly endless," recalled Cliff. "The preeminent auction firm of the day, Stack's...sold about $2.7 million worth of coins at auction in 1972...$5.8 million in 1973...[and] nearly $7.5 million for 1974, including a proof 1875 $3 gold piece for $150,000."

Liberated gold and soaring coin prices carried silver upwards with them. Silver bars in record numbers were sold through every venue from ads in old line numismatic publications to frantic late-night television spots. The speculative bubble in silver bars burst by the end of the year but, in a year in which the federal government had printed 4.8 billion gas rationing coupons, speculative frenzy was not surprising.

Shortages turned up in other places, such as the cash registers of local stores and the printing plants of newspapers. A shortage of pennies prompted Treasury officials to plead with Americans to cash in their penny hoards. They also issued a ban on melting, treating or exporting one-cent coins. Once again, collectors were blamed for removing coins from circulation; once again, the Mint struck some coins minus mint marks, and once again the government produced a flood of coinage — more than 400 billion pennies — that prompted collectors to remove from circulation all the 1974-S cents they could find.

In American printing plants and publishing houses, a shortage of newsprint was causing headaches for production people and driving up the price of all printed material. Newsprint is the rough-textured, low-cost paper on which newspapers such as *Numismatic News* and *World Coin News*, as well as some magazines, are printed. In the early 1970s, all Krause periodicals were printed on newsprint. The covers of Krause's magazines were printed in color, and used coated, glossy stock to put forward a bright, appealing image, but the insides were on newsprint. The newsprint shortage of 1974, attributed to a demand by Canadian logging and papermaking companies for better prices, combined with the oil shortage and the general rate of inflation to hit hard at the publishing industry.

Krause had no choice but to keep page counts at the most cost effective level — 64 pages for the *News*, 80 for *Old Cars*, and *World Coin News*. Gone were the exciting and costly days of the early 1950s when the *News* printed page after page of copy and ads. Instead, Krause had to increase subscription and advertising rates. Subscribers were asked to pay 20 percent more in '74 and were hit with another 25 percent jump in '75. For some the blow was cushioned by the fact that they were getting a lot more newspaper. A subscription to *World Coin News*, for example, which started at $4 for four issues in early 1974, cost $6 for 26 issues in February 1975.

Advertising rates also increased, mainly due to inflation, but also because Krause was delivering more readers to the market. The *News* held steady throughout 1974, with 45,000 subscribers, but hit the 50,000 mark by the fall of '75. *Old Cars* showed a steady gain, with 55,000 readers in '74 and 60,000 by the end of '75. *World Coin News* plateaued at the 16,000-17,000 level in these years. Charges were going up on both ends — to subscribers and advertisers — but Krause was still delivering more of what each of them wanted. Readers found news about the increasingly interesting and valuable world of coins and coin-related collectibles. Periodicals from Iola also kept them up to date on the increasingly volatile prices in national and international markets. They could also read news about antique cars, buy and sell auto-related items through the classifieds in *Old Cars*, and keep up on where and when car shows and swap meets were held. Anyone, whether interested in coins, tokens, and silver bars, or cars, hubcaps or hood ornaments, could find the current price for the item in a Krause Publication. For nearly all readers, the package was well-worth a few more dollars.

Advertisers purchased access to the people most interested in what they had to sell. Krause's readers were true fans of their hobby and, as advertisers soon found out, were willing to spend money on it. *World Coin News*, which showed slow but steady growth in readership in 1974 and '75, had page counts that varied between 64 and 96, but always filled two-thirds to three-quarters of its pages with ads. Its 16,000 readers were truly interested in buying and selling world coins, as Krause's advertisers happily discovered. The success of *World Coin News* in its early days, points out another truism of periodical publishing. Numbers of readers alone do not mean success; having the right readers for the advertising market does.

Krause Publications was growing and a number of people right for the company came on board in 1974. Russ Rulau was one of them. He had spent ten years as an editor at *World Coins*, and, like so many other Krause people, started in the hobby while still a boy. Colin Bruce II, an army veteran and coin dealer who specialized in Oriental and Mexican coinage, also joined Krause in '74. Rulau and Bruce rounded out the company's international team, with Rulau becoming managing editor of *World Coin News* and foreign editor of *Numismatic News* while Bruce concentrated his efforts on *World Coin News* and the *Standard Catalog of World Coins*.

Other members of the class of '74 were Bob Lemke, who started in numismatics but ended up in the Sports Division; Tom Wildermuth, advertising; Suzanne Olkowksi, circulation; Marge Williams, Ramona Wasrud, Judy Schmidt and Carolyn Borth, data entry.

New equipment was also on the way. The IBM System 3 Model 10 data processing system that had so expedited the work of circulation and fulfillment was upgraded with the latest in computer technology — the disk drive. Less then two years later, in the spring of 1976, the disk drive's portable companion, the floppy disk, arrived in Iola.

Improvements in computer technology were steady and incremental from 1974 on, so it is difficult to pinpoint a date on which a particular piece of computer gear brought about dramatic change. Krause became the first publishing company of its kind to use computers when it installed the System 3 Model 10 in 1970, so perhaps that is the most significant date. The arrival of the disk drive, which dramatically reduced the size of the required storage while it increased the speed and capacity of the system in 1974, might also be the really big date. So might October 1975, when the *Third Edition* of the *Standard Catalog of World Coins* became the first Krause publication to use computer-generated page makeup. The following year, 1976, also had its electronic landmarks. In March floppy disk technology opened the door to greater speed and true portability, and in October, the IBM System 3 Model 12 came on line and consigned the punch card to the dustbin of history.

The dates are less important than the process of computerization, which has gone on at Krause for more than twenty-five years. While the company has hired and fired people, built new buildings and additions, started and ended the lives of many periodicals, lobbied with politicians and marketed itself to millions of potential readers and customers, Krause has also continually modernized its computer system. The business computer age dawned, went through its adolescence and entered maturity in the years since Chet Krause mailed out the first issue of *Numismatic News* and Krause Publications has been along virtually every step of the way. It was a subtle, behind-the-scenes process that was simply part of doing business in Iola, yet the ongoing adoption of the latest in computer technology may have been more important to the company's success than anything else it has ever done.

The Franklin Mint capitalized on the vigorous interest in collectible medals and other memorabilia in the 1970s. Krause published Franklin catalogs from 1975 to 1982.

Chapter 24

1975

*"It was a year of golden promise — a
promise that went flat."*   Cliff Mishler

One promise went flat in '75, but many others were kept and they enabled Krause Publications to motor right along. The flat promise involved that newly liberated American gold. The price of the precious metal that bulled its way to the $200-an-ounce level in late 1974, fell precipitously in the new year and cooled the gold fever that could have created an entirely new set of hobby publications in Iola. The signs were very good early in the year, when a special issue of the *News* devoted to gold turned out to be the largest edition produced in either '74 or '75. If not a magazine, at least another tabloid, like *World Coin News*, might have been born to cater to the gold market, but the market did not hold up and the publication did not appear, at least in '75.

Krause continued to find and cater to more specialized markets within the realm of coin-related collecting. The last month of '74 had seen the publication of Krause's first *Guidebook of Franklin Mint Issues*. A second presentation appeared in August 1975 and a third was underway by the end of the year. The *Guidebook* contained approximately 12,000 individual listings of the coins, medals, ingots and other metallic commemoratives struck by the largest private mint in the world since 1965. Chet and Virginia Culver, veteran token collector, elected officer of the ANA, and columnist for *Coins*, co-authored the second edition which sold over 16,000 copies in the last quarter of the year.

Franklin's output was so large, varied and finely struck that it constituted a market niche unto itself. By publishing a catalog of Franklin's issues, Krause was serving that branch of the collecting public that valued and traded the mint's wares.

The company went after a somewhat larger but still specialized market in March 1975 when it brought out the *Standard Catalog of World Paper Money*. It was another massive compendium of information and photos that ran to 720 pages including 20,000 listings complete with valuations, plus more than 4,000 photos of the currency of every sovereign entity from Abu Dhabi to Zanzibar. The *Catalog of World Paper Money* was immediately hailed as the "bible" of its subject and was turning up in just as many "god-forsaken" places as the *Standard Catalog of World Coins*.

The paper money catalog opened up another door for Krause Publications. Not only was the subject matter international, so was the editorial and production staff. The principal author was Albert Pick, with Cliff and Russ Rulau acting as editors. Pick was a German currency expert, and Krause published his book in cooperation with the *Battenberg Verlag* of Munich. The book was typeset and pasted-up in Munich, negatives were shot on Krause's cameras in Iola, with printing and binding performed by the R. R. Donnelley Company. Donnelley, the largest printer in the world in 1975, was appropriately known as the planet's number one producer of telephone directories as large or larger than the *Standard Catalog of World Paper Money*. Krause had worked with Donnelley before so the people in Iola were no strangers in the offices of what was probably the most prestigious printer in the United States.

The Munich connection was invaluable. Albert Pick was one of the most respected experts on currency in the world and *Battenberg Verlag* offered Krause a leg up in Europe, which was, after North America, the world's largest market for collectors.

The companion volume to *World Paper Money* was reissued in '75. The *Third Edition* of the *Standard Catalog of World Coins* was much larger than its predecessors. The "telephone book" that appeared in November included date-by-date histories of the coinage of all the 560 countries, states, provinces and cities that have struck coins since the closing years of the 18th century. It contained 55,000 coins listed by date and valued according to several grades of preservation, as well as more than 30,000 photos of individual coins, and was printed on 1,376 pages of lightweight "telephone book" paper. The first printing was sold out by the end of the year and a second run was completed in January 1976.

The monumental *Third Edition* of the *Standard Catalog of World Coins* was an Iola production. Colin Bruce and Marian Moe coordinated the efforts of 250 consulting numismatists, historians and collectors, while Dave Heise and Judd Aiken performed photographic work. Pre-press work — the equivalent of preparing a year's worth of any other Krause publication — was performed in-house, with printing and binding completed by the now-familiar R. R. Donnelley. The *Third Edition* was marketed primarily to coin dealers, but libraries, reference services and the most thorough of collectors also purchased it.

Despite its size and hefty sales pace, the *Third Edition* was hardly a mass market paperback. Like *World Paper Money* and the *Guidebook to Issues of the Franklin Mint*, it was targeted on a specialty market that may have been large, but was still specialized. The publication of these books enhanced Krause's reputation as the largest and most knowledgeable source of information on coins, currency and coin — related collectibles in the United States, if not the entire world. If you wanted to know about coins, currency and related collectibles, you could, as Casey Stengel used to say, look it up in the "bibles" compiled and published in Iola.

Krause also went after a more general market in 1975. Cliff Mishler, Bob Wilhite and Glenn Wright put together a 196-page "handbook" that supplied "all the essential information required to intelligently buy or sell United States coins and paper money." The *Standard Guide to United States Coin and Paper Money Valuations* presented both wholesale and retail coin and currency valuations. It was "aimed primarily at fulfilling the needs of beginning, novice and occasional collectors, providing reliable side-by-side price information" for those intent on either buying or selling the listed issues. An initial press run of 50,000 appeared in January 1976 for distribution and sales on newsstands.

Valuations was a general guide targeted at the many inexperienced collectors now entering the field, most of whom were more interested in coins and currency for their speculative value in an inflation-ridden, uncertain economy. It represented yet another segment of the collectors' market Krause attempted to serve; and, in the Krause tradition, the title on the cover stated plainly what was on the inside-coin and currency values.

A rundown of the special titles published by Krause in 1975 indicated the size and the variety of the markets that only one branch of its operation served. The most recondite numismatic specialist, the collector of commemorative tokens, the silver speculator and the most casual browser at the grocery store newsstand could find space reserved and a volume designed for him under the Krause tent.

The Krause tent was getting literally larger in '75. "With our twice-expanded quarters downtown bursting at the seams and overflowing into a trio of satellite facilities to accommodate a 68 employee compliment..." Cliff recalled, Krause Publications needed more space. Making what Cliff called "a long range commitment to the Iola community," Krause decided to build a new building on the edge of the village. The 20,000-square foot, $800,000 structure would allow for the consolidation of all Krause's operations under one roof, and the surrounding acreage had plenty of room for further expansion. With 16 acres at first and another 40 to come, the grounds around the new building could also be developed and maintained for the Old Car Show, which was growing steadily with no limit in sight.

There was little thought of severing the company's association with the village. Chet's long-standing commitment to his home community was unshaken and, after twenty-three years, he had proven that an international publishing company could not just survive, but thrive, in a Wisconsin hamlet. The trends of the time were on his side. In the 1970s, the century-old movement of people out of rural areas to cities was reversed. Newly mature members of the baby-boom generation were moving to rural areas, along with retirees and working people in their middle years. Despite the energy crisis and rising gasoline prices, Americans broadened the definition of what they considered a tolerable commute to work and moved to homes well beyond the sidewalks. The countryside around Waupaca County villages like Iola became home to people who commuted to work in larger communities, or who brought their work with them and made a living based on where they lived instead of the other way around.

The new popularity of rural areas only made it easier for Krause to find good people willing to come to Iola, which in turn made it easier for the company to maintain its commitment to the village.

Technology also helped, and not just computerized technology. For example, when Krause published Albert Pick's *Standard Catalog of World Paper Money*, typesetting and page make-up was performed in Munich. Paste-ups of the pages were then packed in a box not much larger than a telephone book and shipped by air to Iola, where they were turned into negatives that were sent to the printer in Ohio. In the letterpress days, the lead-filled forms from which each page of *World Paper Money* would have been printed would fill a semi-trailer and weigh more than a ton. Publishers and printers would laugh at the idea of doing typesetting and make-up on one side of the Atlantic and printing on the other. By the 1970s, the newly developed process of offset printing made international connections between places like Iola and Munich easily possible. This connection was made in the days when computerized publishing was in its barest infancy. In fact, computers played almost no role in the production of *World Paper Money*.

All the improvements that came to publishing through computer development in the years since 1975 have only made it easier for Krause to stay in Iola. "The phone lines run everywhere," as Chet pointed out. The once separate rural-urban division that Chet knew as a boy has been bridged by better automobiles and roads, improved communications and services, and the fact that the world has become a truly smaller place.

The Old Car Show was not getting smaller. What had started with fourteen of Chet's buddies at a chicken roast in 1972 grew to ninety cars and 1,200 dinners in '73. In 1974, 180 old cars lined up for display and 1,700 folks partook of the Lions Club chicken. In '75, the last show held on the grounds of the village park, 409 antique cars were shown and eighty-six vendors rented stalls to peddle everything from a box of Model T radiator caps to whole cars in "restorable" condition. Car owners, vendors and visitors must have been getting hungrier every year for, in 1975, they made the Lions happier by chowing down 2,500 chicken dinners.

Everything was moving up in the realm of antique autos. *Old Cars* continued to grow, with circulation crossing the 60,000 mark. The newspaper, which had become one-of-a-kind in its market, switched from a bi-monthly to an every-other-week publishing schedule that added two issues to the annual workload.

The combination of history, lore, humor, classified and display ads plus show and swap meet notices that characterized *Old Cars* in the '70s — and still does in the 1990s — gave the paper a happy, youthful air. It looked and read as if it was produced by a bunch of precocious young guys who liked to hang out together in the garage out back and whose greatest pleasure in life was to tear down a 1940 Ford engine, clean it up and reassemble it. And when they weren't working on cars, they were talking about them.

The political news, the atmosphere of speculation and possible gain that was evident in the pages of *Numismatic News* was absent in *Old Cars*. The car collecting hobby was still fun in ways that coin collecting had matured beyond. It was as if old cars were fun, while coins were business, even though antique cars had the potential to be just as valuable as collectible coins.

Perhaps the antique car hobby appeared to be more youthful because every generation of auto-crazed Americans cherishes the cars of its youth. The old-timers of the first automotive generation — such as Chet — love their Model Ts and 1930s roadsters. The members of the second generation like the cars of the post-World War II years, like the Chevys of 1955, '56 and '57 that they first fell in love with as boys. The baby boomers who hit their teens in the 1960s and early '70s will carry with them an affection for Mustangs, GTOS and Volkswagen Beetles as long as they live.

The old cars hobby began with that first generation of Model T mechanics, and second and succeeding generations didn't really get serious until the 1970s. In fact, the Antique Automobile Club of America would not allow cars built after World War II to be displayed at its big Hershey, Pennsylvania show. In 1974, Chip Miller and Bill Miller organized what they called Postwar '74 at Carlisle, Pennsylvania, and soon built it into one of the largest old car shows in the country. The Studebakers, Hudsons and Buicks of the late 1940s; the Ford Fairlanes, DeSotos, and, of course, Chevys of the 1950s; the Mustangs, Pontiacs, and Corvettes of the 1960s have all had their debuts at Carlisle and Iola as new generations of fans reinvigorate a hobby that just doesn't want to grow up.

Collectors hoped for a special set of coins to commemorate the Bicentennial of American independence in 1976. They got it, as witnessed by the Silver Proof Set here, with help from prominent hobbyists such as John Pittman and Cliff Mishler.

Chapter 25

1976

*"The Hobby giveth, and Man in his short-
sightedness, taketh away."*   Russ Rulau

The hobby gave its share to the Bicentennial of United States in 1976, and it can be said that most Americans took a few things away from it other than memories. The Bicentennial was the first truly national American festival since the end of World War II, and the nation had changed quite a bit in the three decades since 1945. By 1976, Americans had become so market-oriented that few people looked askance at the flood of commemorative material — both treasure and trash — offered for sale to mark the nation's 200th birthday. Anything was collectible in '76, from men's boxer shorts to women's hair curlers, as long as it bore some semblance of the Bicentennial Seal.

The coins struck for the celebration were, of course, on the list of collectibles and they were already in circulation before the calendar turned to 1976. In March 1975, Mint Director Mary Brooks announced that 1975-dated dollars, halves, and quarters would not be struck. Production of the first Bicentennial coins began at San Francisco in April while Bicentennial halves were placed in circulation and collector sets — containing 1976-dated silver examples of all three coins — were released right after the July 4th holiday. Quarters bearing the figure of a drummer in a tricorn hat flanked by the flame of liberty encircled by stars, halves whose reverse bore an image of Independence Hall, and Eisenhower dollars bearing the Liberty Bell and the moon became part of America's pocket change.

Krause had argued before Congress and in the pages of its periodicals that circulating coinage should also be commemorative and that the Bicentennial was important enough for the United States to redesign all its coins for it. Three out of six new coins was either half-bad or half-good, depending on one's outlook, and the folks in Iola decided to emphasize the positive and call it half-good.

The numismatic press has always benefited from any news related to coinage and the Bicentennial was no exception. The celebration, the special coinage, and the flood of commemorative medals, bars and other materials helped buoy up circulation figures at *Numismatic News, Coins,* and other Krause periodicals for the first three quarters of 1976. By the end of the year, however, a downturn had set in. The slide was most evident at *Numismatic News,* which lost 20 percent of its subscribers and fell to 40,000 readers by the end of the year. A regular series of circulation promotions tied to Krause's upcoming 25th anniversary in 1977 halted the decline and maintained the *News* until another period of oil crisis, silver speculation, inflation and economic uncertainty revived interest in coins in 1979.

Coins had recovered from the slump it had undergone in the late '60s and early '70s and, with over 30,000 subscribers and 80,000 newsstand sales per issue, was truly the quiet giant of the numismatic wing of Krause Publications. *Coin Prices* was selling better than ever, as every unsettling headline about the economy encouraged casual collectors to see if the Franklin halves they had stored in the back of the closet back in 1965 were worth more than fifty cents.

All of Krause's publications were certainly in better shape than two other venerable numismatic periodicals. In January, *World Coins* and *Numismatic Scrapbook Magazine,* pocket-sized monthlies published by Amos Press in Sidney, Ohio, halted publication. Publisher J. Oliver Amos cited "the continuing economic softness in the numismatic marketplace" as the reason for the demise of the magazines. *World Coins* first appeared in 1964, one of many periodicals started at that time to take advantage of the ongoing boom in coin collecting. The *Scrapbook* was the dean of numismatic periodicals. It had been founded by F. Lee Hewitt in 1935 and was unquestionably the most popular coin magazine of its day. Chet and other old-timers at Krause had cut their numismatic teeth on it, and its demise gave every veteran collector cause to reflect on the passage of time.

Russ Rulau's sentiments on the hobby giving and men taking appeared in an editorial eulogy for the two publications in *World Coin News.* His views were truly heartfelt since he had been the founding editor of *World Coins,* and had spent ten years with it. He had also followed Lee Hewitt as *Scrapbook* editor and managed it for six years before coming to Iola. "The staff here at *World Coin News* holds no joy in their hearts at the towel-tossing of the competition. Rather we will miss the good fight."

Rulau had waged it and ended up on the side of the survivor. Despite the ill-fortune of its fellow periodicals, *World Coin News* was far from declining. Quite to the contrary, it was now the only North American publication "devoted exclusively to the international facets of numismatics," and it was growing. In May it became a weekly, which Rulau said was "the wave of the future in numismatic publishing."

It was the old publishing dictum once again illustrated. Given a minimum of readers and advertisers, you can build your publication by bringing it out more often.

At about the same time that *World Coin News* became a weekly, *Numismatic News* also started to publish information its readers wanted to see more often. A totally restructured price guide titled Coin Market first appeared in the *News* in May. This feature resembled the *Standard Guide to United States Coins and Paper Money Valuations* that had appeared in book form in January. The paperback would eventually become outdated, which didn't really matter much to the casual collectors for whom it was produced. Values quoted in the Coin Market section of the *News*, which was read by many truly serious traders, would be right up-to-date. It was described in the 25th anniversary edition of the *News* as, "designed to provide the hobby with its first rapid-delivery coin price guide tuned to the realities of both the wholesale and retail markets in U. S. coins. It supplies both collectors and dealers with accurate guides to the prices being realized by the most popularly traded coins in collector-to-dealer, and dealer-to-collector transactions." Coin Market was yet another adaptation in coverage so the *News* could continue to serve as large a market as possible. Coin prices had always been a matter of interest to collectors and readers of Krause numismatic periodicals, but no more so than in the mid-1970s.

Iola celebrated the Bicentennial, like most American communities, with special events in July, starting with the national observation on Independence Day. A week later came the biggest Old Car Show and Chicken Roast ever held, followed by an open house weekend and dedication of the new Krause headquarters on the outskirts of the village. At least 700 guests and friends attended, including Mary Brooks, director of the United States Mint; James Conlon, director of the Bureau of Engraving and Printing; Virgil Hancock, president of the American Numismatic Association; John Pittman, also of the ANA and one the world's most renowned numismatists; and many other good friends old and new, such as Ed Rochette.

Chet called the new building "a milestone in our planning for the future." It was needed since the company had "simply outgrown our present facilities and rather than attempt to expand, we decided to move out, lock, stock and barrel to a new location, where we'll have plenty of room to expand." The room was surely needed, since Krause had added twenty-five new employees in the previous eighteen months. In that time the staff had grown from forty-three to sixty-eight, and would already just about fill the space available in the new building.

The completion of the new building was indeed a milestone, perhaps even more so than the 25th anniversary that came in 1977. It was vivid evidence of the permanence of the company, of its role as a source of jobs and development in the Iola community, and of its optimistic outlook on the future. It was also a much nicer environment in which to work than the other places the various branches of the Krause operation had called home during its recent period of growth, much to the delight of the staff.

Since the completion of the new headquarters was such a milestone, it is appropriate to pause and present a glimpse at Krause Publications in 1976.

Krause Publications in the Bicentennial Year

The Publications

Title	Began Publishing	Circulation, 1976
Numismatic News	1952	50,000
Coins	1961	115,000
Coin Prices	1967	122,000
Old Cars	1971	65,000
Standard Catalog of World Coins	1972 (3rd Ed.1975)	85,000
World Coin News	1973	16,000
Standard Catalog of World Paper Money	1975	32,000
Guidebook of Franklin Mint Issues	1975	16,000
Standard Guide to United States Coins and Paper Money Valuations	1976	50,000

The Staff

Corporate and Operating Officers

Chet Krause, President and Chairman of the Board; Cliff Mishler, Publisher and Executive Vice President; Bob Strand, Controller and Secretary; Glenn Wright, Vice President, Advertising; Gene Olstad, Vice President, Production; Ben Krause, Second Vice President. Receptionist Margie Blanchard.

Numismatic News

Arnold Jeffcoat, Bob Lemke, Russ Rulau, Trey Foerster, Bruce Smith, Linda Waller, Glenn Wright, Art Christoph, Pat Akey, Joe Jones, Tom Wildermuth, Lynn Erickson.

World Coin News

Russ Rulau, Bob Poeschl, Bruce Smith, Linda Waller, Dave Heise, Glenn Wright, Jim Fulton, Margie Blanchard, Chris Domask, Joan Melum.

Old Cars

Dave Brownell, Terry Boyce, Dave Heise, Bob Lichty, Sally Leer, Pam Moericke.

Coins Magazine

Bob Proeschl, Bob Lemke, Dave Heise, Glenn Wright, Joe Jones, Tom Wildermuth, Pat Akey.

Coin Prices

Cliff Mishler, Glenn Wright, Joe Jones.

Standard Catalog of World Paper Money

Colin Bruce, Marian Moe, Dave Heise, Judd Aiken, Cliff Mishler, Russ Rulau.

Sales Promotion

Dave Gendry, Luella Johnson, Jean Moericke.

Accounting

Bob Strand, Clare Oppor, Rosella Jenson, Alyce Kolden.

Maintenance-Shipping

Herman Gjertson.

School Job Co-op Program

Mary Ellen Bauer, Sandy Domask, Gail Grant, Lana Hardel.

Data Processing

Harry Becker, Suzanne Olkowski, Mona Wasrud, Carolyn Borth, Sondra Haase, Judy Schmidt.

Typesetting

Evelyn Bestul, Sue Davis, Shirley Flaata, Kathy Hines, Judy Kitzman, Marge Knaup, Doreen Mai, Sharon Moore, Marilyn Riddell, Pat Sprangers, Kari Lynn Trzebiatowski, Goldine Wilhelm.

Production

Gene Olstad, Roy Van Epern, Mary Rosholt, Dave Ostrowski, Herb Ward, Debbie Melum, Barb Ambacher, Dave Waller, Jim Olson, Bonnie Webb, Renee Peterson, Bob Nyiri, Lynn Larson, Marjorie Schmidt.

Number of Deadlines To Meet On Time: 148

The first Old Car Show to be held on Krause's new grounds took place the weekend before the Open House, and the staff put together a capsule history of and guidebook to Iola, the Lions Chicken Roast, the Old Car Show and Krause Publications. This portrait of the whole operation appeared in the first issue of *The Iola Car Show and Chicken Roast News*, July 11, 1976.

The first photo in the eight-page tabloid was of a "mighty Duesenberg J," with a caption that read, "less than 500 of these powerful Duesy models were ever built.... Original selling price of the chassis alone when new in the '30s was $10,000." This different version of the *News* also contained a photo of the *Old Cars* staff gathered around editor Dave Brownell's restored Morgan sports car and some of their thoughts on the hobby.

"The only generalization one can make about the old car hobby is that it defies generalizations," read the lead article. "It's a very individualistic pastime...and an exercise for the intellect as well as a chance to hone mechanical and craft skills.

"While the old car hobby has grown explosively in the past 10 years, its roots go back prior to World War II when a small number of collectors, mostly on the east and west coasts, began forming clubs.... The war, of course, brought the hobby to a standstill, but in 1946 the old cars were brought out of mothballs and the hobby began to grow.... Shows and meets were held with greater frequency. Young cars became old cars. The hobby started to grow and diversify from its near-total devotion to pre-1920 cars to the more readily available and less costly Model A Fords, [and] great classics like Packard and Cadillac twelve-cylinder cars, LaSalles, big Lincoln 12s, and Pierce-Arrows ...the crown jewels of automobile collecting.

"As the hobby grew clubs proliferated. A number of national organizations were founded.... Other clubs were devoted to a single make or model of car.... Today such organizations number well in the hundreds.

"The growth of the old car hobby brought with it an upsurge in specialist suppliers of parts and services.... Parts specialists began offering reproduction parts for popular collector cars....

"Today the old car hobby shows no signs of slowing down its remarkable growth...well over 150,000 people are interested in the hobby in this country...in the capacity of a large serious collector, or as historians, [or] collectors of license plates, radiator caps, hubcaps, sales catalogs and technical literature....

The summary listed who read and advertised in *Old Cars*: collectors, suppliers, club members, students, historians, buyers, sellers and traders. Its final sentence sums up what collecting is all about: "All that's required is a sincere interest in the old car hobby."

Every year more people with a sincere interest showed up at Iola, and every year they set a record for exhibitors and attendance. In 1976, 564 cars were on display, 100 vendors had goods for sale, 10,000 spectators poured over the grounds and — much to the delight of the Lions Club — they consumed 3,600 chicken dinners and other refreshments.

Chapter 26

1977

*"Teamwork is the key underlining the
success of Krause Publications..."*
Iola Car Show News, 1977.

Krause celebrated its 25th anniversary in October 1977, but "the key to
success" of the company was stated a few months earlier in the renamed
Iola Car Show News.

The *Car Show News* may seem to be an unlikely historical source, but the
1977 edition offered a thorough yet light-hearted description of the company
in its 25th year. It was unlike the promotional booklet produced for the 20th
anniversary in 1972, less business-like and more personal.

After describing each periodical and all of the major books Krause had published, the article talked about some of the people who had made it possible
for the company to mark its silver anniversary.

It started with David Gendry, sales promotion director, whose work was
"heading the coordinated thrust for media saturation" of the promotion and
marketing department. He was assisted by the "king of creations," Tom Wildermuth, who designed promotional brochures and did much of the "leg
work" at shows. Doug Watson who, "was the first art department" in 1964,
was not working at Krause in '77, so he was not listed in that year's staff rundown. Promotion and marketing created direct mail packages and media ads

The new office building on the edge of Iola opened for business in 1976, and the staff

and promoted all Krause products. "Each product has a specially designed direct mail package used to promote, sell and service it."

Next came Harry Becker, whose job and that of the data processing department was "keeping track of 160 million bits of information and distribution of approximately 400,000 periodicals."

Becker joined Krause in 1963 and in that time mastered nine different data handling systems, including the newly installed IBM System 3 Model 12. Data processing had evolved from the manual typewriter to the computer punch card and had just converted to floppy disks and tapes. The latest innovation was a direct link between the data processing computers and the Compugraphic "Unisetter" which set type automatically without having a person punch a keyboard more than once.

The production department was also using up-to-date electronic and photographic gear. Headed by company vice president Gene Olstad, production had updated its equipment five times in the previous fourteen years. The latest innovation utilized "Compugraphic Unisetters with Automix Keyboards Ultra-Count 200s as input keyboards. The storage system...is the Maxis floppy disk...[for storing] classified ads and calendars, besides additions, deletions, mixes, alphabetizing, and sorting." Olstad and his crew were not only good at production, they also became excellent linguists who could understand what the new jargon of computerdom actually meant.

They were looking forward to more computerization, including "video display units in each editorial cubicle for direct input into the Maxis system. This will enable an editor to write and edit a news story as it goes into the computer system...." These units, later known as personal computers, or PCs, dramati-

lined up in front for a historical portrait.

cally changed communications in the 1980s and Krause showed how forward-looking it was by anticipating them in 1977.

The staff outline continued, starting with the people who produced *Old Cars*. Terry Boyce was the editor in '77. He was a former advertising manager and car nut who had been writing about cars for newspapers since he was eighteen and who graduated from journalism school so he could make automotive publishing his life's work. For fun he owned cars, sixty-five of them as of 1976. Chris Halla was another auto maven, who also worked as an associate editor at *Old Cars*. A Wisconsin native and journalist, Halla also owned several not-so-old 1950s and 1960s cars.

Tim Bauer was advertising manager for *Old Cars*. He interpreted the role of ads as "a direct communication link between supplier and hobbyist," and "under his capable direction, *Old Cars* has set advertising inch records issue after issue."

Bauer learned the advertising ropes from Art Christoph at *Numismatic News*. Christoph was one of the company veterans, who joined the staff in 1957 and was still working the phones, designing ads and servicing accounts in '77. Ads in *World Coin News* were the specialty of Jim Fulton with assistance from Joe Jones, who was a general jack-of-all-advertising. Jones held several titles in his years at Krause, but his work always involved coin-related advertising, whether his accounts bought space in a periodical, catalog or guidebook. The advertising managers were assisted by Joan Melum, Karen Pribbenow and Chris Domask.

Vice president Glenn Wright supervised all the advertising people for all the publications. When he wasn't working, he was enjoying his small collection of vintage Corvettes.

Numismatic News was edited by Arnold "Jeff" Jeffcoat, who was in his eleventh year as a numismatic journalist. Bob Lemke held down the news editor's spot at the *News* and covered the political side of the hobby. As an associate editor at *Coins*, Lemke was also able to bring his knowledge and love of American Civil War history to its feature pages.

Coins, the "top slick in the business," was edited by Bob Poeschel, who had ten years of experience in numismatic publishing at Krause. *Coin Prices*, along with Coin Market, were the responsibility of Bob Wilhite. He had to contend with "interpretations of price increases, decreases, the fluctuation of gold and silver and other items...." He was also one of the authors of the *Standard Guide of U.S. Coin and Paper Money Valuations. World Coin News* was the preserve of managing editor Russ Rulau who "molded the publication into a pacesetter in the field," even though it was still a newcomer.

News stories and ads were the visible part of Krause Publications, but people like Pat Akey, who were less visible, were also vital to operations. Akey, who joined the staff in 1971, kept track of dealer accounts, a meticulous chore, at which she excelled.

Since its first appearance in 1972, the *Standard Catalog of World Coins* and the *Standard Catalog of World Paper Money* had become the largest single publishing jobs at Krause. In '77, they were managed by Colin Bruce, whose work was described as "forging the products from a chaotic accumulation of photos, texts and various contributions by collectors and dealers." He was aided by Fred Borgmann, a specialist in military memorabilia whose German language skills were an asset. The day-to-day work of producing the *Catalogs* fell to Marian Moe. Her work "encompasses revisions, additions, deletions, correspondence and the constant communication with catalog contributors."

"There are many more names on the KP roster," concluded the article. "They work together to ably serve two great hobbies; and are all valued parts of this still highly personalized firm."

The top management team was still organized as it had been in the mid-1960s, with departments reporting to vice presidents or, in financial matters, to comptroller Bob Strand. Except for Art Christoph, no one had been with Krause longer than Strand. He joined the company in 1961, was still on the job in '77, and remained until his retirement in 1988. As the company had grown Chet had become more of a policy maker and strategist, while more of the general management of the company lay in the hands of Cliff Mishler.

Cliff had a distinguished career in Iola and also in the international world of coin and coin-related collecting. He retained his love for tokens and medals and had presided over the Token and Medal Society for several years. He had served as spokesman for Krause Publications and the hobby before Congress and federal agencies, most notably on the matter of Bicentennial Coinage. In 1973, he sat on the Assay Commission, the third representative from Iola to be so honored. He continued to write columns for the *News*, co-authored catalogs and guidebooks, and took great pleasure in traveling around the country to distribute Numismatic Ambassador Awards. In 1975, he was named executive vice President and publisher, which meant he became the general coordinator of all operations, with the work of all staff members his ultimate responsibility.

Cliff was still "just plain" Cliff, however, and he marked the 25th anniversary year with a gesture faithful to the guiding spirit of the company. He tried to help collectors return to the source of their hobby, i.e. the bottom of their pockets. He launched a column in the *News* called "Circulation Finds" in an effort "to excite in our audience the realization that assembling a collection of modern U. S. coins from circulation can once again be an interesting and challenging pursuit." Considering the degree to which the variety of coins in circulation had diminished over the previous decade, the effort was certainly a challenge.

A profile of Chet also appeared in the 1977 *Car Show News*, but a long interview that appeared in the 25th Anniversary Edition of *Numismatic News* the following October was more revealing. For the 20th anniversary in 1972, Chet talked about business. For the 25th, he talked about business, but also about himself.

When asked about "the mystique of the image as opposed to your role in the hobby industry," Chet responded:

"First off, 25 years ago Iola, Wisconsin, was a very remote place in the minds of people in the heart of New York City....

"I guess as I got to be known, both as a name and as a publisher...there has always been, and still is, this thought that Iola is a long way from the civilized world.

"I think a lot of people who aren't familiar with country life, with rural life or modern communications can, just through their own ignorance, fail to realize how easy it is to get to a small town.

"There's no mystery about it in my eyes, but I do understand why there might be a mystique in the general public's eyes....

The mystique of the small town has been both an asset and a liability. The image of midwestern rural remoteness and backwardness is not pleasant, but it is balanced by the equally strong image of hard work and integrity that come with it.

Jimmy Carter had been elected president in November 1976 and comparisons were made between the man from Plains, Georgia, who had won the White House, and the man from Iola, Wisconsin, who had become equally successful in his own field. Chet wasn't interested in the parallel, and when the interviewer alluded to it, he made it plain that he didn't see any connection between himself and the president.

Every so-called self-made man has people who serve as models or heroes. For Chet, his parents would come first. In the hobby, the person closest to a hero for Krause was "Dick Yeoman."

"There are [sic] a multitude of reasons. He was one of the first personalities I met.... His style, the way he talked, a lot of things — and I don't even know if speaking softly and carrying a big club is the way to talk about that.... If I had to point to any one personality, he certainly would look as somebody who has made great strides in the hobby."

It was inevitable that Chet was asked about his "philosophy of business." He summarized it very well. "Just be damn sure what you say is correct and deliver the merchandise on time."

The final question asked about the future, "twenty-five years from now?"

"...Let me say that we've got our feet pretty damn firmly planted on the ground. Yes, we are a senior publishing house. But we don't really plan to sit on our laurels.

"What we have done in addition to physically situating ourselves in a building which can be used advantageously in publishing, we also have kept up on all the techniques as far as setting type, handling names and addresses and subscription promotions. All the techniques that go with the publishing industry are a part of our bank of information....

"If anyone in God's world can adjust to the social conditions and the energy problems and the cost of paper and people and postage, I guess we're able to do it."

Chet and Krause Publications received a carload of congratulations for the anniversary, but none had more meaning to Chet than the Farran Zerbe Award. "I know it was a moving experience for me when I got the Farran Zerbe Award. When you have to walk to the podium with a standing ovation, it gives you something."

The award was the highest honor bestowed by the American Numismatic Association for "distinguished service" to the organization and the hobby. As the citation read, "Twenty-five years ago you started a project that was to become a driving force in the hobby....

"Your integrity and tact has enabled you to correct your friends, maintain good will, and point out the road that should be taken.

"You have enlisted the finest workers available, given them direction and a free hand, and developed a large industry in what was once a small farm community....

"Not content to educate and inform, you perceived the recognition of valued and little known workers in the hobby, and instituted an award to honor these people.

"Ten years ago in Miami you were awarded the ANA Medal of Merit....

"Now we are proud to recognize your total accomplishments, dedication and strong support of the ANA...."

The award went to Chet, but, as the citation pointed out, there were many others involved — the people who purchased and read Krause publications, the hobbyists who worked for the hobby and were themselves honored with the Ambassador Award, and, most importantly, Chet's friends and colleagues who made working for Krause Publications both an avocation and a vocation. Chet's name was on the plaque, but he would admit that they all deserved a share in the award.

It may have been an anniversary year, but the work went on in Iola. The 1977 edition of the *Standard Catalog of World Coins* was published. It covered the issues of 687 countries, states, provinces and cities from 1800 to 1976. Sixty-five thousand coins were listed by date and mint and valued in three grades of condition. The listings and 31,000 photos covered 1,600 pages.

Another edition of the *Standard Catalog of World Paper Money* also came out of the Iola shop. This volume covered the currency issued by 271 countries between 1850 and 1976. Twenty-three thousand notes, with values listed in two grades, shared space on 704 pages with 5,000 photos.

The roll call of heavy volumes continued with the *Fourth Edition* of the *Guidebook of Franklin Mint Issues*. Compared to the *Catalogs*, this was a small book, with only 15,000 listings of Franklin's many items.

In the periodical department, coins were down and cars were up. In the coin market, "there was not a $100,000 class auction," recalled Cliff Mishler. The line on the growth charts for circulation, page counts and ad lineage in the numismatic periodicals remained flat, but *Old Cars* knocked out 80 pages every two weeks and broke the threshold of 90,000 in circulation. Perhaps the best news for the anniversary year came from the Old Car Show, where all the numbers just about doubled: 900 collector cars, 200 vendors, 20,000 spectators, and 4,400 chicken dinners.

*The **Old Cars** "guys" in 1977. In six years, they had built a successful publication that firmly established Krause in a second hobby niche.*

Chapter 27

1978

*"It just shows to what degree we would
go to get products to print on time, every
time."*   Doug Watson

"We sent off a box of film by air to World Color Press in Sparta, Illinois. The next day, we got a call that the film had not arrived. I took off for Green Bay at 3:00 p.m. with a duplicate set of films. All along the way to the airport in Green Bay, I called the printer, asking 'Did the film get there?'

"By 6:00 or 7:00 p.m. I had arrived at Chicago's O'Hare Field, ready to take off for St. Louis, but the flight was cancelled and the next scheduled flight would not get me into Sparta by the deadline.

"So I got up at 4:00 a.m. and drove from Chicago to Sparta. I got there one hour before the deadline, and so did the original set of films. But it just shows to what degree we would go to get products to print on time, every time."

Doug Watson's trek to Sparta took place in the early 1970s, but it could have occurred at any time during Krause's first forty years. The "on time" slogan was and is practical as well as motivational. Missing a printing deadline sets back many other editorial, advertising, production, and fulfillment deadlines. Publications have always come out of the Iola shop like cars off an assembly line. A delay in one place holds up the whole process. Starting in 1978, there were more deadlines every year for the staff to meet "on time."

The adventuresome Watson had returned to work at Krause in 1978 as head of the art department. His comings and goings can serve as mileposts in development of the company in the 1970s and '80s. When Watson left Krause in 1975, the company was still heavily dominated by its numismatic branch, with *Old Cars* the only publication not devoted to coins or coin-related material. By the end of the 1970s, Krause would be well into the period of expansion and diversification that would transform it from a numismatic hobby publisher to a general publisher of hobby, recreational and other periodicals and books.

The process began at *Old Cars*, with the application of principles proven successful in numismatic publishing. The names of the publications, the hobbies they serve and the dates of the events can be changed, but the process has been the same since the early 1960s. In 1978, Krause took its successful collector car periodical and published it more often. *Old Cars* became a weekly in 1978. John "Gunner" Gunnell, who joined the company in '78 and later became editor and publisher of what was now called *Old Cars Weekly*, recalled that at first "it was hard to switch from every other week to weekly. We heard it a lot: 'I don't need it every week.'" The naysayers were in the minority and *Old Cars* has been a weekly ever since.

Next, in what appeared to be 1953 revisited, Krause decided to print the results of the increasingly popular auto auction sales in every issue and set up a system of grading cars reminiscent of the ratings used to appraise coins. Throughout the mid-1970s Terry Boyce and the *Old Cars Weekly* staff worked out a system of evaluating old autos based on five grades. The system remained essentially unchanged until 1989, when a sixth grade was added. "The Car Grading Guide," the first of its kind, was initially published in *Old Cars Weekly*, then became part of another innovation, the *Old Cars Price Guide*.

Price guides were nothing new at Krause, where they had been an essential part of the periodicals since the 1950s. At first, the staff assumed that an annual price guide would be timely enough to report on a relatively stable antique auto market. It would be sold primarily on newsstands, and probably occupy space on the rack not very far away from *Coin Prices*. By the end of 1978, it was obvious that the auto market fluctuated quite a bit in the course of a year and the annual *Old Cars Price Guide* soon became outdated. The *Guide* became a quarterly and eventually a bi-monthly. Right from the start it contained the "Car Grading Guide" along with more than 85,000 price listings for both foreign and domestic automobiles.

Prices were set by a national advisory panel similar to the committee used by *Numismatic News*, but no auctioneers or dealers took part as they did in the original coin price guides of the 1950s. "Pricing can be controversial," said John Gunnell, "so no auctioneers or dealers are in. It may have general hobby experts, restorers, writers, appraisers, for a balanced blend."

The *Old Cars Price Guide* served one segment of the antique auto hobby. Every old car fan was interested in prices to a greater or lesser degree, as were coin collectors, but the number of auto fans interested only in prices was much smaller than the number of coin investors. Many car collectors owned only one car that they had lovingly restored and had no plans to sell. By comparison, coins and coin-related collectibles attracted a large percentage of speculators who cared about little else except buying and selling.

As John Gunnell said, "*Old Cars Weekly* is an editorially driven product, more so than other Krause publications." The history and lore of autos was attractive to readers in ways that the heritage of coinage was not. For example, *Old Cars* was less than ten years old when it had already published two volumes titled *The Best of Old Cars 1971-'78*, containing the most popular articles to appear in its pages. No similar volume on the many fine feature articles on coins that appeared in *Numismatic News* or *Coins* was ever compiled. Throughout the 1980s, *Old Cars* would continue to publish collections of its best feature photos and articles. In 1991, one of its most popular collections was *Antique Car Wrecks*, a 224-page volume featuring photos of accidents involving antique cars from *Old Car Weekly's* "Wreck of the Week" feature.

Although people purchased *Old Cars Weekly* to check the classifieds, display ads, auction results, and the calendar of car shows and swap meets, they seemed to be more likely to read and remember the feature articles there than those who looked at *Numismatic News*.

Once they detected a reasonable market for automobile features, the Krause staff set out to enter it. In '79 the company launched *Car Exchange*, a monthly magazine destined for the newsstands and with an editorial focus on autos of the post-World War II era. The energy crisis and the resulting downsizing of cars, as well as the maturation of the baby boom generation, had stimulated nostalgia for the big old buggies of the 1950s, and *Car Exchange* tried to tap it. "The attractive publication," as it was described in *Old Cars Weekly* in 1981, "features in-depth marque histories, a large classified ad section and a generous use of color photography." The use of color printing was becoming more widespread throughout magazine publishing in the late '70s, and *Car Exchange* used it for "a color centerspread, suitable for framing." Ironically, while readers seemed to enjoy the features about the autos of the pre-World War II era published in *Old Cars Weekly*, they took less interest in features about the first Corvettes and Rancheros, or the last Hudsons and Edsels. "We couldn't get it on track, "Chet recalled. Consequently, by the end of 1984, *Car Exchange* was sold to another publisher. (Actually *Car Exchange* was probably doomed from the start, since its title violated the Krause dictum of naming a periodical as literally as possible. What was a car exchange? A marketplace for ideas and stories, or a trading bench for autos? *Coins* was obviously about coins. *Car Exchange* was about...?)

Another extension of tried and true hobby publishing principles that Krause had better luck extending to antique autos in the late '70s was the *Standard Catalog*. "Chet had the *Standard Catalog* concept in the late '70s," said Gunnell. "We assigned it to several people; it was a tough project." Tough it was, and time consuming. The first volumes of what became an entire family of *Standard Catalogs* did not appear until 1982, but, when they did appear, they were huge successes. "More than half of the readers [of *Old Cars Weekly*] own a *Standard Catalog*," said Gunnell in 1991.

Within two years, Krause had the entire formula for filling a hobby publishing niche underway in the antique auto sector: the weekly tabloid with classified ads, hobby notices, news and features; the feature magazine for sale on newsstands; a periodical price guide reporting up-to-date market values; and the "phone book" compendiums that presented an encyclopedic store of information on different varieties of collectibles. They joined the already-popular *Old Cars Calendar*, first published in 1972, and which was modeled on Krause's popular *Coin Calendar*. The company discovered and published for a market consisting of people who liked to read about and see photos of old cars.

Also in place was a distinct automotive division within the company. It would soon be headed by Le Roi "Tex" Smith as publisher. He was a well-experienced collector car journalist who brought a sunny disposition and a Pecos Bill accent to Iola in 1979. Smith had written for a half-dozen automotive periodicals, as well as producing several books. He had driven race cars and played professional baseball. All in all, he was one of many hobby experts/authors who worked in their specialty at Iola.

Smith was joined by Tony Hossain, managing editor of *Old Cars Weekly*; Richard Johnson, associate editor, *Old Cars Weekly*; John Gunnell, the New York transplant who thrived in Iola, as editor of *Old Cars Price Guide*; Chris Halla, editor, *Car Exchange*; and Bob Lichty, advertising manager for the whole division. Lichty also functioned as chairman of the Old Car Show, which put him in charge of one of the largest old car shows in the country and made him the busiest man in Iola. For one crazy weekend in July, Lichty became the equivalent of a mayor of a small city, ringmaster of a circus with a cast of thousands, and stage manager of the largest show of its kind in the Midwest.

As a tribute to Lichty's abilities, the Old Car Show continued to grow by leaps and bounds. It filled the usually placid countryside around Iola with the unfamiliar purrings and putterings of antique cars and the familiar busy hum of people browsing, bargaining, admiring antique cars and enjoying themselves. For the '78 Show, Krause added fifteen acres to the car show grounds to accommodate 1,200 collector cars and 30,000 spectators who finished off at least 5,000 chicken dinners.

The featured cars were Fords, Buicks and Cadillacs, all celebrating their 75th anniversaries. Chet showed off his 1903 Model A, the 605th Ford ever built, which was also the first auto sold in Waupaca County. A 1908 Model 10 Buick and a 1905 one-cylinder Cadillac runabout represented the other two honored auto lines.

In the numismatic division at Krause, 1978 was the quiet year before the inflationary storm of 1979 and the early '80s blew fresh speculative breezes through the hobby. It was a time for the coin press to rediscover the true nature of its subject and examine again the pleasures of collecting for its own sake. In Iola they tried to focus on collecting by publishing a quarterly magazine called — to no one's surprise — *Coin Collecting*. It premiered in the winter of '78 with 154 pages and a line-up of heavy hitters on the masthead — Cliff Mishler, Bob Poeschl, Bob Lemke, Doug Watson, Joe Jones. The contents of *Coin Collecting* was long on how-tos and material for beginners who were not ready for *Coins* or the *News* and — it was hoped — would pick up the new magazine on the newsstand. The staff hoped that by covering collecting itself, the magazine could bring more people into the hobby. It was an attempt to explore the numismatic niche and test the market, just as *Car Exchange* was probing for space in the collector car niche.

The image of coin collecting had never fully recovered from the political battles of the 1960s and the speculative atmosphere of the early '70s. Chet had touched on this topic in the 25th anniversary issue of the *News*. "Really," he said, "the non-numismatic press has been highly derogatory to coin collecting. In fact, it is rather difficult today to read anything that is favorable to collecting coins. They are prone to write bad things about us."

It was into this atmosphere that *Coin Collecting* was introduced. "I'm not damning investment oriented collecting," Chet continued, "because, with no thought at all to investment, if you just collect nice things in a good orderly fashion and keep your own judgment, by nature, numismatic items are a good investment."

Coin Collecting was intended to help its readers "collect nice things in a good orderly fashion." That was the truly "good investment" that would pay off. But despite the worthy sentiments behind it, *Coin Collecting* didn't pay off. After its introductory issue, it appeared four times each in 1979 and '80, then shut down.

By the end of 1978, the future course of Krause Publications was charted. The company would find a hobby publishing niche and then explore it with tabloids, magazines, price guides, catalogs and calendars. Like any voyage of exploration, the course wound its way through many a tight passage, around stormy headlands and into dead end bays, but it also contained many stretches of smooth sailing and fast currents that stimulated growth and diversity. The ship was ready in '78. All that was left was the launching.

By 1979, the Iola Old Car Show was attracting 35,000 visitors and 400 swappers who looked at 1,200 cars on exhibit. It had already become the largest show of its kind in the Midwest and would soon be the third largest in the United States.

Chapter 28

1979

*"This newspaper is directed primarily to
collectors of paper notes, bonds, checks,
and documents; collectors of wooden
money, ration tokens, wampum, odd and
curious, and other items of a non-coinage
or non-medallic nature...."*

Grover C. Criswell

D iversity was the watchword for Krause Publications at the end of the
1970s, and 1979 was an exemplary year for it.

The company purchased *Bank Note Reporter*, which was founded by Grover
Criswell in 1973 and dedicated to covering the many varieties of fiscal paper
that people have used for money over the years. Krause also purchased Western
Publications, then the publisher of three magazines devoted to the history and
lore of the American West: *True West, Frontier Times* and *Old West*. They were
a genuine departure from Krause's niche in hobby publishing.

Bank Note Reporter was a logical acquisition for the company that already
published the *Standard Catalog of World Paper Money*, and whose numismatic publications covered virtually every aspect of collectibles related to
money. Bob Lemke was named editor of the *Reporter* after it moved to Iola,
with Colin Bruce, Jim Fulton, and Trey Foerster, who was associate editor of
World Coin News, also on the masthead.

Bank Note Reporter had a circulation of about 2,500 in '79, a small but respectable readership for a subject of such narrow appeal. With so few readers, the paper had always struggled to stay afloat on its own, and its coming into the Krause tent probably saved it. Krause could promote it with the readers of its other periodicals, and its sales people could offer marketing opportunities to advertisers that a one-paper publisher could not. *Bank Note Reporter* held its own and by the end of the 1980s, its circulation had doubled and passed the 5,000 mark.

Paper money was only indirectly the source of big news in numismatics in '79, the year of the Susan B. Anthony dollar. Inflation had cut the purchasing power of the American dollar in half in the previous twenty years, and many economists, politicians and — of course — numismatists urged the United States Congress to issue a one-dollar coin that would eventually replace the paper dollar. The design, size and press run for the new dollar was much argued over but, in 1978, Congress passed, and President Jimmy Carter signed, the Susan B. Anthony Dollar Act. It authorized the Mint to issue a new dollar to honor the American women's rights leader, Susan Anthony. Since the coin was intended to be used for general circulation as pocket money, for convenience's sake its size was reduced to about that of a quarter.

Convenience turned into confusion and controversy. Many Americans were reluctant to give up the paper dollar, others did not like the ease with which the Anthony dollar could be confused with the quarter, and the whole attempt to replace the dollar bill with a handy dollar coin bogged down.

"The dollar coin was a good idea," said Cliff in 1991. "It's more durable, more economical than paper and needed in vending machines. A coin lasts twenty-five years in circulation, a bill lasts eighteen months. [The Anthony dollar] was handled in a terrible way. It had no chance of success and failed because the government insisted on continuing to issue the dollar note. They should have set a date for discontinuation of the note and eliminated the half dollar."

The U.S. Treasury and Congress didn't do much of anything to encourage use of the dollar coin, and the clumsy way the whole affair was handled was used by presidential candidate Ronald Reagan as another example of the ineptness of the Carter Administration.

For numismatists the Anthony dollar was another coin to collect. It was made doubly interesting by an error that created a "filled S" mint mark on most of the 1979 proof coins and a more valuable "open S" mint mark on others.

The Anthony dollar fracas was a sideshow compared to the silver boom of 1979. Once again turmoil in the Middle East caused an oil shortage that fueled inflationary fires and kindled fear of economic collapse. The coin market, along with silver, boomed again. Gold, which was out of the speculative picture in the 1960s and early '70s, played a big role in the '79 boom. The price of an ounce of gold rose all through '79 and hit $887.50 in January 1980. As soon as restrictions on gold ownership by Americans had been relaxed, a growing market for collectibles wrought from the precious metal was established. Gold coins, tokens, medals and bars were attracting more collectors who, so it was discussed in Iola, could be the audience for another Krause publication.

A periodical devoted to the gold market did not appear in '79, but there was still plenty to be excited about in the numismatic division at Krause. Silver started 1978 at $5 an ounce, more than doubled to $11 in '79 and hit an all time high of $48.80 in January of '80. The Hunt Brothers of Texas had a hand in silver's rise, but their famous attempt to corner the market was more effect than cause of the increase.

The effect on coin prices and circulation of Krause's numismatic publications was predictable. They surged again, as they had in the early '60s and in 1973. At an Stack's auction in New York City in June, $1.7 million in United States gold coins changed hands. A 1907 ultra-high relief $20 double-eagle, one of only sixteen struck, sold for $225,000, a record for any U.S. coin. Even more common coins were selling at unheard of prices, like the premium quality 1910-D $5 gold piece usually listed in the $500 range; it garnered $2,800 at the Stack's sale.

In this kind of atmosphere, *Coin Prices* became a particularly popular periodical. At the *News*, the staff calmly reported prices for coins higher than they could have possibly imagined a few months earlier, and old-timers reminisced about the return of the good old days. The boom in the gold market would slow down in 1980, and silver would collapse disastrously, but the coin market continued to rise and took Krause along throughout the inflation and recession ridden years of the early '80s.

At Western Publications, they were more concerned with the gold rush of 1849 than the boom of 1979. Western had been founded by Joe and Elizabeth Small in 1953, an interesting date for a number of reasons, and not just in Iola. The Federal Communications Commission ended a moratorium on licenses for television stations in '53 and TV spread to smaller cities, such as Green Bay and Wausau, Wisconsin — which sent signals to Iola. In a few years western melodramas would become the most popular shows on the air and maintain interest in cowpokes and gunslingers that helped Western Publications develop into a successful publishing house.

At the same time, television was bringing about the closing of the era of the "pulp" novel and magazine. In their day, "pulps" were the print equivalent of television, so-called because of the inexpensive low grade wood pulp paper on which they were printed. It was in the pages of the "pulps" that the otherwise ordinary lives of various denizens of the American West — Wyatt Earp, Wild Bill Hickock, the Sundance Kid — acquired heroic status. In the 1910s, these heroes were transferred to the silver screen of the movie house and, in the 1950s, to the little screen in the living room. With the transfer came the demise of many of the books and magazines of the "pulp" trade, and not just westerns but science fiction, mystery, crime and other assorted adventure yarns.

Western Publications was a throwback to the pre-television age and it enjoyed its heyday in the 1950s when the "pulp" tradition was waning but still alive and TV programming was dominated by horse operas. As time passed and the popularity of the "pulps" faded, Western pruned its output from six periodicals in 1958 to three in '79. By then, the Smalls were ready to slow down and they sold their company to Krause, with the condition that they continue to edit their magazines. The editorial offices remained in Austin, Texas, while advertising and production moved to Iola. It was a testimony to the technology of the times that editorial material moved back and forth from Austin to Iola with little trouble. The communications and publishing industries had come a long way since Krause struggled to publish *Canada Coin News* with one set of offices in Toronto and another in Iola.

Krause stopped publishing *Frontier Times* in 1982, but kept the monthly *True West* and the quarterly *Old West* alive. Finding readers for popular western history was tough, and finding advertisers was even tougher. Although collectibles related to the West existed, the hobby wasn't organized in the same manner as was the old car and coin collecting fraternity. The magazines had never been aimed at collectors anyway. "Western Publications wasn't collector-oriented," said Cliff. "It was tied to the history of the country. We were surprised there wasn't more popular demand we could tap."

The Krause team of Jim Dullenty, editor, and Mary Haefner, editorial assistant, who took over editorial work in 1982, was nevertheless able to increase the circulation of *True West* by more than 30 percent. They also did a good job of hanging onto readers. A full 75 percent of *True West's* subscribers renewed. However, the average age of those readers was fifty-eight years, which did not bode well for the future.

Nearly all of Western's advertisers were located west of the Mississippi, and, although the phone lines crossed the river, selling ads from a base in Iola proved to more difficult than anyone anticipated. In 1984, Krause sold Western Publications to publisher Bob Evans of Perkins, Oklahoma. He was located closer to most of Western's advertisers and not very far away from the Cowboy Hall of Fame.

"The Western Publications required a different advertising approach," said advertising manager Randy Clausen in 1984. "In hobby publications, advertisers come to you. You are doing them a service.

"Western required that you actively go out and grab advertising. Our staff was set up for the hobby style."

Krause's venture into western publishing proved to be a voyage into one of the blind bays on the sea of diversification. The exploration continued until 1984, when the last of the western "pulps" rode out of Iola and off into the sunset.

A positive side of the Western Publications adventure was the inventory of books, artwork and other memorabilia that came with the magazines and which Krause marketed. Western Publications was also a source of editorial material which Krause reprinted in the early 1980s especially after it resurrected Western's *Gold!* magazine. The readers of *Gold!* enjoyed the old yarns about gold strikes in the Rockies and lost mines in the deserts of Arizona.

The experiment with Western Publications set a precedent for the coming decade. Krause would continue to diversify, but, at least in the opening years of the decade, would not again wander away from collectibles. As it turned out, the company did not have to wander very far at all to find hobbies where Krause could apply its formula with the greatest success, but not in 1979.

Instead, the last year of the '70s like the last year of each decade before, makes a good indicator for Krause Publications. In 1959, Chet's little operation had doubled its readership from 10,000 to 20,000 and started to take part in the first great coin collector's boom. In 1969, the company was recovering from the hard times of a few years earlier, and was expanding its coverage of coin-related medals, tokens and commemorative items. It had also successfully established *Coin Prices* as part of the hobby publishing niche. In '79, Krause was spreading farther, with two hobby niches filled and with others under exploration. The 1980s would offer great opportunities for growth, and Krause was ready for them.

Starting in the early 1970s, Krause utilized IBM computers, such as the System 3 here, to stay on the cutting edge of electronic publishing technology.

Chapter 29

1980

*"All products interrelate to some degree,
all serve leisure time interests. There's
some cross-fertilization between advertisers and subscription lists of several
publications."*   Cliff Mishler

O ccasionally questions arise about the nature of collecting and collectors.
Is there a single type of person who collects? Are all collectors alike?
Chet Krause, who should know, says that there isn't any one type of person
who collects. "I've known all kinds," he says.

All collectors seem to share a few traits. Most are good students of their subjects. Coin collectors know about coins themselves and the history related to
them. Baseball card collectors know about the players depicted on their cards
and the lore of the era in which they played. Record collectors know the music
they like and are familiar with the cultural context in which it was produced.

Most collectors are collectors first; any gain made from the investment
potential of their hobby is a secondary consideration. If a gain is expected,
it's long term — a nest egg for retirement or a gift to pass down to children
or grandchildren.

Most collectors like to share their knowledge and passion with others. They
like to read and write about it, come together at conventions and swap meets
and talk to each other. Most serious collectors also remain within the bound-

aries of one hobby. Coin people stay with coins and coin-related items. Car nuts are car nuts and rarely stray from the greasy-knuckle crowd. Sports collectors stick to the memorabilia of the playing field.

Finally, almost all collectors are traders. They watch the market and are able and willing to buy, sell and barter to build their collections.

Publications devoted to a collecting hobby are very much like the collectors they serve. They must know their subjects well and plan for the long term. They have to plainly enjoy communicating with their readers and advertisers and they must stick to communicating only what they know best. They must cater to traders and provide a market that spans the distances among people who share the same passion but reside in different locations.

Krause Publications has always followed these general rules. The editorial people, starting with Ed Rochette and Cliff Mishler in the early '60s and continuing to *Comics Buyer's Guide* editors Don and Maggie Thompson in the 1990s, have always been experts in their respective fields. While the staffs of individual publications within a niche routinely work on all the publications in it, rarely do staff people leave a niche. They may all be professional journalists who could conceivably work for any publication, but they prefer to stick with what they know best.

Sticking with what they know best makes it easier for Krause people to be enthusiastic about it. Contradictory as it may seem, there are publications, especially publications with a narrow editorial focus, that do not seem to care whether or not they have any readers. Krause Publications began with the goal of communicating with "isolated collectors" and bringing them together with ads and articles, and it never lost that spirit. It is apparent that the newspapers and magazines from Iola are "'readers' publications."

Even more so, they are "'traders' publications." The gauge of a publication's popularity at Krause is not necessarily the editorial content, but the classified word ads. They are the measure of the marketplace that a publication delivers to its readers. Display ads serve a similar, but not identical, purpose, since collectors like to trade with each other and do it via the classifieds. "We publish 40,000 classified ads a month," said Chet in 1992. "Classifieds are the basis of hobby publishing." And the want ad is for everyone in the hobby.

By 1980, Krause had filled the numismatic niche, but that did not deter the company from trying to expand with a little cross-fertilization between niches. The market for precious metals was as bullish as it ever was, and the name of the gold coin from the Union of South Africa — the "Kruggerand" — was recognized in every household in the United States. The company's numismatic branch was reporting news on gold, and advertisers were offering a growing assortment of gold coins for sale. The time was right for the company to see if the numismatic niche could support a periodical targeted solely on gold collectibles.

Krause had a ready source of editorial material in the news it was already reporting and in an unusual set of feature pieces it had recently acquired. When it purchased Western Publications, Krause also acquired *Gold!* magazine. It was a pulp periodical which printed fact and — probably — fiction related to gold in the American West. Tales of lost gold mines, buried Spanish treasure, and caches of gold stashed and forgotten by various desperadoes were part of the western genre and *Gold!* with the exclamation point, had a mother lode of them. Krause decided to combine the old features with news on gold markets and ads from dealers to produce a revamped *Gold!* The magazine whose advertising once ran to offers for metal detectors and weekends at dude ranches now carried ads for United States gold coins, the Franklin Mint's various gold offerings, and the Krugerrand, along with a special sale on back issues brimful of golden treasure tales.

Distribution of the new magazine was restricted to newsstands and, since it was experimental, the publication schedule of the magazine was irregular. *Gold!* was dated by year and numbered sequentially. It was staffed by some of the regulars from the numismatic team — Cliff Mishler, Bob Lemke, Russ Rulau and Joe Jones — but *Gold!* had a short life. The magazine never grew fatter than 64 pages and the final issue appeared in 1981. As a sign that the end was near, *Gold!* Number 21 carried pieces about how to purchase precious metal mining stock and pointed out that the best investment opportunities for 1982 might be in silver.

The brief life of *Gold!* magazine in Iola illustrates how most of Krause's expansions have occurred over the years. *Gold!* fit into the numismatic niche. The company had staff, editorial material and a display advertising base. It might have been able to build circulation and increase advertising — if gold investors could develop a taste for adventure yarns and if the fans of gold mining tales would start purchasing gold collectibles — and give *Gold!* a future. As it turned out, Krause's resurrection of *Gold!* lasted less than two years. Krause was not shy about experimenting to see if the borders of a niche had changed, and the 1980 probe showed that numismatics had not yet enlarged enough to support a periodical targeted on goldbugs.

Even though *Gold!* was not growing, Krause was. Between 1976 and 1980, forty positions had been added to the staff. The 1975 building, which was meant for a staff of 70, was now home to more than 100 people working in less than comfortable conditions. As a book publisher, Krause had acquired an inventory that had to be stored, with further demands on space. The company that published the "phone books" of numismatics and was working on the equivalent for antique cars, needed a place to store all those weighty volumes.

The march of modernization in the computerized typesetting operation had also continued since '76. An AKI typesetting system was installed in July 1977. It was upgraded to a capacity of 600 lines per minute in May 1978, then to 1,100 lines in September. In January 1979 the IBM Series I typesetting interface arrived, and it set its first classified ad for Krause in April. A second IBM System 3/Model 12 system arrived in January 1980. This new equipment meant greater speed, accuracy and capacity in production, and it also required more room.

To meet all these needs, Krause added a new wing on the southwest end of the 1975 building. It was a 15,500-square foot addition, with one quarter of its area reserved for the cataloging and marketing departments, another quarter for circulation and an expanded direct mail operation, with a full half left for warehousing. The southwest wing was the first of four additions that made the 1980s the decade of the greatest growth in the company's physical plant.

Also growing in 1980 was the Iola Hospital. A new facility, costing $1.3 million, was completed that year. A substantial portion of that money was raised by the Iola Lions, and nearly all of their funding came from the hot dogs, brats, and chicken dinners they sold at the Old Car Show.

In February 1981, the *Lions* Magazine ran a feature on the Old Car Show and it captured well the atmosphere of the event that was already the biggest car show in the Midwest.

"For 363 days a year," the article read, "Iola is a quiet picture book community of 1,000, hidden in the farmland country of central Wisconsin. But for the other two days — the weekend following the Fourth of July — Iola is transformed into the old car capital of the world.

"The 1980 show drew 45,000 visitors. Some made reservations a year in advance at the town's one motel.... Many stayed 60 miles away in Green Bay and Appleton. More than 2,000 pitched tents or staked out a claim in an area set aside for 500 campers, or slept in their cars.

"On Sunday the 80-acre spread was a crush of steel and humanity. 2,700 restored show cars, ranging from a shiny red 1902 Rambler to mid-'70s models. More than 6,000 visitor cars blanketed the show grounds. Another 850 people rented space in a swap meet area to sell old auto parts.

"Lions handle overall supervision...[and] every other Iola civic organization is assigned specific duties. Jaycees from Iola and neighboring Scandinavia...vounteer firemen...American Legion...Hospital Auxiliary...Winter Sports Club...Booster Club...Kiwanis...Boy Scouts. [Everyone expected a record crowd but] "...no one was prepared for what happened the weekend of July 11-13.

"By Friday night, the show car area was already half full and all the camper spaces were taken. On Saturday, the first day of the swap meet, about 15,000 people came to try and find that obsolete fuel pump or old fender they had been seeking. The heat was oppressive, concession sales brisk, and visitors welcomed the cooler air of evening.

"The Lions...were out in force at 5:00 a.m. Sunday.... Half an hour later, cars began to arrive and a long line had formed when the gates were opened at 6:30. During the morning, thousands of cars poured in, and an authentic double decker London bus brought in a group from Appleton. By noon the crowd was so dense that just moving around became difficult. Outside the gates cars were backed up six miles and at 1:00 p.m. the sheriff's deputies began turning hundreds away. But for those who had planned ahead and arrived early, it was a memorable day. The highlight was a special display of cars built in Wisconsin by such pioneer companies as Kissel, Nash, Sternburg and Oneida Truck. Brook Stevens, the noted industrial designer, brought the latest version of his legendary Excalibur sports car. And everywhere there were glistening vintage Fords, Packard phaetons and convertibles, Pierce-Arrows, early Mercedes-Benz, Duesenbergs, a 1927 Belgian Minerva owned by Chet Krause, ancient fire and army trucks, and nearly everything else imaginable from the wonderful world of old cars.

"The weather was again in the humid '90s and several people collapsed from sun stroke. They were quickly treated at a first aid station.... By mid-afternoon...everything had been sold...4,500 chicken halves, 13,000 bratwurst,

10,000 hot dogs, 400 pounds of chili, and more than 1,000 cases of bear and 1,400 cases of soda pop.

"...At the end of the day Lions and other workers hauled boxes of cash to the Krause offices. The tally was phenomenal. After expenses the Lions had netted $50,000 and another $20,000 went to other local organizations. That is a $70,000 profit from a two-day project in a town so small it is difficult to find on a road map."

Media people never stop telling the world that Iola is remote or hard to find, and every year tens of thousands of people have no trouble finding it. The Old Car Show was a success for the company and the community. As part of both, the people at Krause both worked for and benefited from the big show.

The '80 show was memorable for the hot weather and the hot chili. The Iola Antique Fire Company, a collector group heavily populated by Krause people, sponsored a chili cooking contest, an activity assumed in subsequent years by the Scandinavia Fire Department. Automotive division publisher Tex Smith headed a panel of judges recruited for their fine palates and ironclad stomachs to judge entries with names like "Arsonist's Dream" from the Scandinavia Volunteer Fire Department and "Arkansas Red," Bob Wilhite's concoction. "Arsonist's Dream" was named the best-tasting, while "Arkansas Red" took the honors for the hottest chili in Iola.

The Old Car Show was part of the Krause experience. People worked for the company, worked for the community, and enjoyed each other's company. It was community development, corporate promotion and camaraderie among friends all rolled into one.

In the late 1980s, theorists of business management stated that the hierarchal structure of American management was obsolete. They said that workers produced better if they felt that they were part of a team pulling together for a common goal. One of the ways, the theorists said, to encourage team spirit at work is to get employees to mix and work together away from the shop. They encouraged companies to sponsor community projects that their people could work together on and reinforce team spirit.

Maybe they read the theories in Iola, and if they did, the people at Krause were probably gratified to know that the theorists had caught up with what they had been doing for years. Keeping the company a part of the community came naturally to the people who worked there, whether they were raised in Iola or not. It came naturally to Chet because that was the way he was raised, and that philosophy worked its way through the entire operation. The concept of the individuals within a company being part of a community both inside and outside of the corporate walls, and that the company, the employees and the community would benefit from it, wasn't new. The Old Car Show does many things for car collectors, old car periodicals and the community of Iola. That it also improves morale and performance at the company is another benefit that the theorists of business management have only recently discovered.

A few of the "experts" on staff did not see much promise in a 1980 suggestion put forth by Bob Lemke and Doug Watson that Krause diversify into baseball card collecting. The experts were wrong. Led by **Sports Collectors Digest** *and* **Baseball Cards,** *which first appeared in 1981, sports collecting took less than a decade to become the most profitable niche at Krause.*

Chapter 30

1981

"Bob Lemke and Doug Watson came to us for over 6 months to produce the **Coins** *magazine of baseball cards. After 6 months, Chet came into the office and said, 'Maybe they should take a shot...it won't be a success, but it won't cost too much.'"*　　　　　Cliff Mishler

The events of the years ending in "9"-'59, '69, '79 — are good indicators of where Krause Publications had been in the previous decade. The years ending in "1" are indicators of where the company was going. In 1961, *Coins* was born and represented Krause's first expansion within a hobby niche. In 1971, *Old Cars* appeared. It was Krause's first attempt to diversify beyond the numismatic niche. In 1981, the company entered another niche, sports collecting. It would become, by the end of the decade, the largest and most profitable division within the company.

Also in the eventful year of 1981, Krause reorganized its management structure by adding a personnel department, continued to upgrade its data processing and production equipment, and started on another addition to the building. For the historian charting the company's development in the 1980s, 1981 was perhaps Krause's most significant year. It also stands out as a keynote year in which the course of events summarizes the entire operation.

The route that led into a new hobby niche traveled down two familiar pathways. First, Krause gave Bob Lemke and Doug Watson a shot at the *"Coins* magazine of baseball cards." The first issue of *Baseball Cards* magazine appeared for sale on newsstands in the spring of '81. As the masthead read, Cliff Mishler was publisher; Bob Lemke, editor; Doug Watson, ad manager/art director; David Heise, photographer; Marge Williams, classified advertising.

The new magazine followed the standard Krause formula: its title stated exactly what it covered; it had a color cover printed on glossy paper with newsprint inside; it was published as a "one-shot" at first to see how well it sold, with semi-annual, quarterly and monthly publication planned if it was successful; it was sold first on newsstands, like *Coins*, with subscribers as a secondary market.

As Lemke wrote in his first "Coach's Box" editorial, "The premiere issue of *Baseball Cards* magazine...will commence, and the sports collecting hobby will enter a new era — receiving national newsstand exposure for the first time."

He went on to say that "we are not exploiting or commercializing the hobby....the worst complaint we've heard that we will admit to being guilty of is that we do intend to 'wise up' the public about the true nature of the hobby. We heard from some persons...that this magazine would dry up potential sources of 'cheap' baseball cards...any Joe Sixpack...can pick this magazine off the rack and get an accurate idea of what those cards are worth. He is, therefore, less likely to let them go for a song to the first collector or dealer he happens to run across.

"We like to think that while it may be true that some entrepreneur has lost a quick profit from Joe's hoard, the hobby has gained a convert.

"What is all boils down to is that *Baseball Cards*, like the other KP products, is 'For Collectors. By Collectors.'" The last line was literally true. Both Lemke and Doug Watson were avid card collectors who had been trading cards and attending shows for years. Watson was a dyed-in-the-red St. Louis Cardinals fan who had idolized Stan Musial and had an extensive collection of Cardinals cards and other memorabilia. Lemke had been collecting cards for over twenty years — which made him a pioneer in the hobby — and had written articles for and contributed photos to other card collectors' periodicals. Having editorial people who knew and practiced the hobby they covered was also part of the standard Krause formula, and *Baseball Cards* was no exception.

The cover of the first issue featured some of the most valuable cards and some of the most memorable players of all time: Mickey Mantle, Babe Ruth, Willie Mays, and Stan Musial (of course). Dave Winfield, one of the biggest stars of the early '80s, was also featured, and so was the Honus Wagner card that was the most valuable card in the market. A straight-arrow if there ever was one, or maybe just a shrewd businessman, Wagner objected when the American Tobacco Company used cards printed with his image to promote its products without his permission. The company stopped printing the cards and the less than twenty cards known to exist in 1981 were valued at $17,500 each.

Also inside was a "Meet The Team" photo spread that featured Chet, Cliff, Bob, Doug and Dave Heise depicted on mock baseball cards. They were wearing red T-Shirts and the caps of the Iola-Scandinavia baseball team, which bear an S slashed with an I that looks, coincidentally, like a dollar sign.

As Krause well knew, a feature magazine could not stand alone within a hobby niche. A trader's tabloid had to stand with it, and, in fact, carry it along. The sports collectible hobby was young in 1981. It was a popular pastime for nostalgic baby-boomers who were just getting old enough to start reminiscing about their good old days in the 1950s — which is why cards depicting Mickey Mantle, Yogi Berra, Willie Mays, Stan Musial, Henry Aaron and the Brooklyn Dodgers of Gil Hodges, Duke Snider and Jackie Robinson were among the most popular in the trade.

One of the few periodicals devoted to the hobby was *Sports Collectors Digest*, which had been founded by John Stommen of Milan, Michigan in 1973. As Steve Ellingboe recalled in 1991, *SCD* was "set up like Chet Krause 40 years before, [but] the Stommen family didn't have the machinery or the vehicle to promote it properly." The *Digest* was published twenty-four times a year, had a circulation of about 8,500, and was known among collectors as the "bible" of the hobby.

Krause could have started its own tabloid and probably could have competed successfully with *SCD*. Instead, it bought the newspaper, thereby removing the competition, acquiring *SCD's* subscription list and advertising base, as well as its reputation for fine quality and knowledgeable coverage. Krause completed the purchase in August 1981, and sent the first issue out of Iola in September.

Hobbies are reflections of changing times and tastes. In the 1970s, a generation of Americans raised to play sports matured into the world's greatest sports fans. Every major professional sport in the nation — baseball, football, basketball, hockey — and a few minor ones, added more teams to its leagues and more fans to its newly built, colossally sized stadiums. The popularity of major college sports teams rivaled that of the pros, and more members of the "subway" alumni of legendary sports universities such as Notre Dame, Penn State, and UCLA emerged from the underground.

Television was the most important factor in the rise of sports. Every weekend saw an orgy of sports on the air, and on many week nights people who did not like sports had to shut off their sets for lack of anything to watch. Sunday football on TV had become such a part of life that many Americans born since 1960 couldn't fathom autumn weekends without it. In the '70s, special sports events like the Olympics, the World Series, the NCAA Basketball Championship and the Super Bowl took on the significance of religious holidays during which all regular activity stopped so Americans could witness the on-screen rites. Not only were more Americans than ever watching sports, more Americans than ever were playing sports. Sports leagues for adult baseball, basketball — even football and hockey players — were organized or expanded in every community. Americans also became obsessed with physical fitness in the 1970s. Joggers, walkers and bicyclers clogged the parks and highways while health clubs filled with exercise-addicted members. The sports craze was not limited to men, either. More women played, watched and enjoyed sports than ever before.

The 1970s also saw a major increase in the cult of the celebrity. Back in the 1960s, avant garde artist Andy Warhol smirked and declared that every American would someday "be famous for fifteen minutes." That day didn't come in the '70s, but the number of people who were "famous" for nothing except being "famous" mushroomed. Entertainers, politicians and, of course, athletes became leading contenders in the celebrity contest, where value was measured less by accomplishment than by notoriety. As the '70s passed into the 1980s, the concept of celebrity, of valuing fame for its own sake, gained even more credence and marketability.

In this atmosphere, it was not surprising that baseball and other sports cards — tokens of celebrity in a sports crazy land — should become the most popular collectibles in the country. Once again, as in 1971, Krause Publications was ready to help build and benefit from a growing hobby market.

In 1981, *Baseball Cards* magazine was the only magazine of its type on the newsstand. "It exposed thousands of new collectors to the hobby and rekindled the nostalgia bug in thousands of others," said Steve Ellingboe. "People said, 'I had all those when I was a kid.' And suddenly people were scurrying to their attics and basements to look for their old cards."

When they wondered what those cards were worth, how to judge their condition, where to sell them, and buy or trade for more, the new collectors turned to *Sports Collectors Digest*. Just like *Numismatic News* and *Old Cars, SCD* carried pages of classified ads, display ads from dealers, and notices of shows and swap meets. The first Krause issue of *SCD* was just 64 pages and was sent to a mailing list of 7,000. Lemke was editor, Watson was ad manager, Williams handled the classifieds and Harry Becker managed circulation. In another "Coach's Box" editorial, Lemke introduced the new set-up and explained that the new *Digest* was not as thick as the old one, but the pages were bigger. He also explained that Krause did not miss deadlines, and ads that trailed in late would not be run until the next issue. The discipline of the deadline could not be broken, as Dan Albaugh, who joined the staff early in 1982, once told an advertiser, "Not that I don't appreciate your business, but I couldn't accept an ad from my own mother if it came after the deadline."

The ads came in on time and so did all the other material that made *SCD* grow. A year later, circulation had increased to 12,000 and page counts averaged 160, with the August issues hitting 184 pages. Once again following the successful Krause formula, the *Digest* became a weekly in March 1987, and, by 1991 had a circulation of 51,000, with a whopping page count of 312. *SCD* also had a price guide to 30,000 different cards — updated weekly — and a huge calendar of sports card shows. It was targeted at advanced collectors who did not need an introduction to the hobby and who were its most avid buyers, sellers and traders.

The sports collectible hobby grew fast in the 1980s with help from *SCD* and also from *Baseball Cards*. Aimed at newcomers who found it on newsstands, the magazine also contained an updated price guide for cards and, despite its name, other sports collectibles. By 1991, it was a 200-page monthly with an average circulation of 335,000.

Not long after *Sports Collectors Digest* and *Baseball Cards* were established, Krause expanded within the niche. At the start of 1985, the company purchased *Baseball Card News*, a monthly newspaper that combined feature pieces on athletes along with updates on newly issued card sets. Despite its name, *Baseball Card News* also covered football, basketball, hockey and other card sets. By 1991, it was serving 81,000 readers, and was published twenty-six times a year.

As the names of all the sports collectors' publications indicated, the term "baseball card" had already become generic by 1981. Just as the definition of "coin collecting" and editorial coverage of that hobby expanded to include medals, tokens and other metallic collectibles, "baseball card" also refers to cards from other sports and to other sports-related objects as well. Autographed basketballs, bats, annual programs, even boxing gloves signed by Muhammad Ali, can be found for sale in "Baseball Card" publications.

To fill the hobby niche according to plan, Krause also published an independent price guide and a hobby calendar. Krause's first sports collectible calendar appeared in 1985. It joined similar calendars devoted to coins and old cars. In 1988, the company introduced *Baseball Card Price Guide Monthly*. It lists prices in two grades for more than 45,000 cards produced by Topps, Fleer, Leaf, Classic, Donruss, Bowman, Sportflics, Score and Upper Deck, as well as grading/pricing guides and investment columns. By 1991, circulation of the *Price Guide*, sold principally on newsstands, hit 284,000.

Investment potential is a part of all collecting, but in none is it more evident than in sports cards. In 1988, *Money* magazine reported that a selected portfolio of baseball cards depicting the rookies-of-the-year offered a compound annual return on investment of 42.5 percent, compared to 12.7 percent for common stocks, 3.5 percent for United States coins and 3.4 per cent for diamonds.

The number of dealers also increased phenomenally, with an estimated 200 card shops in the United States in 1983 increasing to more than 10,000 by 1988. All of them were potential advertisers and certainly readers of the Krause periodicals. Collectors, casual and avid, number in the millions, with some observers stating that sports cards have become the most widely collected item in the country. If so, Krause Publications can take a share of the credit for the growth. By the late '80s, its four sports collectors' publications were holding down more than 90 percent of their market share, a much larger percentage than most of the other Krause hobby publications could claim in their niches. If good timing and marketing ability are virtues, then Krause is well-blessed. It got into the baseball card market just at the right time and used its standard formula to eventually dominate it. Chet said that in 1981 the company invested $250,000 to get started in baseball cards. In 1991, Krause's sports division grossed $21 million, further proof that the investment return was in the cards.

With the addition of *Sports Collectors Digest* in the fall of '81, the total number of scheduled deadlines at Krause hit 246, only eight short of one for each of the year's 254 working days. In addition to the regular publications, Krause was also putting out *Baseball Cards* and *Gold!* magazines, which would both become quarterlies in 1982.

1981 was also the biggest yet for book publishing in Iola. Eleven titles were already on sale: the *Guidebook of Franklin Mint Issues; Hard Times Tokens; Standard Catalog of World Coins; Standard Catalog of United States Paper Money; Standard Catalog of Mexican Coins, Paper Money, Stocks, Bonds and Medals; Standard Price Guide to World Crowns and Talers; Early American Tokens; Standard Catalog of 20th Century Type Coins; Standard Guide to United States Coin and Paper Money Valuations; Merchant Tokens (1844-1857);* and the *Best of Old Cars III.*

The *Standard Catalog of United States Paper Money* was the latest in a long line of "phone book" catalogs to roll out of Iola. Chet and Bob Lemke were the principal authors, but catalog regulars Colin Bruce and Marian Moe were also on hand. Once again, Krause issued a *Catalog* with impressive statistics: 204 pages, 525 photos, 3,500 listings of currency with issues of the more than 13,000 National Banks valued by type. *Paper Money* harkened back to the company's first book, its 1958 *Guide to United States Fractional Currency*, by including listings for encased postage stamps and over 200 major types and varieties of fractional currency. In its busiest year of book publishing, with more than 175 titles in print, Krause returned to cover the first ground it had walked on as book producer.

Other books were underway in '81. *United States National Bank Notes (1862-1935)* was on-line in the company data bank, but with a lot of work yet to be done. The 2,000-page volume was published in 1982 under the title of the *Standard Catalog of National Notes.* Also projected in '82 was a 3,000-page tome titled *State Bank Notes (1800-1862)*, with 20,000 photos, that would require three volumes, compiled by Jim Haxby. Although it was scheduled, the Haxby book would not actually appear for another seven years. Delays notwithstanding, the publishing process employed to create these books revealed how computerization was changing publishing. Data for all three books was shepherded electronically through the system in Iola by data processer Patti Krause.

A *Standard Catalog of South Asian Coins and Paper Money* was also scheduled for 1982. William Spengler, a veteran of the Foreign Service, and South Asian coin expert John Deyell were the authors working on the new book in Iola.

Also in preparation was the *Standard Catalog of American Automobiles.* New York writer Beverly Rae Kines was compiling information for Volume 1, which would cover autos built before 1942, and John Gunnell would handle cars built since World War II for Volume 2.

In addition to selling its own hobby-oriented books, Krause had acquired a list of about twenty-five western titles from Western Publications in 1979. The acquisition expanded the company's role as a marketer of books it had not produced but were likely to sell in the markets Krause served. Plans were made to expand the line from the 175 titles currently in the warehouse to more than 300.

The expansion of the book production and marketing division, as well as the creation of an entirely new division devoted to sports collectibles, brought more new faces into the Krause line-up. The company recognized how it was developing and that it now needed a separate personnel department. It was organized in the fall of 1981 when Bob Lee was named vice president of administration. Although Lee had never worked in publishing or collecting, he was an experienced manager who knew how to run the people end of a business. One of his primary responsibilities was the creation of the department that became known as human resources.

"It's For You, the Employee," read the headline of the lead article of Issue Number 3 of the *KP Chronicle*, the newsletter which was one of Lee's first creations. The "it" he referred to was the personnel department whose job would be "to centralize the tasks of recruitment and administration of personnel." The new department would interview prospective employees, handle training and discipline, provide wage guidelines, monitor payroll, hire temporary staff, approve employee transfers within the company, manage benefit programs, monitor requests for job-related training, and keep track of the personnel manual.

None of these functions was new or startling. Krause had now reached the stage where the staff and their work had grown so large that it was unfair and inefficient to expect publishers, editors and production managers to handle the specifics of personnel in addition to their primary tasks of putting out newspapers, magazines and books. Once again, Krause's timing was on cue. In the 1980s, the work force would more than double in size, but the company had the administrative system on line to handle it. Luck was not a part of it, but a decision that had long been deferred.

As Chet said in 1991, "I wish we had gotten into human services years earlier. Back when we had fifty employees, people would come in to talk about their problems and at the same time I was wrestling with a million dollar problem of my own." After 1981, neither Chet nor the employees would wrestle with those problems. In fact, the expansion of human resources programs in the 1980s stands with the growth of the company itself as one of the key accomplishments of the decade.

Managing a new kind of work force was also one of the most important working place issues of the decade, one that management and workers wrestled with and theorized over throughout the '80s. Krause would go to extraordinary lengths to accommodate its people. New employees were interviewed carefully to be sure they'd fit into their jobs and the greater Iola community. In the day of the two-career family, spouses were also consulted to see if each one could live and find work within tolerable commuting distance of Iola. Krause also adjusted to the relatively new presence of large numbers of women into the out-of-home work force. Although generalizations about them are inherently flawed, the majority of the collectors Krause served were male. Coins, cars and sports were traditionally male pastimes. At the same time publishing itself, and especially the new computerized systems, have always employed large numbers of women. Integrating female staff people into the male-centered hobbies — as when Mary Haefner Sieber became editor of *Old Cars* and Pat Akey became advertising manager for *Turkey Hunter* and *Trapping And Predator Caller* — would also become one of the administrative tasks of the human resource department.

The tasks of the department ranged from the most substantive to the most trivial. Benefit programs, retirement plans, health insurance, maternity leaves, special project employees, work schedules for three shifts, substance abuse programs, family counseling, training and motivational presentations were all part of the job, as was the purchase of extra coffee machines and reminders that the last staff person to leave at the end of the day should turn off the lights.

All of these were predictable problems of growth. Through its first thirty years, even though it was a multi-million dollar operation with fifty, seventy, even 100 employees, Krause could be run like a small family business. As it entered its fourth decade in the 1980s, as its divisions multiplied, its staff grew, its budgets and needs for capital expanded, Krause developed more standardized and professional management practices while still hanging onto the informality and camaraderie of its earlier years.

The balanced attitude was summarized by Clare Oppor, who joined the staff in 1960 and who, despite a hiatus of about three years, was one of the longest-employed people on staff in 1991. She said, "We've got a personnel department, but most of us still think of Chet as the boss." It's another way of saying, yeah, we're big now and more sophisticated, but we remember when we were still the little guys from Iola and still try to act that way.

One place this attitude was most evident was in the pages of the *KP Chronicle*, the employee newsletter that began with the personnel department in September 1981. The four- or six-page monthly was originally edited by Trey Foerster, then by Arlyn Sieber. It kept employees informed on new acquisitions and ventures, profiled staff people new and old, explained new equipment and processes and told occasionally humorous jokes. Krause had grown too large to rely on the company grapevine, and the *Chronicle* kept people informed accurately and light-heartedly.

The Old Car Show also continued along in its light-hearted, but serious fashion. The statistics were again larger than ever: 3,000 show vehicles; 1,000 vendor spaces; 60,000 visitors; 4,500 chicken dinners. The Car Corral debuted in '81, and inside the enclosure were 300 collector cars for sale. The best buy was probably a 1948 Cadillac limousine that went for $1,500 and one of the most interesting was a token of the muscle-car days, a 1967 Dodge Charger with a rare 426 Hemi engine.

Visitors to the show were used to odd engine sounds, but they heard one of the oddest and rarest in '81. The Central County Flyers, Iola's resident flying club, sponsored a Fly-In for the Old Car Show, and the hit of the event was a 1931 Stinson TriMotor airplane. Trimotor airplanes were among the first airliners to fly in the United States, and the Ford model was familiar to most aircraft buffs. Stinsons were rare, and the model that landed at Iola in '81 was one of only two survivors. It had been more or less hidden in Alaska before being restored and was in fine shape for the car show. A shuttle service via an antique fire truck carried visitors to the airport from the show and the old Stinson carried them aloft to circle the grounds.

This most significant year closed with Krause looking back on its first three decades. The company kicked off its 30th anniversary celebration with an open house in honor of the inaugural issue of *Numismatic News*. Four-hundred people attended and saw the latest additions to the building, the publications and the staff. More than one of them remarked how, after thirty years of life, Krause was still new.

What's happening at:

Charlton
"We're selling our heroes to DC"

Harvey
"We're temporarily suspending"

Warren
"I cannot confirm or deny"

Western
"We're going to print comics"

ISSUE NO. 482   FEBRUARY 11, 1983

A handshake closes the deal transferring ownership of The Buyer's Guide for Comic Fandom and Film Collector's World to Clark Krause (left) from Alan L. Light. Light started Buyer's Guide 12 years ago, putting his first issues together in his parents' living room. Krause began his publishing career 30 years ago, laying out the first issue of Numismatic News on his kitchen table. Each saw their creations grow considerably over the years, until Buyer's Guide became too large for Light's basically one-man operation and more suitable to Krause's modern plant, which publishes books and periodicals for collectors in many fields of interest.

Slimmer Buyer's Guide offers more for readers

Killraven, Dazzler star in Marvel Graphic Novels

"Hotel" fills in for "Doonesbury"

Good timing has played a role in Krause's success. The publisher decided to diversify into old cars and sports cards just as each hobby started to expand. Good timing struck again in 1982, when Krause acquired **Comics Buyer's Guide** *just before the hobby entered its period of greatest growth.*

Chapter 31

1982

"Looking around and seeing the state's governor, two U. S. representatives, state politicians and cars overflowing into a hayfield, and wondering why fate had chosen Iola, Wisconsin as the site for all this."   Arlyn Sieber

A rlyn was reflecting on the 30th anniversary celebration that brought the political leaders and a crowd of about 1,000 other well-wishers to Krause's front lawn.

The company celebrated its 30th with a Weekend In Iola that included a steak fry, pig roast, open house, speeches that Arlyn claimed "were actually fun to listen to," and lots of smiling faces and handshakes.

1982 was a good year to recall the history of *Numismatic News*, although the veterans still on staff — Chet, Cliff, Art Christoph, Bob Strand, Harry Becker, Doug Watson, Mary Rosholt, Clare Oppor, and Rosella Jenson — might have wondered if they were reliving the part that took place in the 1960s all over again.

The deja vu began with that venerable Krause tradition — a coin giveaway tied to a subscription sales offer. The giveaway for 1982 was a set of 31 Lincoln pennies, dated 1952-82, in a custom-made album from Whitman Coin Products. The 1982 collection, and another set assembled in 1984, were complemented by a specially commissioned commemorative medal designed by Frank Gasparro. He was the retired chief engraver of the United States Mint who had designed the reverse of the Kennedy half-dollar as well as the Lincoln Memorial reverse that first appeared on the one-cent coin in 1959.

The job of inserting the 31 pennies in the correct slots of the Whitman album was assigned to the sheltered workshop of Waupaca County's Unified Health Services in nearby Manawa. Through organizations like Unified Health, physically and developmentally disabled people were able to become part of the work force, and inserting Lincoln cents into albums was an excellent use of their talents.

The coin giveaway was publicized in a manner that illustrated the degree of sophistication direct mail marketing had developed since the 1950s and Krause's use of it. In addition to advertising in its numismatic publications, Krause sent letters to collectors in areas surrounding an upcoming coin show that would be attended by staff people and a Krause Publications display. The collectors would get the offer in the mail prior to the show, and receive it again if they visited the display. After all its years in numismatic publishing, Krause had assembled a comprehensive list of hobbyists, and the circulation staff had used its computers to so thoroughly organize it that the company could target a mailing on, say, every collector in and around Pittsburgh. Computer operators could pull out the names by zip code, print them on labels and send them on to the mail preparation people. When the orders came in, the names and addresses were added to the subscription list — with expiration date included — and to the list of collectors sorted by zip code. A label for each coin set was also printed as well as another label for the bill sent to the subscriber.

There is a rationale to this entire system that comes naturally to those who are attuned to it. Chet had always been one of them and, although the computer age came too late in his career for him to really get into its intricacies, he was able to understand their workings and how to apply them. Whenever consultant Ken Nelson or Krause's resident computer hotshots in the late '70s and early '80s, Gary Marx or Roy Van Epern, outlined a new system, Chet wasn't baffled. He often explained a computer system, and the entire publishing process, by harkening back to his days as a carpenter. Back in the 1940s, when he started framing a house, Chet could envision what every wall would look like. He could then pick up his saw and cut every 2 x 4 he would need to assemble the entire house. Tracing the electronic path of a computer system wasn't any more difficult.

In 1982, he and other Krause staffers enjoyed showing off what the new computer equipment could do. During the weekend in Iola, Chet guided Governor Lee Dreyfus and other dignitaries though the system and they all nodded understanding even if they hadn't a clue about what was going on. As Arlyn Sieber put it in his open house retrospective, one of his most memorable moments was, "Repeating the same little speech about KP's electronic wizardry dozens of times...and loving the wonderment it caused each time."

Wonderment was only one reaction to another event that inspired deja vu in Iola in 1982. Once again, as in the 1960s, the seemingly obscure pastime of numismatics was drawn to the front stage of politics.

At issue was commemorative coinage for the upcoming 1984 Olympic Games. The scene was Washington, D. C. in the early days of the Ronald Reagan administration, where sentiments about reducing the size of government, while touting the superiority of the "private sector," were loudly voiced. The players were Armand Hammer, the billionaire founder of Occidental Petroleum Corporation; a heretofore obscure Democratic Congressman from Illinois named Frank Annunzio; Chet, Cliff, Dave Harper and other members of the numismatic staff in Iola.

Hammer, who was once known as the Kremlin's favorite capitalist, had long had business dealings with the Soviet Union and he had convinced the Communists to allow him to market the commemorative coins they struck for the 1980 Olympics. When the United States and other western nations boycotted the Moscow Games, they knocked the bottom out of the Soviet coin program. Despite this setback, Hammer had arranged a similar deal on a coin program for Canada and he also hoped to sign up the United States for the '84 Los Angeles Summer Games.

Hammer's proposal called for the United States to use $260 million worth of gold and silver bullion to strike fifty-three types and varieties of coins with a face value of $325 million. Hammer's Coin Group would have exclusive marketing rights to the coins at a big mark-up. Neither the Soviet Union nor Canada had fared well in their dealings with Hammer, but, in the anti-government atmosphere prevalent in Washington in 1982, his chances for cleaning up on American Olympic coins looked excellent.

In Iola, Chet and Cliff were well aware of the unfavorable consequences of a flood of fifty-three commemorative coins. They also felt some justifiable patriotic pique at Armand Hammer's willingness and power to plunder the national treasury. They brainstormed with Dave Harper and he agreed to write a position paper on Hammer's proposal and to offer an alternative. The Iolans called for the United States to strike seven commemorative coins with sales administered by the Mint.

With help from Krause's newly hired Washington correspondent, Burnett Anderson, and newly elected Wisconsin Senator Robert Kasten, Chet was called to the capital to testify on the issue. He and George Hatie, of the ANA, were the only representatives of the hobby to speak on the issue. In the meantime, Representative Annunzio had introduced a bill in the House that called for the striking of only one Olympic coin — a silver dollar.

Despite Chet's efforts and the opposition of United States Treasurer Angela Buchanan, Hammer's proposal passed the Senate. In the course of Hearings in the House, Annunzio's bill was amended to call for six coins. It passed his subcommittee, but failed to pass the House Banking Committee. The final decision fell to the entire House of Representatives, which was under full assault from Hammer's lobbyists. In addition, the Hammer Coin Group withdrew a pledge of $4 million to the Olympic Committee and *Sports Illustrated* magazine blasted Annunzio as "anti-Olympic."

Krause enlisted as many allies as possible, using its publications to tell collectors to contact their representatives. Wisconsin Congressman Tom Petri made a strong commitment to defeat Hammer, and he joined Annunzio in persuading his colleagues to vote against the measure. The outcome surprised most of the experts. Hammer's proposal was defeated and both the House and Senate adopted the proposal to strike six Olympic coins. The addition of mint marks later increased the number to ten, but the important victory was won, as the $75 million raised from sales of the coins went to the Olympics.

The Olympic coin struggle confirmed the wisdom of a decision Krause had made shortly before the battle began. The company hired Burnett Anderson, who had recently retired as an overseas-based public information officer for the State Department, to act as a Washington Bureau for *Numismatic News* and other Krause Publications. Burnett's son, Lee Anderson, also contributed as Bureau photographer. Burnett Anderson proved to be a top-notch journalist when it came to reporting news affecting Iola's most politically vulnerable hobby and also very helpful when it came to lobbying for collectors. He was a welcome addition to the staff, many of whom were reminded of how difficult it had been to cover controversial news like the Bible Bill, the Bicentennial Coin, and the Susan Anthony Dollar brouhahas of earlier days.

Chet, Dave Harper and Russ Rulau made special trips to Washington during the course of the Olympic coin battle, but travel was a regular part of work for a hobby publisher. Ever since Chet attended his first coin show in Milwaukee in the early 1950s, Krause people have brought their publications to shows, exhibitions, conventions and swap meets. In 1982, it was estimated that the staff traveled 457,000 miles, both near and far, to promote their hobbies. The numismatic staff never missed the national ANA Convention and maintained an aggressive schedule of attendance at regional and state gatherings as well. The Krause display wagon also turned up at many coin shows and club exhibits in the eastern, midwestern, and south central states. Working a coin show at a mall in Joliet, Illinois, is a far from glamorous perk, but part of the job.

The *Old Cars* crew could not pass up the big car shows in Carlisle and Hershey, Pennsylvania and many, many smaller ones as well. They showed up with trailers and trucks emblazoned with the *Old Cars* logo and painted in *Old Cars* colors. They distributed periodicals, contacted advertisers, chatted with readers and, in general, flew the company flag in places where it would be readily recognized.

The big shows for sports collectors in the early 1980s were in suburban Philadelphia, Detroit and St. Louis. In these early days of the hobby, a big show meant 100 dealers and maybe 2,000 visitors. Ten years later a show wasn't really big unless it had 700 dealers and 50,000 people coming through the gates.

There were also special trips, as in 1981, when Tex Smith carried Krause's old car banner to England. He distributed several thousand copies of *Car*

Exchange and *Old Cars* at car shows there and talked to periodical distributors about carrying the periodicals on their stands. Other Krause ambassadors have fled winter in Iola by attending hobby conventions in Florida, Arizona, Nevada, and California, while a few have made it across the Pacific to Tokyo, Hong Kong and Singapore.

One of the most memorable trips, at least for those who were there, was made by Greg Loescher and Randy Clausen in 1983. They ventured to Grand Island, Nebraska, to attend the third annual convention of the Buckle Buddies. Greg and Randy represented Krause's Western Publications and carried a selection of *True West* commemorative buckles that at least thirty collectors purchased. They made the same discovery that all staff people do whenever they attend conventions, whether it be with the three-piece-suit crowd at the ANA, or the greasy T-shirt gang at a hubcap lover's swap meet — collectors are serious but fun to be around, just like all people who are doing something they truly enjoy.

Wherever collectors congregate, they attract the collectors' press, so of course there was a *Buckle Buddies* magazine at the Grand Island Convention. The publisher thought it would be a great addition to the Krause line and offered to sell on the spot to Greg and Randy. Their expense account couldn't handle the acquisition, so they deferred the decision back to Iola. The hobby experts there did not see *Buckle Buddies* becoming another *Sports Collectors Digest* and passed on the offer.

Travelers coming to Iola for meetings with Krause people in 1982 were welcome to enjoy the hospitality of the company's restored 1912 farm home, the Thorson House. Located on property adjacent to the Krause grounds, the Thorson House was a fine example of midwestern rural home design — white clapboard siding, a pillared, wraparound porch and hardwood floors and trim set on a rock — solid foundation. It had been the home of the Martin Thorson family since 1912.

In 1979, when Martin Thorson died, Krause purchased the farmstead and surrounding acreage. The land was used to expand the Old Car Show. In 1982, Patti Krause and Judy Preuss directed the restoration of the Thorson House in the style of 1912, but also thoroughly modernized and redecorated it. Care was taken to find wallpaper, carpets, furniture and furnishings authentic to 1912, but the wiring, plumbing, windows, insulation, heating and cooling were brought up to 1980s standards.

The Thorson House became a place for out-of-town guests to spend a night or two when business brought them to Iola. The house was a quiet, comfortable place for staffers to hold small meetings away from the hubbub of the office. The yard and the rebuilt garage became the site of many open-air receptions and barbecues where Krause regaled the great and the not-so-great with old-fashioned country hospitality. Visitors expected to find places like the Thorson house in Iola, and, although homes like it are actually hard to find, the Krause restoration makes sure they are not disappointed.

The Thorson House was a welcome addition to the Krause operation in 1982 and so were two other acquisitions of that year. In December, Krause purchased the *Buyer's Guide* and *Film Collector's World* from Alan Light of Moline, Illinois and then quickly added *Comics* to the front of *Buyer's Guide*. The comic book collecting hobby had grown with the baby boom generation and Light himself started in comics publishing in 1971, while he was still in high school. Don and Maggie Thompson were already into the field, having published a comics guide called *Newfangles* in the 1960s. The Thompsons were leading authorities in the hobby and contributed a news and review column to Light's *Guide* as long as he continued publishing. Iola was shy when it came to expertise in comics collecting, so Krause asked the Thompsons if they would come to Iola and edit the *Guide*. It was standard Krause practice to hire the experts in a new hobby niche and that meant the Thompsons in 1982. Hiring people such as Maggie and Don to edit a publication wasn't new, but hiring a husband-wife team together was. The Thompsons were the first "couples" team to join the staff. Their hiring was yet another illustration of how the work force had changed over the previous decades.

Doug Watson, who had become the designated shepherd of new publications coming into the Krause fold, was named publisher of both *CBG* and *Film Collector's World*. Bob Schmall, Yvette Pauloski and Alice Wolberg handled advertising for *Comics* and Dan Albaugh and Goldine Mortenson added *FCW* to the ad work they were performing in the baseball niche.

In 1982, *Comics Buyer's Guide* was a weekly with a subscription-only circulation of 7,000 and averaged 64 tabloid pages, but Krause was optimistic about its potential. The *Chronicle* piece announcing the acquisition had Chet stating that "he is expecting the circulation of *CBG* to double in 18-24 months. The comic collecting hobby is presently stronger and larger than baseball card collecting."

Baseball card collecting soon caught up and surpassed the comics hobby, but *CBG* did well enough to more than dominate its niche. In two years, it passed the 12,500 mark and in 1989, its circulation would peak at over 24,000. Page counts ranged from 80 to 120, and, most importantly, the *Guide* commanded its market. By 1991, it accounted for 75 per- cent of the comics collectors market share.

Krause very quickly applied its niche formula to its newest hobby. In 1983, it published the first issue of *Comics Collector*, a quarterly feature magazine for the newsstands. It included a price guide and listings of comic conventions and was patterned on *Coins* and *Baseball Cards* magazines. Its first issue out of Iola, dated Spring 1983, was a theme issue devoted to the hero who started the comic book, Superman. The Man of Steel, so *Comics Collector* said, "single-handedly started the comics business and spawned a multitude of different super-powered characters." Action Comics Number 1, in whose pages Superman first left Krypton for Smallville, discovered his super powers, adopted the guise of Clark Kent, and regularly frustrated the adoring Lois Lane, was valued at $15,000 in 1983. Despite the value in the comics, the hobby couldn't support a feature magazine. *Comics Collector* confronted its chunk of kryptonite and faded away as a Krause product in 1986.

In 1990, Krause tried its formula once again and introduced the *Comics Buyer's Guide Price Guide*. The title was a bit awkward but it upheld the company's tradition of using literal names and its practice of bringing new periodicals into a niche. *CBGPG* was a quarterly which, like other price guides, was sold on newsstands. Also like the company's other price guides, it established grades and valued comics by them. Unique to the *Comics Guide* was a color grading guide that helped collectors assess their comics according to the quality of the printing, which was a bit like helping coin collectors assess a coin by the degree of wear on its surface. It must have been helpful, since, after only a year, *CBGPG* had a circulation of more than 34,000.

Film Collectors World had a different fate. It came along with *Comic Buyer's Guide*, but served a much smaller market of about 4,700 subscribers. Film collectors were interested in 8, 16, and 35-millimeter films of the antique, experimental, and avant-garde genres. When it purchased *FCW*, Krause believed that it could expand the niche to include movie collectors (who are not the same as film collectors) and, eventually wrap them all into a periodical that included the new and growing videotape market.

In 1983, Krause purchased a bi-monthly tabloid called *Video Swapper* that was founded in 1980 and had a circulation of about 5,000. The title was killed and the *VS* mailing list, as well as some of its editorial content, was merged into *FCW*, which had itself acquired a new name, *Movie and Film Collectors World*. As Chet later recalled, "That was a mistake. You never call a movie a film or a film a movie."

Critics, artists and just plain folks who like to sit in the dark and watch images move on a screen have argued for many years about the difference between "film" and "movie." Film is supposedly sophisticated, meaningful artistry, while movies are simple mass entertainment. The work of Fritz Lang, the German director of the 1920s and '30s, is "film." The work of Hal Roach, the American who put Laurel and Hardy and the "Our Gang" comedies on screen, is "movies," at least to those who can discern the difference.

They couldn't do it very well in Iola. The attempt at merging the collectors of on-screen images burned out. Krause switched off the experiment after about a year and sold *Movie and Film Collectors World*.

As Chet said, "We must have pulled the plug on about thirty publications over the years." He wasn't afraid to experiment and that spirit was infused throughout the company. With it came the realization that the purpose of an experiment was to see if something worked. Failure after an honest try wasn't necessarily bad. It was just one possible outcome of an experiment.

Diversification into another hobby niche occurred when Krause acquired **Goldmine,** *the music collector's journal with a reader-friendly unit-advertising system.*

Chapter 32

1983

"The Iola Car Show is now legitimately the third-largest car show in the country, behind only the shows at Hershey and Carlisle.... Most of the gain has been made in the last three years." Roi "Tex" Smith.

The gain wasn't accidental. It was the product of good organization, hard work and continued improvements, including $45,000 in capital improvements prior to the '83 show. The statistics were more impressive than ever: 3,000 show cars, 1,500 swap meet spaces sold, 80,000 visitors, 6,000 chicken dinners, 1,800 cases of *Old Cars* beer specially brewed by the Point Brewery in Stevens Point. The Show grossed $275,000, up quite a bit from 1982's $190,000, and $112,000 of it went to local charities.

The secret to success was revealed by Tex Smith "The most important thing about this show is simple," he said in '83. "Volunteer labor and the donation of the Krause Publications grounds. More than 800 people were out there working that weekend. The car show could simply not exist without that free labor. In addition to the free land...many KP employees perform important tasks...."

The Old Car Show was not the only successful party Krause employees organized in 1983. In March they also had a good time at the Cabin Fever Party II. The event was inaugurated in 1982 to help the staff, which had put in many hours of overtime to meet the incessant and growing deadline pressures, "have a chance to kick out of the winter doldrums." The first Cabin Fever Party had been a great success, in part because the winter of '81-'82 had been rugged even by Iola's standards. The winter of '82-'83 was fairly mild by comparison, but employees were urged to attend Cabin Fever II because "we could have another real stinker of a winter next year, and it will pay to keep in practice."

The Cabin Fever parties, and the annual Christmas parties were great fun, best characterized by the door prize that Marsha Handrich received in 1982- a battered door from an old car. Special employee committees organized the parties and they soon showed that they had work-related interests beyond just having a good time. The party committees were only part of the permanent Employee Committee that would reform many aspects of working life at Krause.

First came the Employee Assistance Program that began in February 1983. It offered comprehensive and confidential assistance to all employees and their families troubled with alcohol or other drug abuse, with mental health problems, or in need of financial or marital counseling.

"A number of these innovations are the result of the work of Bob Lee," said Buddy Redling in 1991. He succeeded Lee as vice president of human resources in 1988. "Lee started a program of cafeteria-style benefits before a number of companies did." Chief among them was the 401K retirement program. Krause people also had the right to pass down the "cafeteria" line and choose the type and number of company-financed benefits they wanted.

They became eligible for an education allowance that paid up to 75 percent of fees for courses related to career advancement. Classes for supervisors were offered in-house, with academic credit awarded by the Fox Valley Technical College. Krause also offered classes in business writing, telephone techniques and personnel management. The need for employee training and career development programs was widely recognized by American business in the mid-1980s, and Krause was right in step with the times. The trend accelerated in the late '80s, and Redling has become an ardent advocate of education and training programs that enrich the staff both professionally and personally.

"We like to advance people from within," he said, "when they're ready to move up." It has become customary for Krause to ask employees who interviewed for a job but did not get it to come back and meet with people from personnel who then explain what they need to do to be successful the next time around. Building a working team from within and making it possible for those already on staff to develop into and manage new roles has become standard policy at Krause.

Workshops on stress management at work and at home, on First Aid/CPR for adults and children, on nutrition, exercise and how to quit smoking have also become commonplace.

"It is very unusual," Buddy continued, "to find a company of 330 employees [in 1991] with tennis courts, a fitness center and courtyards for employees to enjoy breaks and lunches."

Tennis/basketball courts were part of the 1983 construction program and the fitness center was built in 1990. "We're very big in health awareness, we have trainers in exercise and aerobics, at lunch and at night after work. And the company foots the bill," Buddy said.

In the 1980s the company also became the headquarters for a number of clubs, including men's and women's softball, volleyball, bowling, golf, chess, bicycling and cribbage.

Starting in the early 1980s, employee-centered programs and facilities became common in the largest corporations of the American workplace-but not in operations with fewer than 200 employees located in small towns. But in its dealings with its staff, Krause has been, as Buddy said, "a very progressive company."

In 1983, it was also a rapidly growing company. In April, Krause announced the purchase of a periodical that would move the company into another hobby niche. *Goldmine* was a monthly 200-page tabloid focusing on the hobby of record collecting. It concentrated on discs from the golden age of rock'n'roll in the 1950s and '60s but also covered the blues, country/western, and rhythm and blues. *Goldmine* had a solid circulation of 15,000 split between newsstands and subscribers. The acquisition was suggested by numismatic editor Trey Foerster, who collected large vinyl discs as well as small metallic ones, and the omni-collector himself, Doug Watson. Once again Watson was named publisher of a new team and supervised the people who brought another new hobby publication to Iola. *Goldmine* made it three new hobbies into the Krause tent in three years for Watson: sports cards in '81, comics in '82, records in '83.

The original *Goldmine* team consisted of Trey Foerster as managing editor and John Koenig, who came to Iola with the magazine, as advertising manager. Jeff Tamarkin and Lydian Sherwood remained in the *Goldmine* editorial office in New York City. The first issue came out of Iola in June 1983.

By 1991, Greg Loescher was publisher and Jim Felhofer was ad manager and they had helped make *Goldmine* the general purpose publication of the music niche. It was a bi-weekly tabloid averaging 152 pages with a circulation of nearly 30,000. Coverage expanded along with the music industry to include tapes, compact discs, music books and videos, as well as the traditional vinyl discs. Hot items for sale throughout the '80s were collectibles like the original 45 RPM discs cut by early rock'n'roll greats Jerry Lee Lewis and Buddy Holly, LPs like the Beatles' *White Album* or Pink Floyd's *The Wall*, on up to Michael Jackson's pioneering Bad video and, of course, just about everything connected to Elvis Presley.

A listing of record shops sponsoring special events related to collecting is also featured, along with the *Music Mart*, the largest selection of classified ads for music collectibles published. *Goldmine* brought the concept of the unit space ad to Krause. It is an extension of the classified ad, but larger, while still being less expensive than a display ad. A unit ad is a printed and reduced copy of a collector's typewritten listing of the goods he is selling. The magazine prints clearly worded instructions on how to compose the ads and explains how they will be handled on a printed page. One typewritten page, containing anywhere from thirty to fifty listings, makes up one unit. An advertiser who has more listings, types another page and buys another unit. In '83 *Goldmine* charged $27 for a unit and $47.50 in 1992. This is low-cost advertising, considerably less than the regular display rate, and *Goldmine* is able to do it because it does not have to pay for typesetting and composition. A unit space ad is simply reduced to size, added to the page paste-up and printed as is. Nine units — three across, three down — can fit on one of *Goldmine's* big pages.

Crowded and hard-to-read as they sometimes are, the unit space ad exhibits the original spirit of Krause Publications better than any other product. It is the obvious, low-cost link between collectors that Chet intended his publications to be back in 1952. It is the "shopper" for collectors and it still exists forty years later.

As the unit ads point out, *Goldmine* is well-attuned to its market, which is large enough to support one periodical, but probably could not support a magazine spin-off or a separate monthly price guide. Price guides covering a single style of music and published in book form that have done well in recent years. For periodicals, *Goldmine*, with its variety of news, features, display ads, unit ads and classifieds, holds down more than 80 percent of its market share and dwarfs its competition.

Krause continued to look for new hobbies into which it could expand. In the summer of 1983, the company purchased the *Postcard Collectors Bulletin* and the *American Post Card Journal*. Each one was a small periodical vying with the leader in the hobby, *Barr's Postcard News*.

The turn of the century was the heyday of American souvenir postcard production. The railroad had enabled middle class Americans to travel for recreation, and the post office enabled them to boast about where they had been for only one penny. Popular tourist spots such as Niagara Falls, New York; Mackinac Island, Michigan; and Kilbourn, Wisconsin (Wisconsin Dells after 1936) supported an entire industry of photographers, illustrators and printers. Even in less popular tourist spots, such as Iola, photographers shot local scenes and printed the images on cards that carried messages via the mail. Hand-painted photographic images were also in vogue, as were illustrations printed in color and black and white. The subjects on postcards could be very specific, with individual buildings or people featured. Stock cards were also available that could be customized to meet a local needs. Dialect humor was popular in the 1900s and a card printed, say, with a Norwegian-dialogue joke, could be customized to identify the speaker as "coming from Iola, where they speke the Norski dere." Trick photos were also popular, such as a scene from a fishing resort depicting anglers in a small boat struggling to net a pike larger than the boat, or a gang of men rolling a giant melon or potato down Main Street above a caption reading something like, "That's how they grow them in Iola."

By the 1980s, the market for collectible postcards numbered in the tens of millions of cards, many of which were worth a few hundred dollars. Krause's new *Postcard Collector* would be a magazine edited by Diane Allmen, founder of the *The Post Card Collectors Bulletin*, who came to Iola when she sold her publication. As usual with its first publication in a new niche, Krause planned for the *Collector* to be a "trader" periodical, concentrating on classified ads, display ads and listings of postcard shows and sales. If the niche proved to be big enough, a magazine and price guide would follow.

The *Postcard Collector* was not what Chet would call "a barn burner." It did, however, build a solid base for itself within the hobby and also became the keystone of Iola's second hobby publishing company, Joe Jones Publishing.

Joe Jones had joined Krause as assistant to Glenn Wright in numismatics in 1973. "I had graduated from college and was selling windows and doors. I had collected coins, saw an ad for an editor in *Numismatic News* and applied. I was not hired for that position but shortly after that, there was an opening in ad sales and Glenn contacted me.

"I loved it. I was working within my hobby. Chet was an easy guy to work for. I learned a lot about publishing from Chet, especially about business ethics. Chet and Krause Publications are known as straight shooters in the industry.

"Chet also taught me to look at the main objective. Your goal can be achieved. A lot of people look at the little things, important, but trivial in scope. These inhibit them from finishing their goal. I learned to look beyond the details from Chet."

Jones looked beyond the details and purchased *Postcard Collector* in 1988 after he left Krause. He didn't go very far, just down the road into Iola. Joe Jones Publishing puts out hobby and collectors' periodicals and annuals that complement the Krause line. "If companies have best friends, they are our best friends," said Joe. "As you grow you learn to solve small problems and bigger ones crop up. When a new problem comes up and I don't know what to do, I could spend a year worrying or I can call up KP and they'll say, 'Oh, we had that problem ten years ago.'"

When Jones acquired a publication devoted to Piper and Cessna aircraft, he thought about doing a Standard Catalog. He "called to let Cliff know what we were doing. I told him I wasn't sure how we were going to go about it, but wanted his sanction. The next day he sent over every *Standard Catalog* KP has ever done."

Along with neighborliness and integrity, another Krause trait rubbed off on Joe Jones — the practice of keeping up on new technology. "We are the largest publishing company using desktop publishing in the state. We have sixteen terminals networked together and twenty-two employees."

Joe Jones would have probably succeeded on his own, but his course was made smoother by his experience at Krause. He also did not have to stay in Iola, but he did. "Krause has a sixty to seventy times bigger annual gross income than Joe Jones Publishing," Joe said, "but the presence of Joe Jones makes Iola more of a publishing hub and more attractive to businesses that serve the publishing industry."

The twenty-two jobs his company provided for the community in '91, and the likelihood of more in the future, are a significant contribution to its well-being, and a contribution with roots that go back to Chet Krause.

Joe was only one of dozens of journalists, advertising and production professionals who spent time learning publishing at Krause Publications. Most of them were young when they started and used the experience they gained in Iola as a base to launch their careers and move on to more responsible positions. Ed Rochette was one of the first, Joe Jones one of the more recent, and many others on a long list in between.

The broad impact of a company like Krause, most notably the senior managerial personnel, as a mentor is nearly impossible to gauge. How many people have learned and adopted the principles of common sense organization, the willingness to experiment, the receptiveness to change, the focus on employee well-being, the commitment to honesty, the dedication to community service, even the shirt-sleeve informality of the work environment that characterize Krause and applied them in organizations far away from Iola? It's impossible to gauge, but graduates of the Krause school of publishing will be making an impact for many years to come. If they well apply what they've learned in Iola, that impact will be positive.

A few folks didn't leave, and one important event of 1983 involved one of them. Art Christoph became the first Krause employee to mark his 25th anniversary with the company. Art joined Chet at the first office in downtown Iola in 1957 and spent most of his career in the numismatic advertising department. He was honored for his years with a specially mounted set of Krause 30th anniversary medallions, including one in gold.

Other employees honored for long service in '83 were twenty-year veterans Cliff Mishler, Harry Becker and Rosella Jenson, and 15-year veteran Alyce Kolden. Every year following would see long-time Krause staffers, who signed on when the company started to expand in the early '70s, marking ten- and fifteen-year anniversaries.

The veterans had seen many changes at Krause over the years, and in '83 they saw another of what was becoming a regular event for the growing company — an office move. In 1982, Arlyn Sieber characterized it as follows: "There's the car show, the first snowfall of the year, the Scandinavia fair and that other annual (biannual?) observance anxiously awaited each year at KP — a tradition known as rearranging the main office."

In '83, Charlie Plueddeman alerted employees that "we folks in the north end have made our semi-annual migration around the office area."

They moved in the late '70s and in the early '80s, and they would move again in the years ahead. Early on, Krause adopted the movable partition system of office organization. It was an improvement on earlier office design in which a large open room was filled with rows of desks. In the new system, shoulder-high partitions divided the large rooms into work stations, one for each individual or for a few people working together. The partitions increased privacy, lowered the general noise level, and gave an employee a sense of personal space expressed by the motto identifying one work station as "Cubicle, Home Sweet Cubicle."

They are also portable, allowing for easy redesign and moving, which meant they fit well into the restless working environment at Krause.

A company that isn't restless, with staff who aren't moving, isn't growing, and that was certainly not the case at Krause Publications. Part of the growth was due to the constant updating of the computer systems. In '83, more disc drives and video displays terminals were added to the system, but perhaps the most memorable innovation was the arrival of the company's first IBM PC. "The PC system could eventually be used to communicate with other personal computer users around the country," read the caption that accompanied the photo of the first PC in the *Chronicle*. PCs would become so common in the workplace in the mid-1980s that a work station without one would seem barren and non-productive.

In 1983, the company was using its computer equipment to publish many different periodicals in different stages of life. Some were newly arrived in Iola, others were experiments within niches, a few were on their way out of town. The list of publications Krause produced in '83 reveals the extent of its *diversification since 1979: Numismatic News, Coins, World Coin News, Coin Prices, Bank Note Reporter; Baseball Cards, Sports Collectors Digest; Comics Buyer's Guide, Comics Collector; Old Cars Weekly, Car Exchange, Old Cars Price Guide; Goldmine; Postcard Collector; Movie and Film Collector's World; Old West, True West.* Specialty publications included the newly acquired and expanded annual report on coin auction results titled *Auction Prices Realized* for the numismatic niche; another anthology of articles and photos, *The Best of Old Cars IV*, and the *Standard Catalog of American Cars, 1946-75,* for automotive enthusiasts.

A promotional booklet produced that year and titled "The Image of KP," presented a page of statistics describing the operation after four years of growth. It is summarized here:

Number of Subscribers	252,295
Annual Total of Copies Delivered to Subscribers	9,150,706
Annual Distribution	2,462,792
Annual Number of Book Pages Published	4,830
Average Monthly Display Ads Processed	4,130
Monthly Total of Classified Ads Published	12,726
Average Monthly Number of Promotional Pieces Mailed	928,260
Names and Addresses in Computer Storage	1,100,000
Annual Total Employees Hours Worked	265,645
Staff Miles Traveled to Conventions and Shows	588,750
Square Feet of Office and Production Space	47,250
Annual Total of Periodical Deadlines	343

The number of magazine and newspaper deadlines the staff was meeting had more than doubled since 1976 to one-and-one-half for every working day, in addition to book and catalog deadlines. The company was showing some of the consequences of that growth. The continual building programs and office reorganizations, as well as the establishment of the personnel department and the employee assistance program, were all consequences of growth.

Krause also experienced its most serious financial crisis in this period, even though it was as sound as it had ever been. The trouble began back in 1979, when *Old Cars* became a weekly. Shortly after Krause announced that it would double the number of times it would mail *Old Cars*, from bi-weekly to weekly, the postal service raised its piece rates for delivery. It was the first time in Krause's experience that the piece rates had ever been raised so radically and without a prior announcement. The increase was substantial and knocked the profitability right out of *Old Cars*. At the same time, circulation had leveled, even declined, which made the financial pinch hurt even more.

Chet later recalled that this was "the worst thing that had happened" to his company, surpassing even the hard knocks of the mid-1960s. The situation was made harder by the fact that it could have been avoided had the postal service given its customers earlier notice of the magnitude of the rate increase. Krause had been trumpeting the fact that *Old Cars* would appear on a weekly basis and couldn't renege. It had to swallow a big and bitter pill and wait nearly three years until the automotive division again paid its own way.

The situation in the automotive area did not deter Krause from investing in new publications, new equipment and new buildings. The debt load was manageable, and Krause had never missed a loan payment, a payroll or account payable to a trade vendor in all its thirty years. By the early '80s, the company's needs for capital had surpassed the ability of local lending institutions, and Krause was dealing with banks in Milwaukee. One day in 1982, Chet went to a meeting to talk about a new loan but was instead told that the bank was concerned about the company's ability to service its existing loans.

Appearances were deceptive here. Krause's accountants had apparently not been reporting its status in the form the bank required and the loan officers were not getting the right information about the company. It took some time to straighten out the situation, but once the facts of Krause's financial soundness were presented and proven in the right form — which took about three years — the question was resolved. There is some puzzling irony here. Here was a company that had never missed a loan payment. All of its divisions, both old and new, were reporting increased sales of ads and larger circulation, yet somehow, someone considered it a credit risk. "Money is the root of all evil," holds the adage. It is also the source of a considerable amount of confusion.

Missteps on the financial path were a predictable consequence of growth. Krause's problems were minor, considering how the operation had expanded and what many other companies undergoing similar growth had encountered. The standard wisdom on business development holds that its early years are the most dangerous period in a company's life. Nearly as hazardous is a period of large growth in a short time span. Krause more than doubled its output in less that a decade. It entered new fields, bought, merged and sold many publications, regularly invested in new equipment, doubled its staff and office space, and came out stronger, larger and more profitable. Growth may be hazardous, but for Krause, growth was good.

Chapter 33

1984

"It was one of KP's most memorable ANA Convention trips."　　　Arlyn Sieber

Krause Publications was born and raised in numismatics, and the coin hobby sustained the company for its first twenty years. The boom periods in coins enabled Krause to develop its multi-publication niche formula, and the down times encouraged it to diversify into other hobbies. In 1979, coin collecting had entered another of its boom periods. Inflation in 1979 and '80 and recession in 1981 and '82 stimulated the market for coins, precious metals and coin-related collectibles. As always, the boom registered in the circulation figures of the numismatic periodicals at Krause. Except for *World Coin News*, which had been declining since 1975, they all reached their peak years in the early '80s. Coins climbed from 97,000 in 1980 to 121,500 in '82. *Numismatic News* increased from 46,300 in '79 to 56,400 in '81. *Coin Prices* climbed from 108,600 in '79 to 141,200 in '82.

As the economy turned into the years of the "Reagan Recovery," the entire coin collecting niche started a decline that lasted for the rest of the decade. Circulation figures tumbled from their peaks in '81 and '82: *Coins* fell below 100,000 in '83, hit 61,000 in '87 and bottomed out at an all time low of 58,400 in 1989. In 1986, the *News* dropped below 40,000 for the first time since the 1950s, then bottomed out at 35,200 in '89. *Coin Prices* also slid steadily, dropping below 100,000 in '85 and hitting a twenty-year low of 81,300 in 1990.

The tide reversed slightly in 1990 and '91. Following the general rule that hard times for the economy mean good times for the coin hobby, the recession that accompanied the start of the new decade saw circulation increase for all the numismatic periodicals at Krause.

In 1984, the numismatic staff struggled with the decline of the hobby and the resulting loss of circulation and sales in their branch of the company. The editorial team involved consisted of Russ Rulau, Trey Foerster, Arlyn Sieber, Bob Wilhite, Courtney Coffing, Colin Bruce, Kit Kiefer and Dave Harper. The advertising staff was headed by Joe Jones with help from Pat Akey and Jim Fulton.

Rulau had joined Krause in 1974 and served as editor of *World Coin News* and *Bank Note Reporter*. He left Krause in '84, but continued to compile, and Krause continued to publish, his series of books on tokens and medals. Trey Foerster, a specialist in world travelers checks, letters of credit, and other paper artifacts related to checking and credit, worked as editor of *WCN* before switching niches and moving to *Goldmine*. Arlyn Sieber was news editor of *Numismatic News* and became editor of *Coins* and managing editor of *World Coin News* in '84. Bob Wilhite edited *Coin Prices* with assistance from Dave Harper, who also took over as editor of *Numismatic News*. Newcomer Courtney Coffing started as editor of *Bank Note Reporter* in that year. Rounding out the team were editorial staffers Kit Kiefer and Tom Phillips.

With circulation on the skids, 1984 became the year of the subscription premium. Dave Ostrowski and Tom Wildermuth designed a special advertising insert offering an uncirculated 1964 Kennedy half-dollar, a coin that would certainly strike a chord with any collectors who remembered its debut in 1964. The coin was worth $8 but came free with a subscription to *Coins* or *Coin Prices*.

The Kennedy half joined the Lincoln Memorial Cent Set premium. It commemorated the 25th anniversary of the redesign that placed the Lincoln Memorial on the reverse of the penny in 1959. Tom Wildermuth designed this promotion, which in December 1983 and January 1984 brought 7,140 subscriptions to the *News*.

Wildermuth built on this successful program and developed the Susan B. Anthony premium set of three Anthony dollars, from 1979, '80, or '81, for subscribers to *Coins*. The 1981 set was valued at $20 and came only with a three-year sub to *Coins*.

It wasn't a subscription giveaway, but the "Coin of the Year" program was inaugurated to stimulate interest in world coins by acknowledging excellence in design and artistry as well as historical significance and popularity. Krause set up a panel of experts from around the world to judge all the coins issued in a year and reward the best. The "Coin of the Year" for 1982 was the United States Commemorative George Washington half-dollar, the first American commemorative since 1954. Although many new coin designs are released annually, they do not all become generally available until early in the year following their date of issue. Judges selecting the "Coin of the Year" do not vote until late in that following year, and the award is not presented until the next calendar year. Accordingly, the George Washington half-dollar received the award for 1982 in early 1984. The long time span gave Krause plenty of opportunity to publicize the program, the hobby and itself.

The staff made other efforts to reverse the numismatic decline. Back in 1982, Krause had acquired an annual publication titled *Auction Prices Realized*. It documented "the lot by lot action for U. S. coins sold at auction by the country's major numismatic auction firms." The book had been published since 1972, along with a companion guide to sales of United States paper money. Deke Hammit, coin market analyst on the staff, and data processor Bonnie Schimke compiled and kept track of the information to produce the book. *Auction Prices Realized* was a logical addition to the Krause numismatic niche, and the company retained the title.

In 1985, Cliff, Colin Bruce, Arlyn Sieber and Paul Tofte redesigned *World Coin News* so it resembled *Sports Collectors Digest*. The reduction in page size also reduced the ad rates and made the magazine easier for readers to handle. A revamped, easy-to-read *Numismatic News* came along in '86. In 1987, *News* editor Dave Harper began a "crusade" to redesign the nation's circulating coinage. The youngest circulating coin design was the Kennedy half, which did not even circulate in most parts of the country, and was twenty-three years old in '87. The Roosevelt dime was forty-one years old, the Washington quarter and Jefferson nickel even older. Harper found a willing listener in Diane Wolff, a member of the Federal Commission of Fine Arts, and found himself organizing a campaign calling for Congress to authorize new coinage. Cliff committed the company, and coverage in the periodicals included discussion of coin designs old and new. Once again, representatives from Iola flew to Washington to testify before federal agencies and Congress and a flicker of hope that coin collecting might revive stirred in the hearts of numismatists — all to no avail. Congress was not interested in changing the coinage.

Despite their best efforts, the Krause team could not reverse the decline in the numismatic hobby. Coin collectors were, on average, the oldest market Krause served, and they tended to be conservative shoppers, and not the kind of readers that inspire advertisers to buy display space in volume. They were also not doing as much trading as in former days, which meant fewer classified ads.

The numismatic hobby itself had become less democratic. It was all but impossible to collect out of circulation, and a whole generation had matured never really knowing the excitement of finding a valuable coin in pocket change. As Dave Harper pointed out, artistry had also disappeared from American coinage. No matter how noble his visage, the head of a politician on a coin could not compare with, for example, a design by Saint-Gaudens.

In addition, despite the publicity directed at coins because of the Olympic coinage controversy, and even though an issue of *Coins* had been featured in the soap opera, "As The World Turns," in 1983, coins remained out of the news. The same media attention that stimulated sports and other collectibles was rarely directed at numismatics. Collecting was also becoming a branch of modern marketing, with new products introduced and sold as collectibles. The numismatic equivalent of the Cabbage Patch Babies or the Teenage Mutant Ninja Turtles had yet to appear; neither could the first nickel Elvis kept in his jeans be identified, nor a celebrity be found with a passion for coins to rival hockey star Wayne Gretzky's mania for baseball cards. Numismatics, as a percentage of production, circulation and sales at Krause would continue to decline for the rest of the decade.

Krause Publications, however, was no longer tied to any single hobby. Its success and strength was in its publishing formula, and its future would be determined by the niches to which the formula was applied. The great question for the future was, "Where to go now?" The system was running as smoothly as one of the finely restored autos at the Old Car Show. The roads leading out of Iola were numerous. Which one should Krause take? This was the fundamental question in 1984, and is equally fundamental in 1992.

1984 may not have been a good year for numismatic periodicals in Iola but it was a good year for the numismatists there. Dave Harper attended the White House ceremony at which the United States released its $10 gold Olympic coin, and the ANA Convention in Detroit was a veritable tour-de-force for Iolans.

Bill Pettit gave a convention presentation titled "Numismatic Literature-The Key to Making Your Hobby More Interesting," and, along with Art Christoph, was honored for his twenty-five years of membership in the ANA. Arlyn Sieber sat on a workshop panel discussing the future of United States commemorative coins, and Bob Lemke was recognized as the Association's top membership recruiter for the year.

"The icing on the cake came," as Arlyn reported, "at the ANA Awards Dinner when Cliff received the Association's highest honor — The Ferran Zerbe Award for outstanding devoted and distinguished service to the Association and to numismatics." Cliff was totally surprised by the honor and probably would not have attended the dinner had Chet not arranged his travel schedule so Cliff had to be there.

The circulation struggle in numismatics focused attention on another department at Krause Publications. The circulation department had been the domain of Harry Becker for two decades and had become very skillful at promoting periodicals. It was responsible for subscription premiums, direct mail solicitations, and advertising Krause products.

Direct mail was the most effective method for the company to market its products. By 1984, the promotion and circulation departments were shipping more than one million promotional pieces a year to potential customers. By 1992, they averaged about 400,000 per month or nearly five million per year. The packages have come a long way from Chet's original offer of three free issues of *Numismatic News* to every new subscriber. They include premiums, reduced sub rates and combination offers. All are written in compelling prose and packaged in an appealing and persuasive design. Coin giveaways have always been successful but expensive, and giveaways in general do not guarantee renewals. In the mid-1980s, for example, premiums brought thousands of new subscribers to the numismatic periodicals, yet overall circulation declined dramatically.

To be successful, a promotion must be targeted on the right audience. The Krause mailing list, which had already exceeded the 1.1 million mark by '84, started with the names of present and former subscribers to the periodicals. Names were also acquired when new publications were purchased and, in fact, the subscription list was the chief asset of many of the periodicals the company acquired in the '70s and '80s. Names have also been acquired at shows and conventions, and many of the tens of thousands of visitors who come to the Old Car Show are listed in the company data banks. By 1992, Krause was storing 3.4 million names, with only about 520,000 currently subscribing to a company publication.

Names can also be rented from list brokers, with varying degrees of effectiveness. Standard practice in the promotion department is to test a list by renting 5,000 names from several brokers, then measuring and comparing the results to see which brings the best return. Promotional work is an ongoing exercise, not an annual or semi-annual event. A periodical's subscription list is comparable to a hothouse plant. It shrinks, swells, puts out new branches, lops off old growth and requires constant maintenance. For each one of its half-million readers, in 1991 Krause sent out ten pieces of promotional mail.

Feedback from readers and advertisers had always come in the form of letters, calls, complaints, compliments and ads. Classified ads are the best measure of a publication's popularity and performance. If readers are willing to invest their own money on a periodical's promise to deliver a return, they must be convinced that a return will come. For Krause, the more classifieds, the better the publication. In 1984, for all the publications, the typesetters in Iola were keyboarding 1,500-2,000 classified ads a week.

Direct mail marketing has been a part of Krause Publications since its dining room table days. Starting with 600 names in 1952 and later pioneering the use of computerized mailing systems, Krause now has 3.4 million names on file.

In 1984, Krause tried to compile a profile of its customers by surveying readers. Dick Sherry had just joined the company with the title of "general sales manager," after fifteenyears with the Field Newspaper Syndicate. He conducted an "extensive marketing survey," of the readers of *Old Cars Weekly, Numismatic News, Sports Collectors Digest, Goldmine, Coins, Bank Note Reporter, Comics Buyer's Guide, Postcard Collector, World Coin News, and Movie Collectors World.*

Sherry hoped to determine if Krause reached a market large enough to attract national advertisers. At the time the company had 183,000 people who subscribed to at least one publication. If they could be defined in terms of their age, sex, income, spending habits and other variables, Krause sales people could present them as a market to advertisers whose message would then appear in more than one publication. The 1984 survey was a pioneer effort for the company, which, like other publishers, has made extensive use of reader surveys ever since.

Krause continued to develop in other ways in 1984. The Western Publications were sold and editor Mary Haefner started a second career as news editor of *Old Cars Weekly.* The automotive division won two "Moto" Awards for publishing excellence. *Old Cars Weekly* was cited for cover page design and the *Standard Catalog of American Cars, 1946-75* took top honors in the book category. *Car Exchange* inaugurated its own "Collector Car of the Year" award and presented it to Ford Motor Company for the 1984 Mustang GT convertible. The trophy, designed by Bob Lichty, was presented to the car that the staff of *Car Exchange* judged to be the most collectible car in twenty years.

Also in '84, the Old Car Show incorporated as a separate tax-exempt entity under the direction of the Iola Lions and other local civic organizations, and the show itself set another series of records in all categories from total attendance (85,000), to cars in the Car Corral (550), to chicken dinners (5,500).

The company confronted the health insurance crisis by adopting a self-insurance plan that gives the employees more control of policies and rates. "Each individual plays an equal role in helping to control overall claim costs," read the announcement in the *Chronicle.* "If the company has a good year claims-wise, employees gain because the money set aside stays in the benefit plan account, not in an insurance company's bank account." With 130 employees on staff, Krause was now large enough for a self-insurance plan to be feasible.

1984 was also an anniversary year for many employees. Marking their tenth years on staff were Jean Moericke, Russ Rulau, Colin Bruce, Ramona Wasrud, Bob Lemke, Marge Williams, Goldine Mortenson, Tom Wildermuth, Judith Schmidt, Suzanne Olkowski, Carolyn Borth and Sondra Haase. Marian Moe celebrated her fifteenth year with the company, while Mary Rosholt and Clare Oppor marked their twentieth years. Finally, Rosella Jenson retired after twenty-one years with Krause.

Chapter 34

1985

> *"KP employees are some of the biggest col-*
> *lectors anywhere ... their collections ...*
> *range from paper clips to teddy bears to*
> *elephants to something as bizarre as Cana-*
> *dian railroad memorabilia."*
>
> KP Chronicle

They also collected buttons, matchbooks, sourdough bread recipes, marbles, unicorns, paperback horror books, thimbles, old fishing lures and mooseabilia — as well as the more familiar collectibles that appeared in their publications. Every collector quietly nurtures the hope that his peculiar passion will enter the mainstream of popularity and profitability, and who can say that they're wrong? In 1960, few people would have predicted that a set of *American* Football League cards, including Jack Kemp in his rookie year, would be worth anything, let alone $250, thirty years later.

In 1992 and beyond, as cigarette smoking becomes less popular and matchbooks fade away as advertising tokens, will Arlyn Sieber's collection of the increasingly scarce fire starters provide him with a comfortable retirement? Or, as the cult of fans wild for Rocky the Squirrel and Bullwinkle Moose grows, will Colin Bruce's mooseabilia swell in value too? And will either collectible become popular enough to support a hobby publishing niche? Probably not, but who knows?

Bill Pettit, one of the keepers of minor collectibles at Krause, knew that his collection of antique newspapers was part of a magazine, newspaper and paper "ephemera" hobby, and he was glad to see it arrive in Iola in 1985. Once again following the lead of Krause's champion of diversification, Doug Watson, Krause purchased *Magazine Collectors Marketplace*, "America's Leading Publication for Magazine and Paper Ephemera." Circulation was small, coverage was narrow but, as Watson recalled, Krause was "interested because we knew that here was a publication that filled a collecting niche. It also presented us with an opportunity and a challenge."

The opportunity and the challenge was to see how big the niche was and what kind of publications it could support. Ideally, a paper collectors' niche could be developed to include collectible newspapers, magazines, postcards, posters and related ephemera. Accordingly the name of the publication was changed to *Paper Collector's Marketplace*. In the Krause tradition, editorial material was deleted, the classified ad rate was dropped to rock bottom, and typewritten display ads were accepted. The first issue came out of Iola in February, with hopes that it might crack into a new publishing niche.

Paper was attracting attention in the mid-1980s. *USA Today* had interviewed *Postcard Collector* editor Diane Allmen, which brought a small stream of requests for information about the magazine and the hobby. Green Bay TV also did a brief spot on postcards, and an Appleton station featured Bill Pettit and his newspaper collection.

In 1986, Krause sponsored Postcard Day in Iola, complete with an antique card show and a new set of souvenir postcards featuring scenes of Iola shot by Krause's Larry Frank. Also in '86, a creative team consisting of Steve Ellingboe, Tom Mortenson, Dennis Schrimpf and Phil LaFranka created a set of collectible trading cards featuring old cars. The *Old Cars* cards, were, as Mortenson said, "conceived basically as another subscription premium." Two thousand eighteen-card sets were printed and used to promote subs for *Old Cars Weekly*. They were the first subscription premium to be wholly conceived and produced at Krause — the first collectible deliberately created here. They were also a historical throwback to the souvenir cards that were produced decades ago, as well as a nice melding of hobby niches — antique cars and trading cards.

Despite the attention and the promotion, the paper niche remained only a minor pursuit at Krause. When Doug Watson left the company in 1987, Chet offered to sell him *Postcard Collector, Country Sounds*, which Watson had started in '86, or *Paper Collectors Marketplace*. Doug chose the *Marketplace*, put up the purchase price of $1, and moved the publication to his home in nearby Scandinavia. He developed the classified section further and made plans to expand editorial coverage. Building the newspaper "calls into play all the advertising skills and publishing knowledge I learned from Chet," he said in 1991.

Watson, like Joe Jones, wanted to strike off on his own, and *Paper Collectors Marketplace* was his means to do so. "It was just a poor relation at KP," he recalled. "If it died, it died, and no one would come to the funeral." Watson kept it alive. Joe Jones also helped keep the paper niche alive. He left Krause in 1986 and two years later purchased *Postcard Collector*. It now thrives in the nurturing environment of a smaller publishing house.

Krause gave paper collecting a chance to grow before moving out of the niche, just as it had given movie and film collecting its opportunity. By the end of 1984, however, it was obvious that the celluloid niche would not develop in Iola. In January 1985 Krause sold *Movie Collectors World* to Brian Bukantis, who two years earlier had sold *Goldmine* to the Iolans. At the same time, Krause showed which hobby it expected to grow by buying *Baseball Card News*, a California sports collector tabloid. *BCN* came to Iola and the paper reached a circulation of 81,000 by 1991.

Krause also attempted to build the sports collector's hobby by borrowing an idea from the automotive division. Baseball card shows were important vehicles for developing the hobby and had grown along with it. The biggest shows in the country were managed by local promoters in cooperation with the National Sports Collectors Association. In 1985, sports division publisher Bob Lemke organized the Milwaukee '85 sports collectors show. It would be the largest show ever held in Wisconsin, with over 100 dealers and featuring Milwaukee Braves players from the 1950s — Andy Pafko, Felix Mantilla and Joe Adcock. It would also be a tune-up for what Bob hoped would be "a KP-sponsored National Sports Collectors Convention in Milwaukee in '86."

Lemke hoped to organize that national convention with labor from Krause and local volunteer groups, with all the profits going to local charities — just as they did with the Old Car Show. The 1985 card show was held and it was a modest success, but the national show in '86 did not come to Milwaukee. Had it come, 1986 would have been an interesting year for the Krause team. They

The Thorson House is Krause's restored Victorian-era farm house. It offers a comfortable bed and board to visitors as well as pleasant surroundings for company gatherings.

were already full-time participants in the Old Car Show. The 1986 National Convention of the American Numismatic Association was scheduled for Milwaukee and the Iolans were unofficial hosts there and official hosts of a special Open House at Krause later. Had they hosted the sports card convention, too, they would have been intimately involved with three of the largest hobby conventions in the United States, all within a few months.

In the summer of 1985, they settled for a visit from the U.S. Treasurer Katherine Ortega. She was accompanied by the director of the Statue of Liberty commemorative coin program who wanted to drum up support in the hobby media for the coins whose sale would help restore the statue in time for upcoming its centennial. Ortega was one of a long line of government officials who have passed through Iola over the decades. The company philosophy — as preached and practiced by Chet and others over the years — for dealing with senators, representatives, governors, legislators and bureaucrats high and low, says, be courteous, friendly, hospitable — and yourself. In 1992, Chet recalled that in nearly forty years of dealing with government officials, he hadn't met one of whom he felt in awe.

Accordingly, when Ortega and her assistants came to Iola in '85, they were greeted warmly, listened to courteously, given a tour of the premises, and fed a hearty meal of potato salad, beans and steak grilled — because of the threat of rain — in the garage of the Thorson House. "We just wanted to make you feel welcome," said Chet at the time — and they did, in the "just plain" Krause Publications style.

The Krause staff also welcomed representatives from two different visual media to Iola in '85. Early in the year students from the communications department at the University of Wisconsin at Stevens Point brought cameras and film to Iola to shoot a movie that could be used as an introduction to the company for visitors and new employees. Two versions of the ten-minute flick were to be shot. The first covered the inner workings of the company, the second focused on the Old Car Show.

By the time summer arrived, Krause had taken a step beyond film to videotape. A committee of staff people purchased a video camera, VCR and other equipment to produce introductory and training shorts. Videotapes and VCRs soon became as common as television, but in 1985, they were new. Krause soon adopted the standard practice of corporations and produced a series of videos depicting company operations.

The highlight of the year came in September when it was announced that the company had received several awards for excellence. *Coins, World Coin News, the Standard Catalog of World Coins, 1985, Comics Buyer's Guide,* and *Postcard Collector* were all honored by publishing associations in their respective fields.

1985 also saw Luella Johnson, secretary in promotion and production, computer whiz Roy Van Epern and maintenance chief Herman Gjertson complete ten years at Krause.

Chapter 35

1986

"One of the most often asked questions from visitors touring the KP building centers on the location or whereabouts of the printing presses and related equipment. Those asking such questions are often surprised to learn that, indeed, there are no printing presses, gigantic rolls of newsprint or stacks upon stacks of freshly printed magazines on the KP premises."
Mary Ellie, KP Chronicle

In 1986, Krause and the *Shawano Evening Leader* printing company completed the 25th year of their working relationship. They had started together in the old letterpress days and stayed together during a period in which the transfer of words and images to paper, and their delivery to readers, underwent the most profound series of changes in history. The development of offset printing, closely followed by computerized typesetting and page design that started in the 1960s, ranks with the invention of the Linotype, the manufacture of wood pulp paper, and Johann Gutenberg's fabrication of movable type as the most significant accomplishments in the history of print communication.

People involved in historical processes like the progress in print communication rarely think of it as something great — it's their daily work, and so it was with Krause and Shawano. The two companies started working together in July 1961, when *Numismatic News* first rolled off the presses. Twenty-five years later eight Krause publications — *Bank Note Reporter, Comics Buyer's Guide, Goldmine, Numismatic News, Old Cars Weekly, Postcard Collector, Sports Collectors Digest*, and *World Coin News* were printed, collated and prepared for mailing in Shawano. The volume of production was large enough for Shawano to use about 1,500 tons of paper a year for Krause accounts.

Krause has contracted with other printers to handle special printing jobs for everything from small brochures to magazines to the "phone book" catalogs and guides. *Coin Prices, Coins, Old Cars Price Guide*, and *Baseball Cards* were printed by World Color Press in Sparta, Illinois. In the late 1980s, as the company launched new publications or purchased established ones, it dealt with other Wisconsin printers — Ripon Community Printers, Fond du Lac's Action Printing, Sun Prairie's Royal Publishing, and the *Stevens Point Journal*. Out-of-state printers included R.R. Donnelley in Dwight, Illinois and Glasgow, Kentucky, the House of Print in Madelia, Minnesota, and — in the 1990s — Walsworth Publishing in Marceline, Missouri.

The relationship with Shawano has remained solid. Throughout the late '70s and '80s, the *Leader's* top management — Dave McAdow, general manager, and owner John Lavine — were friendly and familiar faces at Krause, and other staff members routinely visit back and forth. An annual tour of the Shawano plant is part of the orientation program at Krause. The most frequent contact between Krause and Shawano takes place alongside the highway just outside Bear Creek. Roughly halfway between Iola and Shawano, Bear Creek Corners is the regular meeting place for messengers from Krause and its printer. In time to meet every deadline, a messenger carrying a set of negatives from Iola meets a messenger from Shawano at the Corners.

The negatives are handed over and taken to Shawano where the images they bear are burned into aluminum printing plates. Each plate is fastened onto the roller of a web printing press that is about as long as a semi-trailer. Rolls of paper the size of sub-compact cars sit at one end of the press. After all the plates for one section of a periodical are mounted, the paper is fed into the press, and alignment adjustments are made. With the webs and images properly registered, the press really starts to roll. In 1986, a typical 80,000 press run of an 80-page *Old Cars Weekly* took about six hours.

The process had changed so greatly over the years that the actual printing of a publication had become one of the least time-consuming. The pre-press work performed in Iola — the writing, typesetting, ad design, page composition and camera work to produce the negatives delivered to the printer — takes much longer than the printing, binding and mailing preparation. By the time the negatives are at the printer, the process of delivering the product to the reader is headed downhill to completion.

Krause Publications has been justifiably lauded for the jobs it has created in Iola, but the economic impact of the operation extends beyond its own work force. Printers in several Wisconsin communities, and the suppliers of hundreds of other goods and services, benefit from the creativity at Krause. The publishing company starts with something intangible — a collector's desire to learn about his hobby, his need to buy and sell collectibles, or a dealer's quest to find customers — and converts it into something real — a newspaper or magazine. So reads the summary of the creative process of economic development. It utilizes resources, requires human labor, and creates something of value that earns a return in the marketplace that is shared by the producers. Krause's ability to regularize the process, to do it over and over again, and for more publications every year, has brought stable economic development to Iola and its suppliers in the industry.

In 1986, Krause's production department was turning out 500 tabloid pages a week with the help of two second-generation Camex computerized typesetting/design stations. The Camexes, which first appeared at Krause in 1982, allowed operators to compose a display ad on screen — with both copy and graphics — by steering a stylus over a pad. They could then send the finished ad into computer storage and print out a camera-ready copy for paste-up. The new system was faster, more accurate and easier to operate than the old typeset/cut-and-paste process, and comparable to the difference between sawing lumber with a handsaw and an electric circular saw.

When Krause adopted the Camex in '82, it was one of the first publishers in Wisconsin to use it. By '86 the old models were primitive and the new gear was on the cutting edge — for at least a few months.

The production department was managed by Pete Ruiz in '86 and among the people on staff were Cindy Spielgelberg, Mary Kay Steffen, Barb Johnson, Cheryl Kell, Wendy Liter, Lauren Borth, Chris Mork, Stormy Kulas, Brian Servey, Kathy Hines, Betty Bessette, Kathy Budsberg, Lori Stertz, Ethel Thulien, Sally Moe and Susie Melum. By 1991, the production department had the largest number of employees of any at Krause. Under the direction of vice-president Pete Ruiz, production required three shifts for keylining, typesetting and computerized ad design. Also in the department were people working on process color, proofreading, advertising services, data entry, calendars, classifieds, subscriptions, samples, purchasing, mailing, shipping/receiving, in-house job printing and two shifts of workers answering the phones of the 800-system.

The production people are never the stars of a publishing operation. The editors and writers, the advertising and promotion people, have the high profiles and are known as the people who "produce" the publications. But their contributions are incomplete without the keyliners and typesetters, the Camex and camera operators, the proofreaders and strippers, who really produce the publications by turning the intangible into the real.

The process of turning the intangible into the real was considerably compressed in 1986 when the numismatic division decided to provide blanket coverage of the ANA Convention in Milwaukee and produce a daily newsletter reporting on every meeting, reception and event. Numismatic staffers compiled a day's worth of information, then gave it to Arlyn Sieber who edited it, dummied the pages, and delivered them to the printer in the wee hours of the morning. The next morning, everyone at the convention, including reporters from other numismatic journals, was anxious to read the latest edition of the *Daily Numismatic News*.

As Chet said about the ANA convention in Milwaukee, "We worked hard to get it here, and we'd like to be good hosts." Krause pulled out all the stops for the convention, sending a staff of 30 to work the show and providing a bus for any employees who wanted to just visit. The company display of Wisconsin numismatic and related collectibles was the largest ever seen at an ANA affair and included 140 cases of merchant tokens, Civil War tokens, currency, bank notes, store cards, plus Chet's own Wisconsin made 1922 Kissel touring car accompanied by a bank note signed by its maker, William Kissel of Hartford, Wisconsin.

Company publications trumpeted the convention throughout the state and Krause showed off its ability to target direct mail promotions by sending out an offer for a wooden nickel worth $3 to collectors visiting the Krause booth. *Numismatic News* banged out its largest issue of the year and *World Coin News* produced 80 pages, the largest number in its history.

The ANA reciprocated by honoring Krause Publications on the commemorative medal struck for the convention. The obverse bore the image of Wisconsin's most prominent numismatists, Henry Granberg, R. S. Yeoman and Chet Krause. The reverse bore the names of Cliff Mishler, Ed Rochette, Russ Rulau, Colin Bruce and Neil Shafer. All the numismatic publications also walked off with awards and honors, most notably the new work by Chet, Cliff and Colin, the *Standard Catalog of World Gold Coins*.

"Krause Publications didn't restrict its hospitality," said a special Chronicle reporting on the convention. The company sponsored receptions, breakfasts, a hospitality room, and gave away tokens, mugs, notepads, subscriptions and sample copies of every periodical — numismatic or not — published in Iola.

The hospitality continued even after the convention ended when Krause hosted an open house for over 200 visitors at another Day In Iola. "Everything that can conceivably be done in Iola was available...London-style double-decker bus tours...including stops at the Norwegian gift shop downtown and the famous Groth Gardens...golf...tours of the building and grounds, with plenty of opportunities to talk numismatics...rides in Chet Krause's antique cars...an ample lunch — more than 80 feet of submarine sandwich down the hatch — at the Thorson House..."

"An entire company mobilized and set aside individual busy schedules to serve its guests."

With its roots still in numismatics, Krause took extra pains and pride to make the coin collectors gatherings — in Milwaukee and Iola — "as memorable as it could."

They were getting very good at making memorable gatherings in Iola. The theme of the 1986 Old Car Show was "100 Years of the Automobile," and the show organizers had gone to some trouble to locate and bring to the grounds replicas of automotive "firsts." They found copies of an 1885 Daimler-Maybach motorcycle, Karl Benz's 1886 three-wheel "Patent Motor Wagon," and an 1886 Daimler-Maybach four-wheel "horseless carriage." Show director Jim Bach reported that it cost Mercedes $6,000 to ship the vehicles to and from Iola.

The weather holds no respect for dollars, antiques or show organizers, and 1986 is remembered as the year it rained on the Old Car Show. As Kit Kiefer reported in the *Chronicle*:

"It rained Friday, soaking setup crews struggling with cars worth millions and drenching school-bus-driving swappers with nothing to their names but a tranny to a '62 Belvedere and three hubcaps salvaged off a median strip....

"It rained Saturday, a string of Woodstock-brand summer thundershowers...and brought out rain gear ranging from tarpaulins to garbage bags....

"It rained Sunday, too, and when it wasn't raining Sunday it was threatening to rain.

"But despite the unthinkable, Iola '86 was a success."

Once again the records fell like chickens ready for the Lions barbecue: 2,500 show cars, 2,6300 swap meet spaces, 90,000 spectators, and 7,000 chicken dinners that raised a $421,000 gross and a $135,000 net profit.

The show continued to grow, even though the old cars hobby had seemingly stabilized. Circulation of *Old Cars Weekly* had fallen from its peak of near 100,000 in 1979 to 81,000 in 1986. *Old Cars* was still running second in the market to its senior rival, *Hemmings Motor News*, even though it took advantage of Krause's production equipment to offer classified advertisers the

Production, "on-time, every time," is the byword at Krause, with the staff meeting nearly 600 deadlines a year in 1992. Here, twenty-year veteran keyliner Kathy Hines prepares material at her light table.

option of running a photo of their car along with the listing. *Old Cars Price Guide* told a different story. Its circulation all but doubled in the 1980s, growing from 56,400 in '79 to 106,900 in 1990.

The numbers reveal a fact about the car collecting hobby, which had become less "editorially driven," over the years. Collectors seemed to be satisfied knowing the price of a car without caring about much else, and the *Price Guide* supplied it. Automotive catalogs were also doing well, and the automotive division issued its first *Standard Catalog of American Light-Duty Trucks*, which quickly became the "bible" of its hobby niche.

In 1986, Krause completed the first five years of its decade of diversification. Since 1981, the company had added fifteen different periodicals to its list. A few of them — *True West, Old West, Car Exchange, Gold, Comics Collector, Movie Collector's World* — had been killed or sold by '86. Some — *Postcard Collector* and *Magazine Collectors Marketplace* — were small but promising ventures, while others — *Goldmine* and *Comics Buyer's Guide* — were rapidly becoming the definitive publications for their hobbies. A few more — *Sports Collectors Digest* and *Baseball Cards* — were already the giants of their niche and, since sports collecting was such a large and expanding hobby, they would also become the giants of Krause Publications. The hobby had grown so fast that circulation of *SCD* had increased by a factor of three to over 24,000 in '86, and *BC* had passed the 131,000 mark.

In 1986, the company also attempted to enlarge the music niche by launching *Country Sounds*. It was based on the premise that country, western, bluegrass, mountain, and gospel music had enough fans to support a collectors' publication. Once again, Doug Watson led a Krause team into unexplored territory. He was accompanied by Trey Foerster, managing editor; John Koenig, advertising manager; Harry Becker, circulation director; Greg Loescher, circulation promotion; Beth Wiebe, advertising and direct mail; Goldie Mortenson, manifesting; Judy Schmidt, circulation. John Lomax, *Goldmine's* country editor, supplied coverage from Nashville, Tennessee.

Despite the experience of this staff, and of Doug Watson, who had taken part in the start-up of all of Krause's new ventures of the previous five years, the music niche was not large enough to accommodate *Country Sounds*. Although country music had a large following, and the industry made much of its heritage as the music of the common people, collectors were not numerous enough to support *Country Sounds*. It died after about one year of life.

Watson himself would be leaving the company in '87. He had been a prime mover in much of Krause's diversification in the first half of the 1980s and coordinated the introduction of virtually every new periodical that came on line in those years. When he left in '87 to found his own publishing operation, he took a large measure of the responsibility for Krause's growth with him.

The roll call of employment anniversaries continued to be called at Krause. In 1986, ten-year anniversaries were celebrated by Bob Wilhite, Fred Borgmann and Alice Wolberg. Alice was in her second stint on staff. She had been the second employee Chet had hired in 1954.

Chapter 36

1987

*"From 1987 through 1990, Krause Publi-
cations saw its revenues grow by 300 percent, and its work force by almost 100.
During that time Krause got into several
new, profitable ventures...."* Chet Krause

The years of change between 1981 and 1986 were only a sampling of what
was yet to come. The pace and volume of growth increased in 1987 and
Krause, prepared by what had happened earlier, was well prepared for it.

"In 1982 through 1984, we were under fiscal stress," Chet told the *Stevens Point
Journal* reporter in January 1991. "In the [early] '80s we were overspending on capital. We had built onto our building and spent money on more capital [computers]."

Krause had invested $1.1 million to upgrade its computer and other produc-
tion systems and added 8,000 square feet of floor space. In addition, between
1981 and '86, the company acquired or started fifteen new periodicals and
hired the staff to produce them. Much of this investment was made while the
automotive division was struggling, numismatics was declining and sports
collecting was growing, but still young. The company was solid, but in a
recessionary economy, a major capital investment always takes some nerve.
Krause had the nerve and it paid off.

"In the '80s recovery period we looked like a genius," Chet continued. The
company had built infrastructure, and acquired the technology and core work

force to handle the expansion that a prospering national economy could foster. In '86, Chet set out in search of a manager to develop and implement a strategy for increased expansion. A *Milwaukee Journal* reporter later quoted Chet as saying that he had hired an executive "headhunter" who was "a bit expensive but quite effective." As a result the company was "beautifully poised with the right talents to roll with it."

Donald Nicolay became the second president of Krause Publications in January 1987. He had served as president of the Farm Progress Companies, a $30 million Illinois corporation that published agricultural periodicals and books and sold insurance. The company was well-known for its Farm Progress Shows, farm trade expositions held annually on farms in Wisconsin, Illinois, Indiana and Iowa.

Nicolay was no stranger to country life and, although he and his wife, Doris, had been living in the suburbs of Chicago, they had no hesitations about moving to Iola. Don became responsible for "much of KP's internal direction," as the announcement of his hiring read. Chet, who would be 64 years old in '87, had no plans to retire — yet. He retained the title of chief executive officer and continued to be a very active manager. Cliff remained as executive vice president and oversaw the numismatic division and the overall production of all publications.

Nicolay set out to reorganize the company internally and pursued what Chet called "an aggressive sales" program. He announced the first of many staff changes in February. John Koenig, who had come to Krause with *Goldmine*, was named publisher of comics and records. Gary Marx became manager of information systems and oversaw the flow of editorial copy, advertising, promotional material, circulation figures, addresses and financial data through the Krause computers. Greg Loescher became general promotions manager and became responsible for total circulation promotions and publication design. Terry Tomsyck took over as corporate controller and Bob Strand stayed on as corporate secretary/treasurer. Pete Ruiz became overall production manager and oversaw typesetting, proofreading, camex, keylining, camera and photography.

In the spring of 1988 Don told a reporter, "We have looked at every major collecting hobby with an eye towards possible entry into new fields. We haven't been able to identify any of these major hobbies as having periodical needs which we can fill, so we're beginning to investigate some of the more active pastimes, such as hunting."

In the course of that investigation, Krause discovered *Gun List*, which Bob Van Ryzin described as "a lazy journalist's dream come true...no editorial content." *Gun List* was just what its title implied, a listing of classified ads placed by firearm collectors who wanted to buy, sell or trade. Michael Tenny and Sue Golden started the periodical in their home while still students at the University of Missouri at Columbia, Missouri in 1984 and — borrowing a page from the book as written by Chet Krause — began by offering free want ads, giving away sample copies, and committing the paper "totally" to the collector's point of view.

By 1987, *Gun List* was as successful as a Krause publication could be, without actually being a Krause publication. Tenny and Golden were banging out 100 tabloid pages a month, 60 percent in classifieds that were no longer free, and 40 percent in display ads that were indexed on the front page and arranged by gun make and model. They had 32,000 subscribers and the option to add 15,000 more when, as Tenny explained, "the continued operation of *Gun List* would have required the hiring of more staff, the purchase of typesetting equipment and increased computer facilities...."

Tenny and Golden decided to sell the paper to Krause. They came to Iola in the summer of 1987 and spent six months coordinating the merger of *Gun List*

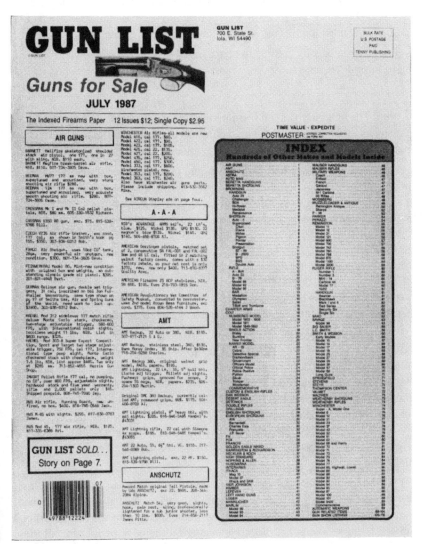

Gun List, the periodical that had all the features of a Krause Publication--but wasn't a Krause Publication--was acquired in 1987. It featured classified ads printed in alphabetical order, an innovation at the time.

into the system. Except for improving the quality of the typesetting and printing, and adding a calendar of gun shows, Krause left the format of *Gun List* unchanged. Krause did use its promotional muscle and, through an aggressive direct mail campaign managed by Tom Luba, nearly doubled the circulation of *Gun List* to 56,000 in about one year. The tabloid received a noteworthy accolade in an August 1988 issue of *Shooting* magazine, where, "because of the ponderous search required to find items of interest in *Shotgun News*, I have recently noticed a trend amongst serious collectors to use *Gun List*, which has a convenient system for finding the listings of specific types or models of guns." Not only was *Shotgun News* the collector's periodical that inspired Chet to start *Numismatic News* in 1952, it was the most popular gun collector's periodical. That is, until *Gun List*, which imitated Chet's style, came along. By 1991, *Gun List*, under the direction of advertising manager John Kronschnabl, was averaging 130 pages, reaching a circulation close to 64,000 and had expanded to an every-second-week publishing schedule.

Gun List had become a force to be reckoned with in its hobby when, according to formula, Krause moved to expand inside the niche by publishing its first *Gun Show Calendar.* Krause had purchased the title and list of Dave Reece's *Gun and Knife Show Calendar* in '87, revamped, renamed and reissued it early in 1988. The quarterly *Calendar* offered the most extensive and accurate list of gun shows in the country and was such a success that both the automotive and sports collecting divisions made plans to imitate it for their own hobbies.

Aggressive marketing had paid off in gun collecting and it also paid off in sports collecting. *Sports Collectors Digest* became the first weekly publication in its hobby and *Baseball Cards* started setting records on a near-monthly basis. With its December issue, *Baseball Cards* became the largest circulating publication Krause had ever produced. With 155,680 copies on newsstands and in the hands of subscribers, *Baseball Cards* was Krause's biggest single product and the most widely read periodical in its hobby. Sports collecting, which had taken off like a rocket in the inflation-vexed and recession-ridden early '80s, grew even more popular in the prosperous mid-'80s. It showed no sign of decline, no matter how the economy jiggered, in the final years of the decade.

1987 was an example of a normal '80s year at Krause. The company moved into a new hobby, enlarged its role in another, and expanded its building — again. The original triangular executive wing, with its distinctive circular, ribbed-walled conference room, was built with only two office suites. Chet transferred his office to Don Nicolay while Cliff retained his quarters, which meant Chet needed a new place to hang his hat. Construction of another executive wing — four offices in a triangle that matched the original — began in spring and was completed in time for Krause's 35th anniversary open house in October.

The 35th anniversary celebration was low-key by Krause's standards. Invitations were extended to friends and family, with no special ceremony scheduled for any dignitaries. Over 200 just plain folks from the neighborhood showed up to see what had been happening on the edge of Iola for all these years, and the staff guides had a good time showing off and explaining their work. The company's new promotional video made its public debut and was well-reviewed by the visitors. The in-house opinion of the company epic was voiced by Dave Harper, who said, "It was marvelous. Some people, people who I never thought possessed any sort of screen presence, came off looking very good."

The catered lunch of hot sandwiches and salads, topped off with a 35th anniversary cake, also came off looking and tasting very good. Staff people felt even better when they opened their pay envelopes that week and found anniversary tokens struck in one ounce of pure silver. Befitting a company that serves collectors who pay close attention to dates and anniversaries, Krause always took pains to well mark its own. The 35th celebration was well marked because it succeeded at being what it was supposed to be — a happy family affair.

Krause had become large enough, and the technology handy enough, to start an in-house print shop. Platemaking equipment and a short-run offset press that could print brochures, letterheads, forms, and the company newsletter was acquired. Susan Stankowski became its first operator. The in-house shop could handle small jobs at about one-third the cost of outside work, and substantially reduce the turnaround time from conception to delivery.

Krause also inaugurated a second shift for production in 1987. Keeping the equipment running an extra eight hours a day increased its efficiency and made it easier for the staff to complete the additional deadlines added to the list during the year.

New technology continued to appear. The significant arrival of '88 was the fax machine, which would enable Krause's far-flung advertisers to ship material to Iola in minutes. The fax is a wondrous device and has often made the difference in whether or not a classified or display ad arrives in time to make a deadline. The near-instant communication it affords can reduce errors, and ease tension between publisher and customer. On the other hand, the fax has also made it possible for advertisers to postpone sending material until just before deadline, which can create a crisis in the production department. Technology has its up and its down sides, and a big part of why humans are so taken with it, is that they themselves are so good at adapting to it.

The fax also made it possible for Krause's "foreign" correspondents to report back to Iola. Most prominent among them was Burnett Anderson, who covered Washington, D.C. for that most political of hobbies, numismatics. Russ Rulau, retired coin editor, continued to produce books on collectible paper and tokens from an office in his home. Neil Shafer lived in Milwaukee but spent a good portion of the year in Iola editing the *Standard Catalog of World Paper Money*. Alan Herbert really was a foreign correspondent who filed articles for *World Coin News* from an island in the North Sea off Germany.

Alan Kaye edited *Baseball Card News* from an office in La Mesa, California and, on the other coast, Jeff Tamarkin covered the music hobby for *Goldmine* from New Jersey. *Numismatics* had long had a representative on the

West Coast in Charlie Colver, who attended shows, distributed samples of Krause products, and in general flew Iola's flag on the Pacific. Bill and Mary Mason were regular *Old Cars Weekly* correspondents from San Ramon, California, who kept track of that state's large store of old car news for the automotive division, and occasionally crossed the mountains and the plains to attend the Old Car Show.

The out-of-town reps were part of an award-winning team in '87. In automotives, the *Standard Catalog of American Light-Duty Trucks* and the *Best of Old Cars Weekly VI* won "Motos" from the Association of Automotive Journalists.

The numismatic crew walked off with a company record of eight awards from the Numismatic Literary Guild in '87. Bob Wilhite, Dave Harper, free lancers Paul Green, Dudley McClure, and Tom LaMarre and other staff people all earned recognition for their work in *Numismatic News, Coins, Bank Note Reporter,* and *Auction Prices Realized.* The entire team was recognized for "35 years of publishing success," when Krause Publications won the Trailblazer Award of Merit. "The only way to beat this year's crop of awards," read the *Chronicle,* "is to take at least nine...at the 1988 NLG presentations." They didn't win nine in '88 but they garnered another eight that year and pulled in nine in '89.

1987 also saw employment anniversaries celebrated by Pat Fischer, ten years; and Art Christoph, who marked his thirtieth year and last full year at the desk of the advertising designer.

Chapter 37

1988

"When it came right down to having to say yes or no, I said no. I just couldn't sell the company." Chet Krause

The year 1988 can be characterized in several ways. It was the year of the changing of the guard, the ESOP and the three T's — turkeys, trappers and toys — each one of which would have been the significant highlight for any year all on its own.

Mary Rosholt retired in 1988 after twenty-four years as a proofreader. She summarized her years with a company for whom building new offices and moving was a tradition by stating, "They always said, 'It'll be different when we get in the new building,' but it never was, because they always bought another publication."

Mary was one of four veterans who called a halt to their working lives at Krause that year. Art Christoph, Harry Becker and Bob Strand also retired in '88. In 1957, Art and Chet were the art and advertising department and, at the retirement party, Chet recalled Art's distinctive method for characterizing advertisers. One file was labeled, "Once a crook, always a crook."

Bob and Harry were the first business professionals to join Krause, Strand as bookkeeper and fiscal manager, Becker as circulation manager. They both brought the company forward from the days of the pen and ink ledger book and the stencil addressograph to computerized recording, budgeting and fiscal

1988 saw the retirement of staffers whose cumulative years of employment totalled more than a century. They gathered with Chet for the camera: (l-r) Harry Becker, Bob Strand, Mary Rosholt and Art Christoph.

management programs, plus mailing systems so sophisticated they could keep track of names and addresses by the million and send a personalized message to everyone.

The retirement of these veterans, plus the recent departures of Doug Watson, Joe Jones and Bob Lee, represented a genuine changing of the guard at Krause. By the end of the year, new people would sit at the helm of nearly every department, and the management structure that would take the company into the 1990s was in place.

Giles Heuer was named executive vice president of finance in February. A colleague of Don Nicolay's, Heuer left the post of chief financial officer of *Chicago*, a slick urban feature magazine, and moved to Iola. Although he was an accountant and fiscal manager, among his first chores at Krause was the planning and supervision of the 1989 building addition.

Don Johnson came on staff in April. English had been his field of study in college and grad school, but Johnson's working life had been spent in sales management for Lee Enterprises and the La Crosse *Tribune* newspaper. As vice president of sales, he became responsible for circulation promotion, bulk sales, advertising design and classified and display advertising.

Roger Case was next. He left a daily newspaper publishing job in Miles City, Montana to become director of numismatic publications at Krause. Cliff and Bob Lemke had shared this chore for years, but the sports collecting division, which Bob also managed, had grown large enough to require his full-time attention. In a subsequent reorganization, Bob became vice president of the sports division. Late in 1989, Roger was named vice president of publishing and oversaw the numismatic, records/comics, trade, automotive, book and art departments.

The year ended with the appointment of Buddy Redling as vice president of human resources. Illness had forced Bob Lee, who had founded the department in 1981 and nurtured it over the years, to stop working. He is remembered as a man who truly cared about and enjoyed other people and tried to make the work experience at Krause as productive and rewarding for the staff as it was for the company. The Employee Stock Ownership Plan, implemented after he left, exemplified the kind of working place benefit Bob believed in.

Buddy Redling came to Krause after a steadily advancing career in human resources with several companies, most recently in Brillion, Wisconsin. He came into a busy job that got only busier. In 1988, thirty-four people were added to the staff, and Krause crossed the 200-employee threshold. By the end of 1990, another 100 would sign on to nearly double the size of the staff in less than three years. Redling rounded out the new management lineup and the VP team was completed when production manager Pete Ruiz was named vice president of production.

At another reorganization early in 1989, Cliff's title was changed to senior vice president operations, and he concentrated his efforts on circulation and production. Roger Case was named numismatic publisher. Chet passed his title of automotive publisher to John Gunnell, and Jim Mohr became publisher of toy and outdoor publications.

Chet's 65th birthday was on the horizon in 1988, and many employees were concerned about the future. Chet was a bachelor with no immediate family on whom he might bestow the company, and Krause Publications was an ideal candidate for a corporate buyout. Rumors abounded in '87 and early '88 that Chet was negotiating with prospective purchasers. After nearly forty years of dedicated work, he could justifiably take his millions and bail out.

The 1980s were the decade of the corporate raider who bought a solid company, ruined it by selling it off piecemeal, and pocketed the profits with no concern for the employees or the community. For an example of this behavior, the Krause people had to look no further than Worzalla Publishing in Stevens Point. It had been a family-owned business, about the same size as Krause, that had recently been sold to out-of-state investors. They used it as a cash cow for their other operations and milked it into near bankruptcy. Worzalla had been saved by the organization of an employee stock ownership plan that bought the company and placed it in the hands of its staff.

Chet resolved to do the same thing for his people. No matter how many promises prospective purchasers made to keep Krause Publications in Iola, he did not feel comfortable leaving its fate — and that of the community — in the hands of strangers. As he told the staff at the meeting outlining the ESOP, "When it came right down to having to say yes or no, I said no. I just couldn't sell the company."

The ESOP would make the employees the owners of the company and masters of its fate. An employee-owned Krause Publications would be a self-perpetuating entity that would last as long and do as well as its people could perform. It was as permanent an arrangement as any human creation could be. The ESOP was also the finest gift Chet could have given to Iola, since it insured the future of the village as well as anything could. It is unlikely but, if a statue of Chet Krause is ever raised in Iola and a list of his contributions is etched in the pedestal, it need be no longer than four letters — ESOP — because the ESOP provides a high degree of assurance that everything else Krause has given to the community — the jobs, the tax base, the donations, the Old Car Show — will continue after he is gone.

According to the terms of its charter, the ESOP began when 30 percent of the stock owned by the Krause family and a few others was sold to the company. It was held in a "suspense account," and each year a percentage of the stock was transferred to each employee's ESOP account. Upon retirement, an employee sells the stock back to the company for cash or an annuity and it can then be reassigned to other employees. The partnership began with 30 percent of the company's stock assigned to the partnership, with more to come in the future.

The ESOP also replaced the old Krause retirement plan and improved on it, since the capital accrued in stock is usually worth more at retirement than standard benefit plans. The standard wisdom also holds that ESOPs pay better retirement benefits because the partners who own the company take a greater interest in making it profitable. Those profits are also kept within the company. For Krause in the late 1980s, the gain would have been significant. "If we had this five years ago," said controller Terry Tomsyck then, "I can't quantify it, but we'd all be shocked at how much our little slot would be worth."

The job stability the partnership brings to employees enables them to invest in houses and other community assets, knowing full well that their jobs are secure. It is a subtle, but by no means insignificant, additional benefit of the ESOP. Dean Listle, then ad manager of *Baseball Cards*, summed it up when he said, "Of all the avenues the company could have taken, this is the one that benefits us the most."

The ESOP preserved the benefits for employees. Production and growth, which was also well underway in '88, created them. The search for hobby fields in which to expand had led to the very successful acquisition of *Gun List*, and Krause continued to explore the realm of outdoor sports for new venues. In July, Don Nicolay announced the purchase of two periodicals from the Spearman Publishing Company of Sutton, Nebraska — *Turkey Hunter* and the *Trapper and Predator Caller*. "We feel these two magazines will make ideal additions to the hobbies we already serve," he said, "perfect companions" to *Gun List* and *Gun Show Calendar*.

Turkey hunting was one of few varieties of hunting that was increasing in popularity in the United States. States in the south-central part of the country, such as Missouri, had good turkey populations with an established sport, and many northern states, such as Wisconsin, had recently reintroduced the birds and a hunting season on them. By comparison, all other kinds of hunting, especially small game and waterfowl hunting, were enjoyed by a smaller number of participants every year. If Krause wanted to move into a hunting niche, turkey shooting was a good one.

Started in 1983, *Turkey Hunter* was published eight times a year, fall to spring, with an average circulation of about 16,400. Gerry Blair, who worked out of offices in Flagstaff, Arizona, edited *Turkey Hunter* and continued to do so after it came into the Krause tent. Krause upgraded the format of *Turkey Hunter*, placed it on newsstands, and turned it over to its promotion department. With the marketing system running full bore, the circulation of *Turkey Hunter* nearly doubled to 32,000 by the end of 1989. The promotion staff fine-tuned its marketing campaign by acquiring the names of people purchasing turkey hunting licenses. In 1989, for example, Pat Stull, who came from Spearman Publishing to coordinate *Turkey Hunter's* integration into Krause, went off to Jefferson City, Missouri, to supervise a team of temporary workers who collected the names and addresses of Missouri's 94,000 registered turkey hunters. The names came back to Krause's data bank, a promotional mailing was designed and shipped, and *Turkey Hunter* acquired a few thousand more subscribers in a state with one of the largest number of turkey hunters in the country. By 1991, *Turkey Hunter's* circulation had surpassed the 59,000 mark.

The *Trapper and Predator Caller* covered what its devotees call "America's First Industry," the trapping of fur-bearers, and its allied sport, coyote hunting. Since trappers spend a lot of time in the woods, and coyotes can be either trapped or shot for their pelts, many trappers are also coyote hunters. Both turkey and coyote hunters bring their quarry into shooting range by means of a calling device. Some calls are simple wooden, bone or whistle-like devices, some are tape recordings, and sometimes they work. The art of calling added to the editorial content and the advertising base of *TPC*, which also included trapping and hunting how-tos and where-tos, as well as supplies for both. *TPC* was also the official news medium of many state trapping associations, and printed the minutes of meetings and notices of their conventions.

Coins dragged hobbyists into politics, adults-only comics offended some self-appointed guardians of public morality, and "gas-guzzling" antique cars unequipped with modern anti-pollution exhaust controls upset the custodians of the ozone layer, but trapping was probably the most controversial hobby Krause had ever entered. It was, and is, a legitimate pastime, and those who enjoy it were well-served by *TPC*. Early in 1991, Krause published a book titled *The Illusions of Animal Rights* by Russ Carman. As the company catalog stated, the book was a "clear and concise presentation of information [that] supports the hunter, trapper and farmer as necessary herdsmen for keeping nature balanced."

Despite it efforts Krause has experienced some problems holding onto readers. In 1988, *Trapping and Predator Caller* had a circulation of more than 58,000; by 1991, the number had fallen to 44,500.

It wasn't for lack of trying. Pat Akey, after fifteen years in numismatic advertising, became ad manager for *TPC* and *Turkey Hunter*. Pat, Don Johnson and Don Nicolay plunged right into the sport in 1988 when they attended a trappers' convention in Illinois. Pat later reported that she met some very nice folks, one of whom sold her a pair of snakeskin cowboy boots. Don Johnson picked up a skill indispensable for a sales manager. He attended a workshop at the convention where he learned how to mimic the call of a dying rabbit.

The third "T" of 1988 appeared in August. *Toy Shop* was a Krause introduction in the tradition of *Gun List* and the early *Numismatic News,* but with all the benefit of thirty-plus years of marketing savvy. Jim Mohr was named advertising manager of *Toy Shop* early in the year, with Brenda Mazemke as assistant. Mohr spent the better part of six months traveling to toy trade and hobby shows talking up the publication, whose first issue had yet to see any printer's ink. His efforts were reinforced by a direct mail campaign to toy collectors and dealers.

The result was that, even before its first press run, *Toy Shop* had a list of subscribers and advertisers, both classified and display. The initial press run, projected at 7,000, was actually 18,000, 5,000 of which went to paid subscribers. The first *Toy Shop* ran 48 pages, carried 2,600 classified ads and 115 display ads. Nearly 80 percent of the display ads were on contract, which meant they would run in more than four issues. *Toy Shop's* format was virtually identical to *Gun List's*: Ads were classified alphabetically and indexed, editorial material was absent, but the articles for sale were hardly the same. Instead of Remingtons, Rugers and Colts, *Toy Shop* offered Tonka trucks, character collectibles and Barbie dolls.

The differences between collectibles did not matter, and Krause's success in two diverse niches only points out how well it had refined its formula. Collectors wanted the same kind of information, whether they were the stereotypically beefy and beetle-browed gun nut or the little old lady types whom people outside the hobby perceive as the typical toy collector. The fact is that all kinds of people collect all kinds of stuff. They all want the same kind of information, and Krause supplies it.

The introduction of *Toy Shop* also pointed out how far Krause had come since Chet sent his first sample issue of the *News* off the dining room table, and even how far it had come since the introduction of *Old Cars* in '71. Provided the hobby was right, Krause could now produce a complete periodical, with subscribers and advertisers, and without printing a pilot issue, but instead using only its own promotional know-how. A powerful tool had been forged in Iola. It had only to be aimed at the right target in order to strike the bull's eye. *Toy Shop* hit it. By 1991, with Brenda Mazemke as ad manager, it was a 100-plus-page monthly with a circulation of 18,500 and growing.

The success of the quarterly *Gun Show Calendar* encouraged Krause to try the idea in other niches. The *Baseball Show Calendar* appeared with the start of the baseball season in April '88, featuring 100 pages of dates, locations, attendance figures and the names of the stars who would be autographing collectibles at a show. It was intended to be a handy guide for hobbyists, but it was too specialized. Card collectors could find much of the same information in other Krause publications, along with additional material they wanted, so they passed on the *Calendar*, which stopped publishing in 1989.

The *Baseball Show Calendar* may have struggled, but the new *Baseball Card Price Guide Monthly*, which also debuted in April, was a grand slam success. Introduced with a paid circulation of 50,400, it climbed to 123,000 in 1990 and hovered in the 112,000 range in '91.

In addition to bringing out new publications, Krause also spruced up its oldest number. Facing a decline in subscriptions, the numismatic team revamped *Numismatic News*. Page size was reduced, the weight of the stock increased and a reduction in the number of columns from five to four helped improve the presentation. Harkening back to its roots, the *News* also announced that it was offering free classified ads and introducing a unit ad system similar to that used in *Goldmine*. The goal was to increase the number of want ads and thereby reinvigorate circulation. The promotion staff employed a newer tactic. They prepared a special 16-page issue of the revamped *News* and mailed it to approximately 1,500 advertisers across the nation.

The battle to reverse the decline in numismatics continued into 1989. *Coins* was the target of a special marketing campaign, and *WCN* was redesigned and its frequency of publication cut back to twenty-six issues a year.

The book division continued to turn out the massive volumes for which Krause was noted, and a project inaugurated in 1979 was finally coming to its end. Jim Haxby, a pharmacy student at Oregon State University, spent the better part of ten years completing research and photography for the *Standard Catalog of U. S. Obsolete Bank Notes*. The 2,700 page presentation, in four hard-bound volumes, with 20,000 photos, was finally published in 1989.

Another long-awaited book was completed when Courtney Coffing's *A Guide and Checklist of World Notgeld, 1914-1947*, was published. The 184-page volume, which Courtney worked on for fifteen years, provided an overview of the emergency money, *notgeld* in German, issued in times of war and other upheaval in seventy-eight countries around the world. The first printing appeared in February and was sold out by June.

The 15th edition of the *Standard Catalog of World Coins*, the second edition of Russ Rulau's *United States Trade Tokens, 1866-1889,* the third edition of the *Standard Catalog of American Cars* and another *Auction Prices Realized* also came out of the Krause shop.

New works included the *Standard Catalog of Baseball Cards* edited by Dan Albaugh; *Old Cars Auction Results 1987*, an annual report on auction prices actually paid for antique autos; and the *Trapper and Predator Caller Yearbook*.

Books in progress in '88 and scheduled for publication in the first half of 1989 included: the second edition of Colin Bruce's Unusual World Coins; the fifth edition of *A Guidebook of Mexican Coins*, by Clyde Hubbard and Theodore V. Buttrey; *Old Car Auction Results, 1988*; and the third edition of *Sports Collectors Digest Baseball Cards Price Guide*, by Bob Lemke and Dan

Albaugh. Don and Maggie Thompson were also working on the *Official Price Guide to Science Fiction and Fantasy Collectibles*, to be published by Random House/Ballantine in '89.

The Thompsons' book, published by a major New York house, pointed out another growth industry in Iola. People on staff were acquiring ever larger national and international reputations as experts in their fields. A sampling of staffers consulted, referred to or quoted in '88 includes: Bob Wilhite on gold coins for investment in *Money* magazine; *Comics Buyer's Guide* in *Money*, the *Cincinnati Post, USA Today* and *Playboy*; a reference to *Sports Collectors Digest* as the "Bible of Baseball Cards" in an investment newsletter titled *"Personal Finance"*; Bob Lemke and the baseball cards staff featured in a Green Bay TV piece on collecting and interviewed for pieces in *Advertising Age*, the New York *Daily News* and a spot on *MTV; Goldmine* in a *USA Today* article on investment in records; *Old Cars* in *USA Today*; and so on.

Goldmine and *Comics Buyer's Guide* became hot media properties in '88. The definition of an investment collectible had broadened tremendously in the '80s and investors who once would have scorned a 1960s Jethro Tull album or a Spider-Man comic — or a baseball card — now thought about adding them to their portfolios. As Maggie Thompson reported, "...Between the middle of '86 and the beginning of '88, the value of comics sold annually doubled [from $125 million to $250 million]."

Publicity helped and *Goldmine* got it in 1988 when Elvis Presley rocked into Iola. No, contrary to rumor, he was not spotted wolfing down Lions Club chicken at the Old Car Show. He did appear in one of Goldmine's semi-annual Elvis issues and the event pushed the collector's tabloid to the front page of the national consciousness.

Goldmine publisher John Koenig received a phone call from a man named Ed Leek who revealed that he had a 1953 studio tape of Elvis singing "That's When Your Heartaches Begin." It was a one-of-a-kind tape Elvis had paid $4 to record as a present for his mother. Leek was an *Old Cars* reader who knew that Krause also published a music collector's periodical. Because he trusted *Old Cars*, he believed he could tell *Goldmine* about his tape. Koenig talked Leek out of placing a little ad and instead convinced him to let *Goldmine* publicize the find. Kit Kiefer told the story in the August Elvis special issue and Greg Loescher included it in a promotional package that went to 800 newspapers and radio stations around the country.

A few days passed until the New York *Daily News* ran a piece on the discovery, with full credit to *Goldmine*. Then, as Kiefer wrote in the *Chronicle*, "The phone didn't stop ringing. First it was the Associated Press then it was the London *Daily Mail*. Then it was *Entertainment Tonight. USA Today* called.... The Associated Press moved the story on its wire. NBC News...-picked up the story...United Press International jumped.... Then it was Fox Broadcasting.

"Never before had so many major media outlets come to KP looking for information on a story. Never before had KP scooped the country so spectacularly."

It was spectacular, but like most "instant" success stories, the Elvis scoop had a long history. It evolved out of a thirty-seven year tradition of trust and honesty. Ed Leek came to *Goldmine* because he saw the integrity of Krause Publications displayed in *Old Cars*. The integrity there traces back to the concern Chet showed for mail bidders and classified advertisers in *Numismatic News* in 1953. Leek was confident that the straight-shooters in Iola would not have, as the old rock song says, "done him wrong." And they didn't.

Comics Buyer's Guide, despite the often bizarre aspects of its subject matter, was also helpful to the fans of the superstars who appeared in its pages. Back in 1984, two comic artists, Kevin Eastman and Peter Laird, who occasionally submitted work to *CBG*, ran an ad in the *Guide* for a 40-page black and white comic depicting the adventures of four creatures named Michelangelo, Donatello, Leonardo and Raphael — the Teenage Mutant Ninja Turtles. Eastman and Laird had conceived the quartet as a parody of more conventional super heroes and scraped up $1,500 to pay for an initial printing of 3,000 copies.

Based on the ad in *CBG*, the first edition of *Teenage Mutant Ninja Turtles* was sold out in three weeks. The artists plowed their profits into more comic ventures, and the Turtles soon entered the pantheon of American promotional success alongside the Cabbage Patch dolls and the pet rock. By 1989, copies of the first Ninja Turtle comic were selling for $300. The Turtle story illustrates the power of the right idea placed in the right medium and the ability of a mere hobby periodical to stimulate a national craze.

The national craze for baseball cards also received some stimulation in Iola. *Sports Collector's Digest* ended the year by sending out a 120-page holiday gift catalog to 100,000 non-subscribers, who were also asked to subscribe, and Sears put the *1989 Baseball Card Calendar* in its Christmas catalog. *Baseball Cards* started the year as the largest circulating Krause publication in history and ended the year by getting even larger, with circulation hitting 210,000.

The number of employee anniversaries observed also set a record. Cliff Mishler crossed the twenty-five-year threshold; Marge Larson and Alyce Kolden marked twenty years; Kathy Hines and Pat Akey registered fifteen years; and Dave Harper, Susie Melum, Lori Anderson, Darlene Kriewaldt, John Gunnell and Peggy Morey marked ten years at work.

*Acquired in 1989, **Rural Builder** was Krause's first non-hobby publication. The controlled-circulation journal, which also sponsors a trade show that Krause now manages, is aimed at professional builders.*

Chapter 38

1989

"The philosophy is to try to find maga-
zines or books that will utilize our current
assets, which are the ability to efficiently
handle large volumes of name-and-
address records and advertising copy. . . .
We have a production facility that is sec-
ond to none." Don Nicolay

"During October [1988] keylining
churned out 2,920 pages for monthly and
weekly publications." KP Chronicle

The production facility that "churned out" all those pages was growing and modernizing — again. A 15,000-square foot addition was completed in '89, the fifth addition since 1975, and work on the Central to the planning of this addition was the development of a totally new area with the former production area being remodeled into a central conference center. The addition expanded the company quarters to a total of 68,000 square feet.

A new computer system to replace the now ancient eight-year old IBM System/3,with an interim Model 38 upgrade, was installed early in '89. The new AS/400 could handle 200 users and 480 work stations and combined the word-processing system used to write articles and ad copy with the data-entry system that contained names, addresses and other information. The new system was faster and had improved word processing and graphic capabilities. It could even diagnose glitches in its circuitry and automatically place a call for service.

A new laser camera also came on line early in '89. It allowed photos to be stored digitally so the Camex operators designing the pages could call them up on-screen as they worked on a page, then crop, reduce or enlarge the image to fit the design. The new Autokon 1000 Laser Graphics System, combined with Krause's other computerized production equipment, essentially put all production basic work on-screen. The days of cut-and-paste, X-acto knives, and T-squares on light tables were passing as the era of the Linotype had gone before. Computerized page make-up transformed the work of physically putting together nearly 3,000 pages a month of printed material. It was now faster, easier and less prone to error.

Krause's commitment to new, top-flight equipment, and the abilities of the people who have used it, have kept its products neat and relatively error-free. Seemingly simple errors such as misplaced editorial copy, uneven spacing, headlines that run downhill, missing page numbers, typos, crooked borders, boxes with corners that don't meet, and a hundred other basic mechanical errors, rarely appear in Krause publications. A Krause product is simple, neat, presented in straightforward fashion — and accurate. The motto of the shop — "on time, every time" — could justifiably be modified to read, "on time right, every time."

In 1989, two shifts of production workers were getting it right, every time, for 440 publication deadlines. Books on schedule for the year included *Auction Prices Realized, 1989; Standard Catalog of World Coins, 1990, Unusual World Coins II; Standard Guide to Cars and Prices* and the first edition of *Truck Prices*, which contained 144 pages of prices for pickup trucks, vans, panel vehicles and sports pickups. In August, 75,000 copies of this latest "bible" were shipped to newsstand distributors.

In addition to the books, the production department helped several periodicals produce their biggest issues ever. A special supplement containing a national directory of baseball card dealers pushed the page count of the Feb. 24 issue of *Sports Collectors Digest* to 264 pages and the March 3 issue of *Baseball Card News* to 132 pages. These records had a short life, since *SCD* and *BCN*, along with *Baseball Cards* magazine and the *Baseball Card Price Guide* all knocked out record-size issues for the National Sports Show in Chicago in July.

The May issue of *Gun List* shot to a record 196 pages and then went ballistic with a 204-page tally in October. *Goldmine* spun off its largest take with 152 pages on Sept. 22. Although it didn't set a record for size, the May 17 issue of *Comics Buyer's Guide* was special for several reasons. First, it was devoted to the 50th anniversary of Donald Duck and, second, it marked a circulation increase of 137 percent for the tabloid since its arrival in Iola.

The promotion department, the magnitude of whose efforts can be easily overlooked, also continued its high level of output. In January alone, 200,000 promotional pieces were shipped to potential subscribers of *Turkey Hunter* and over 40,000 pieces went out in pursuit of new readers for *Coins.*

Promotions also got into the periodical business when it developed *Contact, a closer look at Krause Publications.* Introduced in the summer of 1989, *Contact* was described by Don Nicolay "as the newest addition to Krause's growing family...the conduit that connects us to you, our business friends and associates." The newsletter, printed in four colors on heavy coated stock, was sent to advertisers, suppliers and other professionals in the trade and the hobbies. "Your name," as Don addressed his readers, "was hand-picked by a member of the Krause staff to receive this special quarterly publication."

Contact presented Krause in a first-class manner, showing off its design abilities — as displayed by the art department's Beth Mortenson — as well as demonstrating the company's diversity. The pioneer issue ran articles about old cars and the Old Car Show, *Toy Shop* (illustrated with a photo of a collectible featuring Robin, Batman's sidekick, that also made the comics connection), a short piece about the 1989 mint mark error on quarters, and an advertiser profile of Alan Rosen, the "Mr. Mint" of baseball card collecting. *Contact* also covered the ESOP and introduced receptionist Lori Hauser, "your first KP contact." In what was becoming a habit in Krause publications, *Contact* also introduced a new building addition, a new book — *Truck Prices* — and a new acquisition — *Rural Builder.*

Krause had grown enough for its very size and diversity to be a marketing asset. By telling an *Old Cars* auction advertiser that the company also published the leading periodicals for sports collectors and was also expanding into the building trade niche, Krause showed that it was a lot more than just old cars. By talking about its connection with people who turned up in the national media — such as Alan Rosen — Krause was enhancing its image by linking it with a celebrity, and sending a message to advertisers hinting that some of the glitter attached to Mr. or Ms. Famous might rub off if they did business in Iola. Finally, *Contact* helped achieve the first goal of salesmanship — getting the name of the product in front of the buyer on a regular basis.

Getting a product in front of a buyer at least once was the goal of Krause's newest automotive publication. Proving that old dogs can learn from pups, the car team launched a periodical that obviously came out of the same kennel as *Gun List* and *Toy Shop*. It was called *Car Corral*, after the famous sale enclosure at the Old Car Show. It followed the format developed by *Gun List* of printing only carefully organized and indexed classifieds and display ads, then adding a calendar of auto-related events. It was introduced like *Toy Shop*, with Krause signing up subscribers and advertisers before the first word was typeset. The newly named publisher of the automotive division, John Gunnell, headed up a team made up of Paul Katzke, ad manager; Becky Wade, classifieds; Steve Rapp, promotions; and Kristine Schafer, assistant.

Car Corral debuted in August, with 150,000 copies shipped to subscribers and bulk distributors. "The magazine will be aimed at attracting advertisers who are not using other KP automotive magazines," said Gunnell. Two semi-loads of *Corrals* were shipped eastward for distribution at the big car shows at Carlisle and Hershey, Pennsylvania, but the publication survived only for about a year before Krause dropped it. "Nobody has been able to make an automotive shopper go," Gunnell said in 1991. "We were competing against ourselves." The automotive niche was full and Krause was occupying as much as the market could bear.

By comparison, the sports niche seemed to be opening wider. In June the sports division revived a title it had purchased in 1984, and reissued *The Trader Speaks*, as a monthly supplement to *Sports Collectors Digest* focused on classic cards. It was a tabloid targeted at the advanced collector, but it never really caught fire, and it died within a year. The *SCD Baseball Card Phone Shop*, which started taking calls in July, was a combination advertising and telephone sales service. Callers used a 900 number to hear ads from dealers and could immediately place orders.

The *Phone Shop* was a Krause Publication transferred to a different medium. Subscribers paid to get the message and then choose to patronize advertisers. A visionary could claim that the *Phone Shop* was a step on the way to the hobby periodical of the future. All that was needed was a video screen to actually see what was for sale. In time to come the equivalent of a tabloid page of ads could flash on screen, buyers could scan it quickly and punch out an order on the phone. Considering Krause's record of keeping up-to-date on technology, when the videophone is perfected, a video shopper using it will probably beam out from Iola.

The last expansion of the sports niche in '89 left Iola via the traditional print medium. It was a "one-shot" magazine titled *Baseball Card Boom!*, and was released in mid-December to serve as an end-of-the decade recap of the sports card collecting spurt of the '80s. The hobby truly had boomed, faster and larger than any other hobby covered in Iola and perhaps faster then any other hobby anywhere, ever. Testimony to the growth is provided by the circulation figures at Krause during the '80s. *Sports Collectors Digest* multiplied by a factor of six; *Baseball Card News* and *Baseball Cards Price Guide* by five; and *Baseball Cards*, which started big, by a factor greater than two, to cross the quarter-million mark and become the largest volume publication Krause ever produced. Whether it was due to good luck, good judgment, or a bit of both, Chet's decision to let Doug Watson and Bob Lemke move Krause into sports card collecting was one of the best business decisions he had ever made.

In 1989, Krause Publications made the decision to expand into yet another publishing niche and purchased *Rural Builder*. It looked like a long reach out of the company's traditional domain but appearances were deceiving. Krause was a specialty publisher, attuned to meeting the needs of a limited audience with specific tastes. It was also an accomplished direct mail marketing house, equally attuned to identifying a market and aiming its sales message at it. So acquiring *Rural Builder* was not as great a departure as it appeared. *RB* was a controlled-circulation trade publication targeted on — as the title says — people working in the specialized field of construction in rural areas.

The magazine was founded in 1967, when what was then called the pole shed-style of building was developing into the dominant design for agricultural and commercial operations that needed to enclose a lot of space at low cost. Pole building was an adaptation of traditional post-and-beam barn construction to the use of modern materials such as rot-resistant, pressure treated wooden posts, lightweight structural steel framing, and sheet metal siding. The style had evolved over the years into its own specialty, with its own designs, tools, materials and equipment — all of which defined a niche for a publication.

Rural Builder was published eight times a year and had a circulation of about 25,000 when Krause acquired it. In addition to the magazine, *Rural Builder* also published an annual buyer's guide with the names of 1,300 suppliers, ran a direct mail program and a reader-information service — all of which were familiar services in Iola.

Rural Builder also sponsored a trade show, which brought hundreds of builders to workshops and scores of exhibitors offering goods for sale to them. Running a show was also nothing new to Krause, although a professional trade show was a bit different from the down-home carnival of the Old Car Show. On the other hand, Don Nicolay had for years managed Farm Progress Shows that closely resembled the building shows. All it required, as Chet was fond of saying, was "organization and scheduling." The Iolans would get their shot at it, for they would be running the 23rd Annual *Rural Builder* Show in Orlando, Florida in the spring of 1990.

In the meantime, they worked on developing the magazine. Promotions had to be sharply targeted to not dilute the quality of *Rural Builder's* circulation. Sheer numbers of readers matter less than the right readers to any advertiser, but especially to advertisers in trade publications. If *Rural Builder* suddenly acquired 100,000 new readers, the numbers might be impressive, but, unless those readers were good purchasers of the goods and services advertised, they were of little use.

"The idea," as Bob Van Ryzin explained in the *Chronicle*, "is that...[the] publication is keenly targeted at an audience that the advertiser can rely upon as being in a position to purchase merchandise being offered and who have a direct need for it.

"Each year, a private firm will conduct what is known as a Business Publications Audit, which will verify *Rural Builder's* circulation totals. These numbers are, in turn, relied upon by advertisers in adjusting marketing programs."

Consequently, Krause carefully targeted its marketing and built circulation. By 1991, with Rick Groth as publisher/ad manager and Erik Stottrup as editor,

Rural Builder's circulation had increased to 35,000, and accounted for about one-third of its market share.

The trade show that came with *Rural Builder* was, coincidentally, only one of several shows that Krause was actively supporting or sponsoring. First, there was the Old Car Show, the grand summer homecoming of automobilia that brought 100,000 car mavens to Iola, gave collectors a chance to exhibit their pride and joy on wheels, presented backyard car restorers with a chance to find the parts they needed to turn a clunker into a king's carriage, and asked thousands of unsung pullets to make the final sacrifice for a good cause.

Next came the "Milwaukee All-Collectibles Show" in September. Virtually every Krause division had an interest here, and so did good neighbor Joe Jones, who was co-sponsoring the Milwaukee Show on the same weekend as a big RV Show there. It featured "dealer tables from almost every hobby imaginable including baseball cards, coins, records, stamps, postcards, dolls, toys, antiques and paper ephemera," and served as a means for collectors to sample new hobbies and perhaps strike up a new fancy. It was a good vehicle to stimulate interest in hobbies and one in which Krause continued to take an interest itself.

One hobby that didn't need much stimulation was baseball card collecting. In '89, Krause cosponsored its second major card show in conjunction with the Chicago *Sun-Times* in Chicago. The *Times* Baseball Show featured a number of attractions related to the sport, including Krause's 200-dealer card show, a memorabilia auction, and an autograph session with baseball stars. The entire show was a charity event, with proceeds going to the *Sun-Times* Charitable Trust and the ALS Foundation. ALS — amyotrophic lateral sclerosis — is more commonly known as "Lou Gehrig's disease," the debilitating and deadly malady that killed one of baseball's greatest and most-loved stars of the 1920s and '30s.

Virtually the entire Krause sports team and much of the sales staff worked the Chicago Show, and the Iolans had an exciting time in the big city. The line-up for the team working the show on behalf of Krause's largest and most profitable division then included Bob Lemke, Steve Ellingboe, Don Johnson, Tom Mortenson, Mark Larson, Kit Kiefer, Greg Ambrosius, Hugh McAloon, Dean Listle, Duke Tuomi, Steve Madson, Jeff Kurowski, Greg Loescher, Steve Raap, Susie Melum, Barb Johnson, Lauren Borth, Pat Klug, Betty Aanstad, Chet and Cliff.

In the same month the sports card team was enjoying the Chicago show, the numismatic crew was acquiring a show of its own. In September, Krause announced that it had purchased the Chicago International Coin Fair. The 14-year-old show was one of the largest and most prestigious shows in the country dedicated to world coins, one that Cliff described as "a bellwether of activity in the world-coin field." The first Chicago International Coin Fair under Krause's management took place in March 1990.

Running trade and hobby shows was a logical expansion for Krause and one that many publishing companies were well into by the 1980s. With its marketing power, both through its periodicals and its direct mail department, Krause could bring a mountain of marketing muscle and savvy to a show. The 1990 Coin Fair not only was promoted heavily in the Midwest, but also nationally and internationally, and proved to be the largest in its history. Shows like the Coin Fair were another component of the hobby niche that Krause moved into in the late '80s and one that would see more activity in the '90s.

Attending shows was a familiar activity for Krause employees, and many were the jokes told about staff people who undertook the painful task of spending a February week in San Diego, Las Vegas or Orlando. Equally painful were the overseas trips to working meetings in Hawaii, Europe or Asia. One of the most arduous treks undertaken by any Krause employee was Cliff's three-week numismatic tour around the world in 1988. Jokes aside, the collecting niche did not stop at the Iola village limits, nor even the border of the United States. By 1989, Krause publications were shipped to 118 countries, and the company was a full-fledged participant in the global economy.

Most of the more than half-million miles that Krause people traveled every year were to less-than-exotic destinations such as Lakeland, Florida for the Central Florida Auto Fest, Cincinnati for the Frame Builders Show, and Indianapolis for the Indiana Sports Collectors Association show.

"At least three people leave here every week," said Lisa Morgan, executive secretary in charge of travel arrangements. In a 1989 *Chronicle* interview, Lisa pointed out that the West Coast was the favored destination of baseball and sports collectors, while coin people preferred to travel west and south. Car people went east, mainly because of the two big car shows in Pennsylvania. Automotive staffers also tended to travel more in the warmer seasons since many of their events took place outdoors. Depending on the distance and the destination, and how much stuff they had to bring along, staffers either drove or flew to their shows, but the boarding gates at the Green Bay and Appleton airports were a familiar sight to most Krause travelers.

Each hobby had its own set of show displays, both freestanding and table-top, to suit its exhibit. Tom Kepler kept track of the displays in '89 and also made sure each departing Krause representative knew what was packed where, how to find the display at the show site, and also how to set it up. Adventure yarns and misadventure stories of lost luggage, bad weather, and the unusual happenings of life on the road are part of the workday lore at Krause. For, no matter how modern the communication equipment and how personalized the direct mail message, Krause is in the people business and, when dealing with people, there are times when nothing is more effective than a handshake, a smile and a few friendly words spoken face-to-face.

When those words couldn't be spoken face-to-face, there was Luella Johnson. Luella worked in customer service, which meant she fielded the phone calls from unhappy customers, tried to convince them to put their complaints in writing, forwarded the grievances onto the advertisers — and then found herself smack dab in the middle. Most of the time unhappy customers just needed to know that someone was willing to listen to their complaints. If a number of callers complained about an ad, and the advertiser offered no recourse, Luella's job was to turn the name over to the post office for investigation and advise the advertising sales manager concerned so advertising privileges could be revoked.

This type of customer service has been part of the company since Chet's early days with *Numismatic News*. In '89 Luella handled a complaint from a subscriber to *Trapper and Predator Caller*, who was unhappy with a shipment of bear gallbladders he ordered from an advertiser. Luella worked it out and both participants in the deal were satisfied. In terms of Luella's and Krause's role, an unhappy customer was an unhappy customer whether he was buying a Wonder Woman comic, a restorable 1957 DeSoto, a Gabby Hartnett baseball card, or bear innards.

Phone work became increasingly important in the 1980s, when the 800 sales number came into its own in Iola. Subscription sales by phone were the number one item, but books, calendars, and other material could also be ordered. In 1989, the Krause phone order department was still in its infancy and consisted of Shelley Potratz, who had recently followed Kathie Heise in the position. Shelley was as enthusiastic about her end of the phone line as Luella Johnson was about hers.

"I think most people think that I just sit on the phone, taking orders all day," she told Debbie Kellom in a *Chronicle* article. "But I have to have a great attitude and pleasant speaking voice all day. I'm projecting an image of the company.

"I need to know details about each product on a split-second's notice-prices, codes. I don't feel people know how much patience it takes," she continued.

Shelley's busiest week came in January with 754 calls that followed a big promotional push for *Turkey Hunter*. She took all those orders by hand, since her "department" had yet to be computerized. She confessed that she hadn't once lost her patience with difficult callers — the harried New Yorkers who hate to repeat what they've said, no matter how unintelligibly they said it, the hobbyists who want information but use the ordering number to save phone charges, or the folks who say they want a magazine, but don't know which one. Shelley seemed to tolerate the phone foibles, even thrive on them, but even she was not totally unflappable. After a day's work, she never answered the phone at home. Friends and family were warned to call only on weekends. "I just have no urge to talk on the phone after work." Shelley's reaction was similar to that of the journalist who never writes a letter to his mom, or the sales manager who can't bear to dicker with a car salesman.

1989 ended with the staff preparing to move into the newest addition, with the circulation, data-entry, proofreading, and pre-press departments leading the way. It was a fitting ending for another one of those "9" years that serve as a summary for their decade. In 1989, there was growth, diversity, new technology and construction. The particulars were different, but it was the Krause refrain sung once again.

The anniversary story was also told again: twenty years for Marian Moe; fifteen for Bob Lemke, Marge Williams and Colin Bruce; ten for Sue Krause and Gary Marx.

Krause's Greatest Period of Growth, 1989-1990

	1989	1990
Number of Subscribers	404,000	535,465
Annual Total of Copies Delivered to Subscribers	2,100,000	3,092,050
Annual Newsstand Distribution	6,000,000	11,604,914
Annual Number of Book Pages Published	52,656	57,000
Average Monthly Display Ads Processed	6,870	10,424
Monthly Total of Classified Ads Published	15,433	26,132
Average Monthly Number of Product and Promotional Pieces Mailed	896,666	896,666
Names and Addresses in Computer Storage	1,700,000	3,000,000
Annual Total Employees Hours Worked	440,000	604,193
Square Feet of Office and Production Space	47,000	68,000
Annual Total of Periodical Deadlines	424	526

Flanked by Governor Tommy Thompson, Chet accepts his award as Wisconsin Business Person of the Year for 1990.

Chapter 39

1990

"It's really their award."   Chet Krause

Chet Krause was named the Wisconsin Small Business Person of the Year in 1990. Don Nicolay and Greg Loescher, following up a suggestion by Small Business Administration Board Member Tom Godfrey and Iola attorney DeLyle Omholt, prepared the nomination papers for the SBA. The process moved so fast that Chet was selected even before he knew he was nominated. He received the award at an SBA banquet in Milwaukee, where, in typical fashion, he credited his success to the staff in Iola.

The criteria for the SBA Award provide a good summary of how Krause Publications had developed overall since 1952, and particularly in the 1980s. In 1952, Chet had *Numismatic News*. At the beginning of 1990, Krause had twenty-four periodicals with a total circulation of more than 1.1 million and nearly forty book titles with total annual sales of $125,000. Since 1981, the staff had grown from 133 to 237 employees. Since 1984, company revenues had nearly tripled from $10.5 million to over $30 million. Return on average net worth for 1989 was estimated at 39.5 percent.

No business is truly successful unless it has overcome a few hard knocks. Krause survived the decline of the only hobby it served in the 1960s and used the adversity as a spur to build stability through diversification. At the same time, the company showed its commitment to innovation. It was a genuine pioneer in the computerization of data processing and readily adopted other new publishing technology as it was introduced.

The SBA Award winner also had to display initiative in a area of national interest, and Krause's decades of political activism on behalf of numismatics and hobbyists in general was more than enough to meet the requirement. A commitment to the home community was also important, and Krause's support of virtually every charity, volunteer group and good cause in the Iola area impressed the judges. Finally, Chet's adoption of the ESOP as a means of preserving all that he and his staff had built over the years capped his achievements.

Krause was still growing in 1990, with the marketing of books leading the way. Twenty volumes were scheduled for 1990, ranging from the 17th edition of the venerable *Standard Catalog of World Coins* to the new sports book, *Sport's Collector's Digest Hall of Fame Autographs.* The automotive division extended its series on cars by publishing, in separate volumes, a *Standard Catalog of American Cars* for Chevrolet, Ford and Chrysler. Other hobbies also expanded their book lines, as the music division issued *Goldmine's Price Guide to 45 RPM Records*, outdoors produced *The Winchester Model 42* and the toy staff produced *Popeye the Collectible.* Krause published more books in 1990 than in any previous year.

The company also introduced more new periodicals, and many older ones set records for page counts. The still-booming sports collectors hobby was a logical niche for expansion, and Krause did it with several venues. First came the "one-shots" starting with *Baseball Card Boom*, which actually hit the stands in December, 1989. *Boom!* was followed by *A Beginner's Guide to Baseball Cards* in spring and the *Football Card Price Guide* in late summer. They were magazines destined for newsstand distribution and intended to introduce their hobbies and Krause to newcomers. They also initiated a series of specialty publications related to different aspects of the sports collecting field that Krause continued to publish in '91 and '92.

The term "baseball card" had become generic, but the card-collecting hobby had grown large enough for Krause to single out individual segments of it and aim a publication at them. At the end of 1990, the company introduced *Football, Basketball and Hockey Collector* to focus on these mini-niches within the general "baseball card" niche.

As America's oldest professional spectator sport, and the most popular for nearly a century, baseball was the foundation of the card-collecting hobby. By the late 1980s, however, polls showed that football had surpassed baseball as America's favorite pastime. Hockey was the sport whose popularity had grown the fastest in the 1980s, while basketball had also gained many new fans. Since they were not as popular in the 1950s, fewer cards were printed for hockey, football and basketball than for baseball, but their scarcity did not make them any less collectible. Prices for early 1950s Gordie Howe hockey cards compared favorably with those for Mickey Mantle cards from the same period. Also, as the card hobby grew, more publishers were producing cards for these sports, including retrospective editions featuring athletes from the days when fewer hockey, football and basketball cards were issued.

In 1990, the volume of cards available from these sports could not justify a separate periodical for each one. They did very well together, though. When the sports team of Bob Lemke, Steve Ellingboe, Don Butler, Hugh McAloon and Duke Tuomi launched *Football, Basketball and Hockey Collector*, they started with a circulation of 44,000, nearly all on newsstands. A year later, circulation, still chiefly on the stands, hit the 62,000 mark with page counts for the magazine averaging 128.

It has been said more than once that the real game of baseball isn't played on the field, but in the scorekeeper's booth. No sport keeps more statistics, no sport uses numbers more to measure its players' performance, and no sport lives more in a fantasy world of totals and percentages than baseball. In fact, in the 1930s small town radio broadcasters — Ronald Reagan was one — used to "broadcast" major league games by embellishing the bare facts they received in their studios via the teletype. The game the listeners heard was a combination of statistics and fantasy.

Given the demonstrated possibilities, it is not hard to understand the birth of what was known as rotisserie, statistical league or fantasy baseball. By 1990, it was, as Steve Ellingboe described it, "one of the fastest-growing sports pastimes in America." The game was invented in the late 1970s at a Washington, D. C. restaurant called the *Rotisserie*, and in its earliest days was known as rotisserie baseball.

As Ellingboe continued, the game "...involves a group of fantasy managers who draft a roster of major league players and then tabulate points based on their players' daily performance on the field.

"The fantasy teams play against one another in weekly head-to-head competition, and season-long standings are kept.... At the end of the year, winning managers share in prize money...."

Fantasy baseball creates what the writers of comics call a parallel universe. It uses the facts of the game played on the field but puts them to its own uses. A committed fantasy baseball fan studies the performance of players, keeps records, and digests the day's box scores as soon as they are available. The game developed a large audience in the 1980s, but, as Ellingboe wrote, "there has never been a specific publication to serve fantasy-league players — to provide the information and specialized stats....

"That's where *Fantasy Baseball* comes in."

Introduced prior to opening day in 1990, Krause's *Fantasy Baseball* was a logical expansion of the sports niche. Krause was already reaching several hundred thousand baseball card collectors, many of whom were involved in fantasy play, and who would give the new magazine a circulation base. Although it didn't involve collectibles, the new hobby needed a publication that would deliver a lot of information in the form of brief listings, along with advertising for the many reporting services that delivered the daily statistics on which play depended. Krause had been delivering just this kind of information to other hobbies for years.

With Greg Ambrosius as editor and Dean Listle as ad manager, the first issue of *Fantasy Baseball* had a circulation of 156,000, almost all on newsstands. Started as a quarterly, the magazine switched to bi-monthly in 1991, then switched back to quarterly in '92. It found a market niche with circulation in the 105,000 range.

The hobby *Fantasy Baseball* served was in its bare infancy, so new that the magazine had to be subtitled "a winner's guide to rotisserie and statistical league play," since the game had yet to select a single name for itself. The May 1992 issue ran 132 pages and, in his "First Pitch" editorial, Greg Ambrosius mentioned that ESPN cable television was launching a TV show reporting daily statistics and *Fantasy Baseball* might be involved. Having a network television show designed for it was testimony to the growth of the new sport. Television, with its ability to deliver simple information fast, was the ideal medium for fantasy baseball, since true fantasy fans need daily bulletins about their players. Krause might have been concerned about a rival medium stealing its audience, but, as Greg wrote, "The more the merrier. If there's any way to get the public to accept this hobby for what it is — a kid's game played by adults for pure, unadulterated entertainment — then I'm all for it." The young editor of a new magazine speaking in 1992 sounds like Chet Krause in the 1960s, when he pointed out that any news about the hobby of coin collecting was good for *Numismatic News*.

Krause was truly getting in on the ground floor of a hobby here and whether it can help build a new pastime and a profitable publication to serve it will be one of the stories to be played out in the 1990s.

One story that played out very briefly in 1990 covered *Music Mart*. The music division had been successful with price guides on collectible record albums and jazz records and its new guide to 45 RPMs was doing well, so the team brought out "an indexed, all-advertising monthly publication" similar to *Gun List* and *Toy Shop*. "The record field is expanding because of CD's and digital technology," said *Goldmine* Publisher John Koenig. "I watched *Toy Shop* and *Gun List* grow and I thought there was a potential for this market."

Music Mart didn't have it. The music collector's niche wasn't large enough for another publication. Once again a successful Krause publication did not leave room in its niche for another publication — Krause's or not — and *Music Mart* died. Its word ad section was incorporated into *Goldmine*, where it proved to be an asset. Unlike the music hobby, the comics niche could support a regularly issued price guide. Also launched in 1990, the *Comics Buyers Guide Price Guide* established itself as a quarterly with a future.

Krause also saw potential in expanding its new trade division. Considering the relatively small number of Americans who farm, the farm press has been large and diverse. In 1990, Wisconsin alone had three newspapers covering farming, several magazines, and numerous special journals devoted to agricultural specialties ranging from dairy breeding to potato cultivation. *Agri-View* was one of the more recent additions to the field.

Founded in 1975 by Gerald Petcher and James Brayer, *Agri-View* was a weekly with a circulation of 50,000 to active Wisconsin farmers. It provided local coverage by publishing six different editions, each one focusing on a different region of the state. It attempted to cover the entire agricultural niche in a state where, despite its reputation for dairying, farming was quite diverse.

"We purchased *Agri-View* because of its leadership position and preference among Wisconsin farmers and advertisers," Don Nicolay said. "We felt that *Agri-View* offered timely local farm news every week for this all-important section of Wisconsin's diverse economy." Don also felt that *Agri-View* would complement *Rural Builder*, and it would, but only on a limited basis. *RB's* market was national and focused on building. Only a few of its advertisers would consider *Agri-View* a useful medium to reach it.

Purchasing a farm periodical when the farm economy was in recession, and when the number of Wisconsin farmers had been declining drastically for years, was a bold move. However, Krause felt that the declining farm market base would not be able to support all the periodicals currently in it and a weeding out was in the offing. *Agri-View* had a good base of readers and advertisers. Krause could use its marketing power to build on the farm newspaper's strength, and perhaps insure that, when the agricultural publishing niche contracted, *Agri-View* would still be in business. How this story plays out — whether a hobby publisher serving national markets can pump life into a specialty newspaper with a limited geographic base and serving a diminishing market — will also make for interesting news from Iola in the 1990s.

In 1990 itself, growth itself continued to be the most interesting news in Iola. In February, *Sports Collectors Digest* started a record-breaking climb that started at 244 pages and hit 380 in May. The Feb. 16 issue carried a 32-page ad for a Leland's auction, the largest ad to ever run, not just in *SCD*, but in any Krause publication. The May 25 issue, *SCD's* 500th, threatened to hit the 400-page mark, which would be the largest section the Shawano printing plant could handle, but settled back to only hit a record size of 380 pages. It was one of three times in 1990 that *SCD* batted 380.

The largest-ever issues of the *Baseball Cards Price Guide* also appeared in spring 1990, passing the old record of 148 pages and pushing on to 164 pages.

The sports division also saw another record tumble when the April issue of *Baseball Cards* crossed the circulation threshold of 300,000. As Bob Lemke said, "This marks the first time in Krause's history that any periodical has had more than 250,000 circulation...and it went way beyond that mark."

Also in February, a revived *Numismatic News* started to run a string of four 100-page issues and then set a record by publishing 196 pages for the ANA convention in August. *World Coin News* also set a record with its own 88-page ANA issue.

In March, *Turkey Hunter* banged out its largest issue, 92 pages on coated paper with four-color ads. In the same month, *Gun List* hit 216 pages and carried a record 15,000 classified ads. It switched to bi-weekly production in May and publisher Jim Mohr cautiously projected page counts of 64 per issue. In fact, the first "64" pager ran to 136 pages and held that level through the fall. *Toy Shop* set its own records of 136 in September and 152 pages in October. *Goldmine* kept pace in the summer with a 180-page edition, followed by two issues that ran to 204 pages, the biggest yet. Finally *Baseball Cards* finished the year with two 212-page issues in a row. One reason those periodicals grew was that the number of classified ads Krause published was rising by 40 percent, from 30,000 in '89 to 42,000 in 1990.

In addition to setting records for size, *Turkey Hunter, Goldmine, Baseball Cards*, and set new marks for subscriptions. Periodicals earn revenues in three ways — advertising, subscriptions and single copy sales. Of the three, advertising is the most profitable, followed by subscriptions. In 1990, Krause's fastest growing publications were excelling in the most profitable part of the operation, advertising and subscription sales.

Many of those subscriptions were sold via the 800-phone system, which had also expanded by leaps and bounds since early 1989, when operator Shelley Potratz was hooked into the computer. By September 1989, the three-phone department took an average of 741 calls a week. In a single week in September 1990, the department — which had grown to six phones — handled a record 2,016 calls. The total number of calls increased from 31,000 in '89 to 48,000 in 1990.

All these records affected the entire operation. They meant more promotional pieces were designed, printed and shipped; more sales calls were made and received, more new accounts opened and old ones served; more supplies were ordered and delivered; more film shot and processed; more employees hired and hurriedly trained to produce; more negatives delivered to at least five different printers in four states and more books shipped directly to purchasers. By mid-November the Krause team had produced, on time — every time, a total of 57,000 pages of books and periodicals. It was an increase of 40 percent over 1989 and — in terms of sheer volume — the most productive year in Krause's history.

All these records had not been set without a cost. In late 1989 and early '90, many staff people, especially the production crews, had been working 60-hour weeks for up to four months. As Arlyn Sieber put it, "An addition of 40 or 50 pages is like buying another periodical." Krause had not only added 40 and 50 pages, but hundreds more, and brought several new publications into production. For the first time in its history Krause had a serious morale problem and some production workers started talking about organizing a union to redress their grievances.

The idea of a bargaining agent intervening between him and his employees did not sit well with Chet. Something had gone wrong; the "just-plain-Chet" style of management was no longer operating, and changes had to be made.

"The company was growing very fast," recalled personnel vice president Buddy Redling. "Over the past five years there had been constant change, with acquisitions, growth of products and stress levels." The turnover rate for employees climbed to 28 percent in 1988, fell to 18 percent in '89 and 16 percent in '90. "In a mature company with 300 people, it would be high," said Redling. "But there were 90 new people in one year alone."

Chet put the issue to rest. As Buddy recalled, he met with employees and explained that the intention of the ESOP was for the company and the employees to grow together. As owner/partners, they would be unionizing against themselves. "Everything is not perfect," Chet said, "but we are doing the best we can; we were never this large before."

"That reassured everyone," said Buddy. "There is a strong loyalty to and respect for Chet...and they needed that reassurance."

Chet also did more than talk. The man who believed in organization examined the operation he had built and found a kink he could quickly mend. "I walked around the place," he recalled, "and immediately saw what was wrong. We bought five new Camex 'Breeze' make-up terminals and that eased the strain."

The new equipment was a quick fix that eased the work load, but more was required. Krause added a third shift, which kept the lights burning and the computers humming all night, but also reduced the burden of overtime. A reorganization of the production process and management based on the recommendations of publishing consultant Dan Goldman also eased the strain. He suggested that Krause help its advertisers prepare better ads so the production people did not have to strain so hard to keep them accurate. A guidebook for advertisers was prepared so the material coming into the company would be easier to handle. For the same reason, Goldman also suggested that Krause upgrade its fax machines so they would deliver more legible copy. New positions were also created: Ad coordinators were assigned responsibility for a small group of publications which they supervised through the in-house production process; assistant production managers added to coordinate production flow, so supervisors were free to manage the flow of ads through their departments. Another improved Camex system came on line, along with another upgraded computer system that would increase the speed of processing by one-third.

More people were hired to handle what had become a higher plateau of productivity. Between the fall of '89 and the fall of 1990, Krause added 100 people to its workforce, a near 50 percent increase that would push the employment role to 320 people. Training programs for these new people became mandatory. They could no longer be allowed to sit down cold at the computer console and learn simply by doing, nor could they be expected to understand how the whole production process worked by taking part in just a small piece of it. New orientation and basic training programs were instituted to help new people learn their jobs and to understand how they fit into the entire operation.

An increase in production, much of it unforeseen and unplanned for, had created an unpleasant working environment at Krause. It wasn't surprising that a 40 percent increase in output in one year would stress the people involved. The pleasant part was Krause's reaction to the situation, and the measures taken to ease the work load and make growth more tolerable. One of those measures was immediately popular — a 5 percent pay bonus that said "thanks" for the extra effort. It was the first and only such bonus Krause has ever paid. The cumulative effect of Krause's response to the growth crisis of 1990 was positive, as recorded by the employee turnover rate. It fell to 13 percent in early 1991 and continued to decline through 1992.

Almost lost in the flurry of new production in 1990 was a very significant anniversary. Krause marked its 25th year of association with the Kable News Company of New York City. Krause and Kable started together with the March 1965 issue of *Coins*, and by 1990 the distributor was handling *Coins, Coin Prices, Old Cars Price Guide, Truck Prices, Baseball Card Price Guide Monthly, Baseball Cards, Fantasy Baseball, Baseball Card Boom!, Beginner's Guide to Baseball Card Collecting, Football Card Prices* and *Turkey Hunter*. *Baseball Cards* alone sent 263,000 magazines into the Kable network every month, and the distributor handled a total of 8.2 million copies of Krause titles every year. Kable provided the means, especially when a new periodical was introduced, to put a publication in the hands of a reader just about anywhere in the country.

"We have enjoyed a long and mutually beneficial relationship with Kable," Cliff said at the time. "Kable's willingness to help us launch successfully new products such as *Baseball Cards* in the early '80s and more recent titles such as *Fantasy Baseball* and *Truck Prices* helps us achieve our goal of continued growth through diversification." Getting the product in the hands of readers is the goal of the publishing process. Kable has been doing it for Krause for many years, and the length of that relationship bespeaks its quality.

Even a distributor as good as Kable cannot deliver products everywhere. In order to meet its own special marketing needs, Krause has developed its own bulk sales department, which was also growing by leaps and bounds in 1990. Regan Pourchot, with help from Marge Ertl, made up the department that year, and they marketed and delivered more than twenty periodicals to retail outlets ranging in size from large regional retail chains to small hobby stores and weekend conventions.

As KP *Contact* reported, "The idea is to get Krause Publications' products before the public eye...bulk distribution terms are basically risk-free for the retailer or wholesaler who is willing to provide shelf space.... Terms such as 30-day payment period and a 90-day return period are aimed at making bulk-sales orders attractive...."

"We are finding that the volume of bulk sales is constantly growing," said Regan. "We get nearly 50 requests through mail per week for our bulk-sales information."

Conflict between Krause and Kable over bulk distribution is avoided because each one handles different kinds of retail outlets.

Kable puts Krause products on the big newsstands in grocery, drug and discount stores. If a reader finds *Baseball Cards* at a Wal-Mart, for example, Kable probably put it there. If a reader buys *BC* at a small hobby shop, Krause most likely delivered it. Large distributors handle thousands of periodicals and serve the general market. They are interested in large volume sales. A specialty publisher can better serve its own special market by also distributing its own periodicals. A large distributor is not interested in delivering five copies, and only five copies, of Coins to a small shop, but Krause is and will deliver them. Regan Pourchot's bulk sales department helps Krause fill its niche by serving all of its market, no matter how small the outlet.

1990 ended with another changing of the guard at Krause. Don Nicolay left Krause in the summer to pursue other publishing interests, and Chet reassumed the president's title. Don left behind a new management team, a policy of aggressive marketing and a record of unprecedented growth.

At the 1990 Christmas party, Chet announced that the new president of Krause Publications would be Cliff Mishler. Cliff had refused Chet's offer for the job in 1986, but accepted four years later, because, as he said, "We couldn't find anyone better qualified outside the company." Cliff's understated reaction was typical of the man who had spent twenty-seven years working at Krause. He characterized himself as "production-oriented," as opposed to "sales-oriented," and, considering the jump in production Krause had just made, that orientation would prove useful. His list of qualifications for the job was long, but perhaps the best endorsement he could have received came from the staff. The Christmas party, like all Christmas parties, was a fairly raucous, irreverent event but, when Chet announced Cliff's appointment as president, everyone stopped joking and rose to give Cliff a standing ovation. Applause from one's peers is a better job recommendation than a twenty-page resume.

Also receiving cheers at Christmas in 1990 were the employees celebrating work anniversaries: Jim Brayer and Roy Van Epern, fifteen years; Phyllis Beyer, Ken Buttolph, Mary Johnson, John Koszewski, Sally Moe, Kathy Quinlan, Arlyn Sieber, ten years.

The employment record-holders at Krause Publications in 1992: (l-r) Clare Oppor, Marian Moe, Margaret Larson, Chet and Cliff.

Chapter 40

1991

> "...it's the single publication that dealers
> and collectors rely on for business news
> and price info...it's probably a good idea
> to keep the last half-year's or year's worth
> of issues stacked in your basement for ref-
> erence.... Remember the nation's dealers
> religiously read Sports Collectors Digest
> and this is where the prime market is
> made."   Alan Rosen, Mr. Mint.

Sports collecting celebrated its tenth anniversary in Iola in 1991, and Bob Lemke and his crew had much to take pride in. As Bob wrote in *SCD's* anniversary issue, "...*Sports Collector's Digest* remains the flagship publication in the KP sports lineup and still enjoys its proud reputation as the hobby's leading news source and number one marketplace.... Each and every week more than 50,000 devoted hobbyists, dealers and investors depend on *SCD* for essential industry news, feature stories, columns, news — issue reports, nostalgia pieces, investment tips, price guides, show calendars — and the most dependable and diversified advertising in the hobby." With that sentence Bob listed what his publication brings to its readers and summed up *SCD's* success.

It was a success story that extended throughout the niche and included *Baseball Card News*, *Baseball Cards* magazine, *Football, Baseball and Hockey*

Collector — which tripled its circulation in its first year — and *Baseball Cards Price Guide Monthly,* whose circulation had surpassed the 250,000 mark.

Still, the sports team continued to probe the size of the niche. They spent part of 1991 preparing a special publication that harkened back to Krause's experience in the 1960s. *Canadian Card Collector* made its debut in the spring of 1992, twenty-nine years after Krause introduced its first periodical aimed north of the border, *Canadian Coin News.* "We think the Canadian market offers us a real opportunity," said sports publisher Steve Ellingboe. While Canada has only two major league baseball teams, it has its own football league with cards and probably the most enthusiastic collectors of hockey cards in the world. Communication technology has changed so much since the 1950s that the sports staff will encounter few of the problems their numismatic predecessors confronted decades ago, but a Canadian hobby periodical will still face one wrinkle. "The price guide section will present a special challenge for us," said Steve, "because all of the pricing data will have to be converted to Canadian dollars."

Steve's concern is legitimate because it speaks to the heart of the product Krause presents to its readers. "This is a traders' publication," Chet told his readers back in 1953, and its ability to serve traders well — no matter what the hobby — has been the company's strength.

Comics Buyer's Guide Price Guide typifies that strength. Introduced in February, the *CBG Price Guide* was designed to meet the needs of comics collectors — in terms of its content, page design and size. "We designed it to be stored and used easily in their collecting," said Don Thompson. "It's a comic-book-sized magazine that can be stored with comics, carried with comics, and easily referred to."

The information on prices is also clearly displayed and the numbers match the figures comics traders will find in their own communities. "No single source can provide a universally acceptable value guide to comics," said Maggie Thompson, "so we've designed the *CBG Price Guide* to reflect the prices collectors can expect to pay in comics shops. We've tried to aim it at the comic-store customer." Aiming a publication at the right market, providing a service for people who need it — for coins in 1952, cards and comics in 1991 and beyond — that is what Krause does best.

Another example of a publication doing its best could be found in Wisconsin. In the 1970s, one of the state's most successful publishing ventures was an outdoors magazine titled *Wisconsin Sportsman.* It dominated the outdoor scene in the state with fine reporting and an outstanding presentation that attracted a solid advertising base. *Wisconsin Sportsman* built its marketing program on the powerful premise that it was the magazine about Wisconsin outdoors published by Wisconsin outdoors people — as opposed to competing magazines with offices out of state. Therefore, it came as a shock to many *Wisconsin Sportsman* fans when the publisher announced that he was selling the magazine to a corporation based in Atlanta, Georgia. (This is just what

Chet Krause, whose publishing company was much larger than *Wisconsin Sportsman's*, could have done, but didn't.)

It is testimony to the quality of the old *Wisconsin Sportsman*, and the power of its appeal to its readers' identification with the state, that many of its greatest fans refused to accept the idea of a "Wisconsin" magazine published in Atlanta. One of them was John Beauchaine of Green Bay. He revived the old *Sportsman* in the guise of a new magazine called *Wisconsin Outdoor Journal*. The new *Journal* looked much like the old *Sportsman*, hired many of the *Sportsman's* writers and marketed itself as the Wisconsin outdoors magazine written for and by Wisconsinites.

Despite the call to Badger loyalty, Beauchaine's magazine struggled to compete with the *Sportsman*, which had changed little other than its corporate address and its marketing program. By 1990, Beauchaine recognized his need for more publishing muscle and sold *Wisconsin Outdoor Journal* to Krause. With Bob Lemke as publisher, Steve Heiting as editor and Pat Akey as ad manager, *WOJ* has maintained a bi-monthly circulation of about 40,000, with *Wisconsin Sportsman* still dominating the market.

WOJ represented a marketing challenge similar to that of *Agri-View*. Both publications served a niche limited by geography and both faced stiff competition for a market that was no longer expanding. As the baby-boom generation aged, interest in hunting, fishing and allied activities leveled off, and restricted the market for general purpose outdoors magazines.

Despite the contrary demographic trend, Krause's outdoor marketing people did not level off their activities. They spent the better part of '91 working on two outdoors annuals. Early in 1992, 60,000 copies of *Wisconsin Fishing '92* went to subscribers and stands and set a single-copy record for *WOJ*. *Wisconsin Hunting '92* was scheduled to appear in late summer where it would face a more difficult task than its fishing cousin. The hunting market is much smaller than the fishing market and it is already served by many specialized periodicals — such as *Turkey Hunter* — that make stiff competition for general outdoors periodicals. How *Wisconsin Outdoor Journal* competes in its field and how Krause develops this segment of its larger outdoors niche will be another development worth watching in the years to come.

1991 was a dull year by Krause's recent standards — or it could be termed a year of consolidation. Only one new periodical was acquired and only one new one introduced. But twenty-eight books — new and revised editions — came out. On the other side of the scale, consolidation dictated that the plug be pulled on two of 1990's experiments — *Music Mart* and *Car Corral*.

The company's show operations stabilized in '91. The National *Rural Builder* Show "turned a corner" in the eyes of Rural Builder publisher Rick Groth. "We have now firmly established Krause Publications' credibility with the magazine's present and potential advertisers and the show's exhibitors." Nearly two-thirds of the exhibitors reserved space for the 1992 show to be held in Nashville, with its country music attractions. Under Krause's management, the building show changed. "By making certain that builders knew it would pay off for them to attend the educational programs as well as walk the trade show floor," said Al Hauschild, *RB's* ad manager, "we de-emphasized the partying 'convention atmosphere' that diminishes many similar events and concentrated on business...."

Concentrating on business paid off in '92. "It may not have been the biggest," reported Rick Groth, "But many, many builders and suppliers were kind enough to tell us that the 1992 National *Rural Builder* Show was the best ever." Show coordinator Kathie Heise reflected that "the construction market has been hard-hit by the recession, and we consider it an achievement to have delivered a show as well attended as our [1991] Louisville event.... In a year when virtually every other construction trade show is down, we're very pleased with our 22 percent booth increase." As a newcomer trying to find a market in a recession-strapped industry, Krause's success at establishing itself in the building trades niche was a real accomplishment.

Krause management was also established at the Chicago International Coin Show. It was "a big deal," as Colleen Spindler reported in the *Chronicle*, "to foreign coin collectors it is a major event." About 1,200 collectors attended and about 115 world coin dealers set up tables for trade. The numismatic staff also sponsored another Day In Iola following the ANA convention in Chicago. It was the Association's centennial, and the staff produced a special edition of *Numismatic News* that covered highlights of the hobby over the years and included the revival of two coin publishing landmarks. Chet penned the first copy of his "Chet Chat" column to appear in the *News* in twenty years, and Cliff revived his memorable "Coin Carousel."

Whether it was a time of consolidation or not, the year could not pass without another building program at Krause. The 1991 project was a 14,000-square foot warehouse that would eventually be used for expansion of the promotional, printing and mailing departments.

1991 was also the year when the employees became majority owners of the company through their ESOP. Through a regular program of stock sales, Chet had slowly given over custody of the operation he had built and nurtured to those who would carry it into the next century. They were very pleased with the arrangement, at least according to a survey conducted by Steve Vander Ark, who was researching the effect of ESOPs compared to other business structures on the attitudes of employees. Questionnaires returned by staff people reported positive feelings in terms of willingness to "put in a great deal of effort beyond that normally expected to help this organization." They also reported that they "really care about the fate of this organization," and were "proud to tell others that I am part of the organization." Krause also "really inspires the very best" for a high percentage of employees.

Vander Ark's study also pointed out how the employment situation had stabilized since the crisis of 1989-'90. More than 42 percent of employees had remained on staff for more than six years. The last figure is significant considering the number of people Krause had hired in 1988, '89 and '90.

Many of them would have echoed the sentiment voiced by new president Cliff Mishler, now nearing his 30th anniversary at Krause. At the 1988 Christmas Party, when he marked twenty-five years, Cliff reflected on the cumulative result of his day-to-day experiences by saying, "Though there have been many challenging days, which have caused me to release a deep mental sigh of relief when I closed the office door behind me and headed home, never has there been a morning that I was not happy to be opening the same door to face whatever challenges that new day might offer."

Many others have been happy to come back in the morning. In 1991, Bob Wilhite, Fred Borgmann, Neil Luepke and Alice Wolberg celebrated fifteen years with the company. Ten-year work anniversaries were marked by Lori Schoenick, Chris Mork, Sandy Yenter, Barb Johnson, Jim Christoph, Steve Ellingboe, Greg Loescher, Doris Beier, Sue Harvey, Cheryl Hayburn, Cheryl Kell and Nancy Trommer.

When he began in 1952, Krause's products covered no more than one corner of the din-
ing room table. 1992's output smothers the boardroom table and stacks up into an arm-
rest for the man who is still "just plain Chet."

Chapter 41

1992

*"Our niche is the efficiencies developed
within these walls."*   Chet Krause

Chet has worked in the field of mass communications since before the term was invented, but he has never considered himself an extraordinarily eloquent man. Nevertheless, no one has more eloquently and simply defined Krause Publications. Krause covers coin collecting, the sports card craze, the comics collecting realm, a segment of the construction trade, hunting, fishing and farming plus gun, music, toy and car collecting, but what it publishes is less important than how it publishes. Krause's true niche is not in the subject, but in the system.

At the turn of the last century, Henry Ford was one of a thousand shade-tree mechanics tinkering with automobiles. The cars he turned out of his first factories were no better or worse than most of the other products of their time. Were it not for Ford's greatest invention, his cars would be remembered as typical primitives and displayed with other artifacts of the earliest days of the automobile age at events like the Iola Old Car Show. Ford's cars put America and the world on wheels because of the state-of-the-art manufacturing and marketing system Henry Ford and his co-workers developed. So it was with Krause Publications.

Chet and his staff did not merely build a specialty publishing company. They created a publishing system whose niche was determined by its own system of "efficiencies." This is what has really been accomplished in Iola in the last four decades and what should be celebrated in this anniversary year.

As the company entered its fortieth year, the system was operating in its traditional style. It was experimenting to see it if could enlarge established hobby niches with new magazines such as *Canadian Coin Collector* and *Comics Retailer*. It tried to strengthen a new niche by buying another specialty outdoors periodical, *Deer and Deer Hunting*. Special publications were also created — the *Investors Guide to Trading Cards*, the *Wisconsin Outdoor Journal Annuals, Fantasy Baseball's Guide to Fantasy Baseball*. Another shelf full of books was on schedule, including *Sports Collectors Digest Football, Basketball and Hockey Price Guide; Goldmine's 1992 Annual;* the *Standard Catalog of Imported Cars, 1946-1990* and the 20th edition of the *Standard Catalog of World Coins*. Periodical deadlines numbered 548 — two for every working day — and the number of pages published annually crossed the 60,000 mark.

The promotions department continued to release its flood of marketing material at the rate of nearly 400,000 pieces a month, and, of course, there were giveaways. The most notable subscription premium was *Goldmine's* CD sampler, featuring selections from a number of contemporary artists, that new subscribers to the record collector's tabloid could purchase at a deep discount. *Old Cars Weekly* was stepping up its marketing program, and the 800 phone department extended its hours to accommodate the anticipated increase in calls.

The editorial and production departments were sampling another new computer system, DuPont's Whirlwind. Krause was one of the first publishers in the country to experiment with the system that combined text, ads and graphics on screen. DuPont routinely referred potential clients to Krause, and staff people demonstrated their use of Whirlwind in real publishing conditions to visitors from around the world. After working on the system in Iola, a DuPont representative told an industry conference that Krause "was the smoothest, most organized operation we have ever been with."

Krause would display its smoothness at a series of events to mark its 40th anniversary year. Days in Iola, open houses, plant tours, shows on the Old Car Show grounds, and cookouts at the Thorson House, would all be used to mark the milestone. 1992 was also the 20th anniversary of the Old Car Show, and the automotive staff planned to help make this year's event another in a long string of "biggest and best" shows. Chet, who was most intimately connected with both anniversaries, planned to celebrate them just as he had marked earlier passages in time — by sharing them with a few thousand of the many friends he has made along the way.

Technically, Chet had retired in 1991 when he passed the presidency onto Cliff, but he still showed up at the office whenever he was not out of town representing the company at trade or collector's shows. He was also compiling a history book in the form of a day-by-day accounting of the activities of his old World War II antiaircraft unit and working on his latest collection — World War II antiaircraft artifacts and memorabilia. The collection, which includes Jeeps, trucks, searchlights and artillery, were displayed on the grounds of the Old Car Show at a special military vehicle and collectibles show he organized for the weekend after the Old Car Show.

Chet was also maintaining his and the company's involvement in community affairs. Krause was again one of the sponsors of the Badger State Games in 1992 and has committed itself to maintaining the skijump at Iola for use by participants in the Badger State Games. Staff people are regular contributors to local causes ranging from the high school band fund to the senior citizen's center, but their greatest gift comes through the Old Car Show, where they have helped raise over $1 million dollars for the community over the years. Chet himself has become a major contributor to the Rawhide Boys Ranch, which offers a helping hand to young men in need, and to the Marshfield Medical Research Foundation.

Chet did not hesitate to remove himself from the daily management of his company. "In the early years, I was in complete control," he recalled. "When I was confronted with a situation I did something. I seemed to have batted 51 percent. The people I surrounded myself with also batted 51 percent. If I've been as good in selecting staff, we have nothing to worry about."

The appointment of Cliff as president was a crucial decision but one that Chet did not ponder over. He had already asked Cliff to become president in 1986.

"Cliff and I relate as a team," Chet said. "We've been together a long time. I was a mentor, he was a good student. But we didn't spend a lot of time talking at work on weekdays. We talked on weekends, traveling together, or at shows."

For Cliff, his association with Chet "was the best thing that happened...he made sure a lot of things have been happening." As for himself, Cliff says, "I'm just a transitional president. I don't intend to be sitting in this chair ten to twelve years from now. When the right person develops inside the company, he can have it...."

Cliff, like Chet, leaves his suit coat and tie at home when he comes to work. To a stranger, it is an arresting sight to see the "president" of the company stand at a podium and reel off a multi-million dollar financial report while wearing a short-sleeved shirt with an unbuttoned collar. It is not unusual at Krause. Throughout his working life, the "president" has always been comfortable with the "just-plain Chet" style, in his approach to both business and personal bearing.

As for the future of the company, both Chet and Cliff plan on doing just what they have been doing, i.e. applying their proven formula when the occasions arise. "We hope," said Cliff, "to see more of the same."

"But there are no guarantees," said Chet.

"There aren't a lot of hobbies out there that appear to offer substantial growth opportunities that aren't served by ourselves or someone else," said Cliff. "We've capitalized on our opportunities."

Although these two men have accumulated more than seventy years experience in hobby publishing, neither is willing to venture a guess on the future. They both look towards further development within existing hobbies, like music, guns or toys, with further refinements and specialization within niches. They are also looking for new opportunities, for the 1990s equivalent of sports card collecting. Possibilities include, but are certainly not limited to, wheeled toys, farm toys, trading cards not related to sports, golf collectibles, militariana and Elvis Presley memorabilia.

"We're looking," said Chet. The search is a bit more scientific than it was in the 1970s and even in the early 1980s, when a hunch on the part of Bob Lemke and Doug Watson turned into a multi-million dollar inspiration.

The development of technology is easier to predict, at least in part. New software and hardware will continue to change the print production process. In only a few years, the Whirlwind system that is now on the cutting edge will be obsolete and Krause will make the decision to replace or upgrade it. If past performance is any indicator, newer equipment will come on line on a regular basis.

Replacing production equipment inside the plant is not the most difficult technological challenge Krause will face in the future. "It's totally under your control," said Cliff.

"But now [technology] also reaches out to the consumer," he continued. "So how do you choose the one that will be used in the future?"

The situation is comparable to the pioneer days of the telephone, when different companies competed and consumers who bought into one line could not talk to their neighbors if the folks next door were connected to a competing phone system. In about ten years, communications systems may be so diverse that, until one system develops the monopoly enjoyed by today's phone system, neighbors may be as electronically isolated as some phone users were 100 years ago.

"The problem will be interfacing with different vehicles of delivery," Cliff projects. "There will be different electronic means, different mail delivery systems." The team running Krause in the opening years of the next century will wrestle with delivery systems that include satellites, cable video, fiber optics, more sophisticated fax systems, video phones, package delivery services that compete with the U.S. Postal Service and the U.S. Postal Service itself. Improved communication technology will, of course, make it easier for Krause to remain in Iola (it has never been especially difficult anyway). In time, the Krause office will probably become the hub around which even smaller producers — "publishing and communication cottage industries," as Cliff identifies them — will cluster. Electronics will overcome geography and link a writer or marketing person working at home to the office. "They will be more economi-cal," says Cliff. "That's the good part. Loss of control is the bad part."

New technology might also make it easier for Krause to compete in interna-tional markets. "Right now I don't see it as a market of serious potential," said Cliff. Although English is the second language of the world, a periodical reader understandably prefers to use his native tongue. Also, international delivery systems of printed matter are often too slow to deliver information in a timely manner. But, as Cliff points out, "it works with books. A serious col-lector can look at a picture and handle enough of the language to understand subjects, conditions and prices, but not with periodicals." Cliff has just explained why Krause's many *Standard Catalogs* enjoy worldwide circula-tion, but the tabloids and magazines are largely limited to the United States.

"Down the road," Cliff speculated, "if you can deliver electronically and translate...but I don't anticipate it. It's a totally new environment."

New as the environment will be in the next century, it is intriguing to specu-late on the possibility of a collector in Asia calling up the latest electronic edi-tion of the *CBG Price Guide* to see and/or hear the latest quotes translated into Tagalog or Urdu so he can decide if the time is right to trade his antique 1980s *Ninja Turtles* comics.

The factual base for the fantasy is that new technology will create new mar-keting and information delivery options in years to come. It is also a fact that the people working at Krause will — of necessity — be better trained than the people working there now. In 1992, about three-quarters of the Krause work force had graduated from or at least attended a college, university or technical institution after completing high school. The people joining the staff will be better trained but in-house training and enrichment programs, which are already in place, will expand in years to come. Chet has often said that Krause's greatest resource is its people. Their adaptability and willingness to learn new skills and work together as a team is the company's best assurance for the future.

The hardest of Krause's first forty years were the mid-1960s when, as Cliff said, "the coin hobby took that hellish plunge." It was also tough in the early 1980s, when a period of growth was followed by financial stress and again in 1989-90, when even greater growth prompted a staff crisis. It speaks well about a company, when two of its three crisis periods were not the result of decline, but of growth.

Memories of the best times are different, but more revealing. For Chet, the man who realized his life's dream, the most satisfying moment came when he "laid down the hammer" and became a full-time publisher. After making that decision, Chet's life was charted out for him.

For Cliff the best day came early in his career, when he "learned that Chet was truly a man of his word." When he hired on, Cliff had been promised a $10 a week raise after a year with the company. A year passed, but the raise did not appear on Cliff's check. He went to Chet and said that Ed Rochette had promised him a raise. Chet said, "If Ed said you'll get it, you'll get it." He got it with his next check.

That kind of simple integrity has become infused in the Krause system, and it left its impression on the man whose impact on the company is second only to Chet's. It was there in the struggling days of the early 1950s when Chet declared he would not take ads from mail bid sellers who would not publish their results. It was there in the 1970s when Joe Jones and Cliff confronted an advertiser who had been placing full-page ads in *Numismatic News* for "brilliant uncirculated" coins. He took orders, but shipped coins of inferior quality. Cliff and Joe met with him, proved that he was dishonest and — although it cost them pages of advertising — no longer accepted his business. The integrity is evident again when John Koenig affirmed *Goldmine's* policy of banning advertising for "bootleg" recordings. Its impact was illustrated in 1987 when Bob Lemke announced that the sports publications would no longer accept advertising for "unauthorized collector issue baseball cards."

[It] "...will cost us thousands of dollars of advertising per year but [it is] in the best long range interests of the hobby," Bob told the readers of *SCD*. He went on to say that "...unauthorized collector issue baseball cards are bad for the hobby...they siphon money away from legitimate collectibles, the authoritative baseball cards that have formed the backbone of this hobby for more than a century."

Thirty-five years had passed since Chet Krause told his first readers that he was "just plain Chet." Thirty-five years hadn't diminished his or his company's commitment to straight dealing; nor would the next five years of growth that brought the company to its 40th anniversary.

Krause has consistently made another commitment and it is also revealed by an incident involving Bob Lemke. As Cliff told it, in the late 1970s, *Coins* published a story about the bank notes used to ransom the kidnapped baby of Charles and Ann Lindbergh in the 1930s. The baby was never found and most of the ransom money was lost. One day after the article appeared, Bob received a phone call from a reader who said he had popped the inner lining off the door of a 1930s car and found bank notes with numbers identical to those reported in the Lindbergh story. Was this the famous Lindbergh ransom? The call started Lemke's collector's juices flowing and he excitedly embarked on an effort to get his hands on one of those notes and share the information with the hobby.

After the joke had gone as far as anyone could take it, Joe Jones revealed that he had made the call and there were no Lindbergh banknotes. Everyone laughed, including Lemke, but Cliff could not forget Bob's "enthusiasm for the notes. It illustrates his inherent appreciation for the meaningfulness of a collectible."

Appreciation of that meaningfulness has always been evident at Krause. "I am a collector too," wrote Chet when he founded the company, and the people who have joined him over the years have also been collectors of a sort. They are not all professionals, investors or traders, but they understand the "inherent meaningfulness of a collectible" to the people they serve.

It's a simple perception, straightforward and honest, and it became the foundation of a successful enterprise in a place that strangers consider unlikely. It didn't take a major investment banker, junk bonds, a leveraged buyout, a flock of consultants, a helping handout from the government, or a scheme of questionable legality. All it took was a man of spirit, integrity and common sense followed by people who came to share his philosophy. To build Krause Publications, all it took was the man who called himself "just plain Chet."

Number of Subscribers	520,694
Annual Total of Copies Delivered to Subscribers	29,484,674
Annual Newsstand Distribution	9,739,000
Annual Number of Book Pages Published	60,100
Average Monthly Display Ads Processed	6,870
Monthly Total of Classified Ads Published	36,696
Average Monthly Number of Promotional Pieces Mailed	395,000
Names and Addresses in Computer Storage	3,400,000
Annual Total Employee Hours Worked	663,979
Square Feet of Office and Production Space	82,000
Annual Total of Periodical Deadlines	572

1992 KRAUSE PUBLICATIONS
EMPLOYEES

Betty Aanstad, Randy Aanstad, Pat Akey, Dan Alfuth, Greg Ambrosius, Juliet Amundson, Darrell Anderson, Diana Anderson, Lori Anderson, Lori Anunson, Joyce Angst, Carl Babino, Audrey Barabas, Jaci Bartel, Ann Bauer, John Beauchaine, Mark Beauchaine, Doris Beier, Krystal Beil, Chris Belson, Grace Bergen, Annette Bergen, Melissa Beyer, Phyllis Beyer, Michelle Bolen, Pam Bolen, Jennifer Bonikowske, Jenny Bonikowske, Justine Bonikowske, Michelle Bonikowske, Connie Boone, Fred Borgmann, Carolyn Borth, Lauren Borth, Brad Bowling, Mary Brasel, Jim Brayer, Margaret Brewer, Paul Brewer, Diane Brown, Colin Bruce, Kandy Bruce, Kathy Budsberg, Millie Burdick, Jackie Burns, Jim Buroker, Don Butler, Ken Buttolph, KC Carlson, Bob Bydynkowski, Terri Carlson, Roger Case, Faye Cerasoli, Keith Chamberlain, Claude Chmiel, Melissa Christianson, Jim Christoph, RaJean Civik, Barb Clayton, Jenny Colligan, Wayne Conner, Barb Cramer, Krisann Dailey, Jackie Daniels, Norman Denney, Bruce Denny, Mark Desremaux, Ed Devilbiss, Eric Dingman, Mary DiSalvo, Shelly Domask, Laura Donlevy, Sherry Dopp, Bea Doss, Al Doyle, Judy Driebel, Steve Duberstein, Merna Dudley, Merry Dudley, Tom Dupuis, Pat Durkin, Rebecca Eberhardy, Joel Edler, Deb Ehrenberg, Mary Ellie, Steve Ellingboe, Tina Ellingson, Carol Ertl, Loretta Farina, Jim Felhofer, Rick Felts, Missy Fenn, Marcia Ferg, Pat Fischer, Judy Floistad, Lori Forbes, Jennifer Fossum, Richard Fredin, Carol Fredrickson, Barb Fritz, Jane Fyksen, Chris Gagliano, Reeny Gagnow, Jill Ganzel-Redlin, Linda Garbe, Paul Gerhardt, Fred Gibbs, Herman Gjertson, Dave Griena, Rick Groth, Leggie Gullixon, Jonn Gunnell, Donna Hagen, Dan Halverson, Tom Hammel, Richard Hare, Dave Harper, Barb Hartfiel, Sue Harvey, Lori Hauser, Cheryl Hayburn, Kathie Heise, Steve Heiting, Heidi Helbach, Alan Herbert, Giles Heuer, Kathy Hicks, Kathy Hines, Rick Hines, Sharon Hines, Marsha Hitzke, Tina Hoffman, Sue Homeyer, Tom Hultman, Shirley Jackson, Barb Johnson, Deb Johnson, Don Johnson, Jean Johnson, Karen Johnson, Mary Johnson, Ron Johnson, Shirley Johnson, Dee Jones, Judy Jones, Lois Kamke, Jane Karpinski, Paul Katzke, Cheryl Kell, Scott Kelnhofer, Kit Kiefer, Carol Klopstein, Pat Klug, Debbie Knauer, Audrey Kohel, Kris Kohel, John Koszewski, Ron Kowalke, Gordy Krahn, Sam Krainz, Gena Kranzusch, Chet Krause, Sue Krause, Darlene Kriewaldt, John Kronschnabl, Greg Krueger, Stacy Krull, Barbara Kundrat, Bob Kurkiewicz, Jeff Kurowski, Gretchen Laatsch, Phil LaFranka, Barbara Lane, Blaze Lanoue, Dave Larsen, Marge Larson, Mark Larson, Bob Lashua, Barb Lefeber, Bob Lemke, Jim Lenzke, Al Lewis, John Lindgren, Wendy Liter, Luann Loberg, Jill Lodewegen, Greg Loescher, Tom Luba,

Neil Luepke, Angie Lund, Mary Lutz, Jim Lynes, Steve Madson, Mary Lou Marshall, Debbie Martin, Julie Mattson, Linda Maurer, Brenda Mazemke, Hugh McAloon, Joel McNair, Carla Melum, Denise Melum, Joan Melum, Lori Melum, Susie Melum, Kerry Mesar, Tom Michael, Kristie Milanowski, Bonni Miller, Larry Mishkar, Cliff Mishler, Marian Moe, Sally Moe, Tina Moerschel, Peggy Morey, Wendy Morey, Chris Mork, Patsy Morrison, Tom Mortenson, Cheryl Mueller, Dave Mueller, Donna Mummery, Dave Natzke, Tom Nelsen, Kathy Nelson, Steve Nelson, Sandy Ness, Tammy Nieman, Wes Niemi, Therese Niemuth, Tim Nies, Don Nobs, Mary Nutter, Patti O'Connell, Mary Okonski, Stacey Olkowski, Suzanne Olkowski, Theresa Olson, Clare Oppor, Tom Ostrowski, Lori Owens, Kristine Oxley, John Pagel, Andrea Peplinski, Carol Peters, Kim Peters, Ron Peterson, Anne Phillips, Cindi Phillips, Jerry Potratz, Shelley Potratz, Regan Pourchot, Dave Pulvermacher, Kathy Quinlan, Steve Raap, Jodi Rader, Jackie Radies, Tracy Radies, Jennifer Radley, Sally Raisler, Sue Rasmussen, Jenny Readel, Buddy Redling, Shawn Reilly, Mary Ann Rice, Wendy Rice, Marilyn Riddell, Patti Roberts, Michelle Roe, Mary Roloff, Mike Ross, Jill Ruesch, Peter Ruiz, Sharon Rustad, Kathy Rylski, Joan Sanstadt, Jeanette Sawall, Becky Scharf, Steve Scharf, Tom Scheid, Debbie Schellin, Kim Schierl, Jeanette Schmidt, Judy Schmidt, Francis Schnider, Lori Schoenick, Mike Schoepel, Lynn Schrader, Paul Schroeder, Sandy Schultz, Gerald Schweiner, Guy Scudella, Nora Sebora, Cindy Semrad, Ingrid Seversen, Cathy Shanklin, Dick Shaver, Arlyn Sieber, Mary Sieber, Jo Sieckert, Bo Smith, Greg Smith, Susan Sorenson, Chris Sparks, Sandy Sparks, Wendi Sparks, Colleen Spindler, Mary Kay Steffen, Rowene Steffen, Tina Steinbach, James Stiebs, Erik Stottrup, Bob Strand, Mary Strom, Julie Stuempfig, Pat Stull, Connie Tesch, Tana Tessen, Bonnie Tetzlaff, Andrew Tews, Brian Thern, Randy Thern, Sharon Thern, Beth Thompson, Don Thompson, Maggie Thompson, Jacki Thorn, Bonnie Thorne, Liz Thorne, Ethel Thulien, Mary Timdal, Debbie Tischendorf, Paul Tofte, Terry Tomsyck, Kate Townsend, Chris Trinkner, Nancy Trommer, Carol Trudell, Duke Tuomi, Kevin Ulrich, Amy Van Deest, Dawn Van Epern, Roy Van Epern, Mark Van Hoof, Bob Van Ryzin, Mark Vold, Jeff Walker, Deon Wanner, Cari Wasrud, Mona Wasrud, Kathy Watters, Joey Wenzel, Mark Wenzel, Toni Wenzel, Sarah Werbelow, Daryl Wermedal, Allen West, Jennie Wierzba, Deb Wilhelm, Bob Wilhite, Ted Willems, Chris Williams, Mark Williams, Kathy Wise, Jay Wojcik, Alice Wolberg, Bruce Wolberg, Sandy Yenter, Jeanne Zietlow, LuAnn Zimmerman, Michelle Zwicki.

1992 KRAUSE BOOKS IN PRINT

Numismatic books

Complete Encyclopedia Mexican Paper Money
Illustrated Coin Dating Guide
Standard Catalog Depression Scrip
Standard Handbook Modern U.S. Paper Money
Unusual World Coins
U.S. Postage and Fractional Currency
Standard Catalog of World Coins
Twentieth Century World Coins
Standard Guide to South Asian
Guidebook of Franklin Mint Issues
Standard Catalog Mexican Coins/Paper Money/Medal
Rome's Gold Edition 1972-78
Rome's Silver Coins, Vol. 1, 1917-78
Rome's Silver Coins, Vol. 3, 1972-78
Rome's Copper Coins, 1972-78
Rome's Prices Realized 1979, 1981
Standard Guide to US Coins and
    Paper Money Valuation
Standard Guide to Crowns and Talers
Harrison Fisher
Token of Gay Nineties
Standard Catalog World Gold Coins
Medallic Portraits of Washington
Guide Book of Mexican Coins
Spink's Catalog Col/Common Coins
Guide to World Notgeld
U.S. Trade Tokens
Standard Catalog of Obsolete Bank Notes
Discovering American-Coin Collecting
Standard Catalog World Paper Money Gen
Early Paper Money of America
Standard Catalog Nation Bank Notes
U.S. Merchant Tokens
Standard Catalog World Paper Money Spec
Confederate States Paper Money
Early American Tokens

Large Size Silver Coins of the World
Standard Catalog of U.S. Paper Money
North American Coins and Prices
Striking Impressions
Auction Prices Realized
Latin American Tokens
Hard Times Tokens
Forgotten Coins of North America
Collecting World Coins
Standard Catalog of World Crowns

Automotive

Best of Old Cars, Vol. 1-6
Standard Catalog Commercial Vehicles
Standard Catalog of American Cars, 1946-1975, 3rd Edition
Standard Catalog of American Cars, 1805-1942, 2nd Edition
Car Value Guide, 1st Edition
Standard Catalog of American Light Duty Trucks, 1st Edition
Old Car Auction Results, 2nd Edition
Standard Catalog of American Cars, 1976-1986, 2nd Edition
Standard Guide to Cars and Prices, 5th Edition
Antique Auto Wrecks, 1st Edition, Standard Catalog of Chevrolet, 1st Edition,
Standard Catalog of Chrysler, 1st Edition
Standard Catalog of Food Cars, 1st Edition
Police Cars, 1st Edition
Standard Catalog of Buick, 1st Edition, Standard Catalog of Cadillac, 1st Edition
Standard Guide to Automotive Restoration, 1st Edition
Standard Catalog of Imported Cars, 1st Edition
Fabulous '50s, 1st Edition
Standard Catalog of 4x4's, 1st Edition

Firearms

Winchester Model 42, 1st Edition
Winchester Model 21, 1st Edition
Standard Catalog of Firearms, 2nd Edition
Winchester Model 94, 1st Edition
Winchester Slide Action .22, 1st Edition
Rugers at Random, 1st Edition.

Outdoor

Battle of Bunker Hill, 1st Edition

Tales of the Golden Beaver

Illusions of Animal Rights, 1st Edition

Hunting Coyotes East and West (video), 1st Edition

Turkey Hunting With Gerry Blair, 1st Edition

Trout at the Walnut Tree, 1st Edition

Trapper Yearbook 1991, 1st Edition

Fish Wisconsin, 1st Edition

Hunt Wisconsin, 1st Edition

Musky Mastery, 1st Edition

Game Wardens and Poachers, 1st Edition

Sports

SCD Baseball Card Price Guide, 6th Edition

Standard Catalog of Baseball Cards, 2nd Edition

SCD Baseball Card Pocket, 3rd Edition

SCD Baseball Autograph Handbook, 2nd Edition

SCD Football, Basketball, Hockey Price Guide, 1st Edition

SCD Sportscard Counterfeit Detector, 1st Edition

Fantasy Baseball, 1st Edition

Team Baseballs, 1st Edition.

Music

GM Price Guide to Record Albums, 2nd Edition

GM Rock 'n Roll 45 RPM Price Guide, 2nd Edition

GM Jazz Price Guide, 1st Edition

They Called It Rock, 1st Edition

Goldmine Annual 1992, 1st Edition

Doo Wop, 1st Edition

GM PG to Collectible Jazz Records, 1st Edition.

Comics

Popeye Collectibles, 1st Edition

CBG Annual, 1992, 1st Edition

1991 KRAUSE PUBLICATIONS
TOTAL CIRCULATION FIGURES

Date Begun at Krause	Publication	1991 Total Circulation
1990	Agri-View	52,978
1979	Bank Note Reporter	5,700
1985	Baseball Card News	80,900
1988	Baseball Card Price Guide	299,658
1981	Baseball Cards	339,552
	Canadian Card News	N/A
1967	Coin Prices	81,948
1961	Coins	65,794
1983	Comics Buyer's Guide	20,100
1990	Comics Quarterly	34,289
1992	Deer and Deer Hunting	135,000
1990	Fantasy Baseball	103,844
1990	Football, Basketball, Hockey Collector	62,219
1983	Goldmine	29,200
1987	Gun List	59,658
1987	Gun Show Calendar	7,600
1952	Numismatic News	45,600
1973	Old Cars News and Market	70,300
1978	Old Cars Price Guide	113,661
1989	Rural Builder	35,375
1981	Sports Collector Digest	54,200
1988	Toy Shop	18,545
1988	Trapper and Preditor Calling	38,747
1990	Truck Prices	42,892
1988	Turkey Hunter	53,946
1991	Wisconsin Outdoor Journal	37,148
1973	World Coin News	9,000

IOLA OLD CAR SHOW AND SWAP MEET
STATISTICAL HISTORY

Year	Attendance	Show Cars	Swap Spots	Car Corral
1972	600	14	---	---
1973	1,200	98	---	---
1974	1,700	180	---	---
1975	2,500	409	86	---
1976	10,000	564	100	---
1977	20,000	900	200	---
1978	30,000	1,200	400	---
1979	35,000	1,800	560	---
1980	50,000	2,700	800	---
1981	60,000	3,000	1,000	300
1982	70,000	3,000	1,300	400
1983	80,000	3,000	1,500	475
1984	85,000	2,900	1,700	550
1985	80,000	1,700	1,909	194
1986	90,000	2,000	2,097	500
1987	100,000	2,000	2,295	500
1988	100,000	2,000	2,682	400
1989	105,000	2,200	2,700	800
1990	120,000	2,200	3,100	1,000
1991	124,000	2,300	3,600	1,000

Index

P

R

ABOUT THE AUTHOR

Michael J. Goc, an award-winning journalist and historian, has lived his entire adult life near Friendship, Wisconsin, just sixty miles from Chet Krause's birthplace.

He is the author/editor of more than twenty historical books and the recipient of three Awards of Merit from the State Historical Society of Wisconsin. Mr. Goc is also the founder of New Past Press Inc., a publishing company specializing in community, organization and business history.

His collecting energies have been focused on pre-1965 U.S. coins, vintage historical books, antique woodworking tools and parts for a 1966 Kaiser Jeep under restoration. He and his wife, Barbara Weade, live in rural Friendship with their two children, Nathan and Rachel.